ST PAUL
HIS LIFE, LETTERS, AND CHRISTIAN DOCTRINE

ST PAUL
HIS LIFE, LETTERS, AND CHRISTIAN DOCTRINE

BY

A. H. M^cNEILE, D.D.

REGIUS PROFESSOR OF DIVINITY IN THE UNIVERSITY
OF DUBLIN, CHANCELLOR OF ST PATRICK'S, FELLOW
OF SIDNEY SUSSEX COLLEGE, CAMBRIDGE

WIPF & STOCK · Eugene, Oregon

Wipf and Stock Publishers
199 W 8th Ave, Suite 3
Eugene, OR 97401

St. Paul
His Life, Letters, and Christian Doctrine
By McNeile, A. H.
Softcover ISBN-13: 978-1-6667-3447-8
Hardcover ISBN-13: 978-1-6667-9035-1
eBook ISBN-13: 978-1-6667-9036-8
Publication date 8/25/2021
Previously published by Cambridge University Press, 1920

This edition is a scanned facsimile of the original edition published in 1920.

PREFACE

THE Christianity of to-day is broadly speaking the Christianity of St Paul. The influence which he has exercised on the hearts and lives of men is unequalled by that of any other writer in the world's history. The Apostolic Scriptures to which appeal was made in the perilous times when the early Church was holding her own against Gnosticism were, in the first instance, the Gospels and the Pauline Epistles. 'The extent to which "the Apostle," ὁ ἀπόστολος, dominated through the New Testament Canon the Church of the second century has not been adequately realised[1].' Through the third and fourth centuries Christian thought, and Pauline thought in particular, was gradually formulated with increasing distinctness, until it received at the hands of St Augustine the systematized shape in which it was preserved in western Europe, and is largely preserved to this day.

It is natural, therefore, that the Apostle's life and writings have occupied the attention of innumerable thinkers and scholars. This little book is not intended to vie with larger works, but to form an introduction

[1] Turner in Swete's *The Early History of the Church and the Ministry*, p. 103.

to them, by gathering together in a small compass the best that has been written on the subject in recent years. The line of thought, however, in Part III is not directly borrowed from any other work on St Paul's doctrine. I have tried to map out, as briefly as possible, the great area of his teaching in the form which suggested itself to my own mind by independent study.

A. H. M^CNEILE.

DUBLIN,
July, 1918.

CONTENTS

PART I

THE LIFE OF ST PAUL

CHAP.		PAGE
I.	St Paul's Character and Person	1
II	Classes of Christian Converts	8
III.	St Paul's Conversion	11
IV.	St Paul's Movements after his Conversion	17
V.	St Paul at Antioch with Barnabas	21
VI.	St Paul's Second Visit to Jerusalem	23
VII.	The Dedication of Barnabas and Saul to wider Work	28
VIII.	St Paul's First Missionary Tour	29
IX.	The Apostolic Council at Jerusalem	40
X.	St Paul's Second Missionary Tour	50
XI.	St Paul's Third Missionary Tour	76
XII.	St Paul at Jerusalem	95
XIII.	St Paul's Imprisonment at Caesarea	102
XIV	St Paul's Journey to Rome and his Work there	109

PART II

THE EPISTLES OF ST PAUL

		PAGE
	Introduction	121
I.	I Thessalonians	123
II.	II Thessalonians	129
III.	Introduction to I and II Corinthians	135
IV.	I Corinthians	149
V.	II Corinthians	162
VI.	Galatians	168

viii   CONTENTS

CHAP.		PAGE
VII.	ROMANS	181
VIII.	COLOSSIANS	203
IX	PHILEMON	211
X.	EPHESIANS	213
XI.	PHILIPPIANS	225
XII	THE PASTORAL EPISTLES	241

PART III

THE CHRISTIAN DOCTRINE OF ST PAUL

SECT.		
	INTRODUCTION	265
1.	ESCHATOLOGY	268
2.	THE HOLY SPIRIT	274
3.	THE CHRISTIAN'S TRANSFERENCE INTO THE MESSIANIC KINGDOM	276
4.	THE NATURE OF MAN	279
5.	THE WORK OF THE SPIRIT IN THE CHRISTIAN	282
6	THE SPIRIT OF CHRIST	283
7.	'IN CHRIST'	284
8.	CHRISTIANS	286
9.	DELIVERANCE FROM SIN AND LAW	289
10.	RIGHTEOUSNESS, GRACE, AND FAITH	293
11.	JEW AND GENTILE	295
12.	THE CROSS	298
13.	THE SACRAMENTS	303
	LITERATURE	308
	INDEX	313
	MAPS illustrating (1) St Paul's life to the end of the First Missionary Tour, (2) the Second Missionary Tour, (3) the Third Missionary Tour and the Journey to Rome	*at end*

INTRODUCTION

1. APART from Jesus Christ, St Paul is the greatest figure in the history of Christianity. His character, his preaching, and his letters made Christianity a world religion. The fountain of the water of life, offered first to Jews, ran to Gentiles through channels cut by him. He appeared, in God's providence, a very few years after the crucifixion of our Lord, when the mind of the Church was still young and plastic, and laid his impress upon it for all time.

Nevertheless none of his contemporaries attempted to write his biography. The book of the *Acts* is not a biography, but a summary sketch of the spread of Christianity from Jerusalem until it reached Rome, the head and heart of the Empire. St Paul indeed figures largely in the latter half of it, but in the former half St Peter holds the principal place. It is the 'Acts of the Apostles,' not the 'Acts of Paul,' much less his Life. No records survive of his childhood and youth; and for an account of his death we are dependent upon patristic tradition from the close of the first century and onwards (see pp. 256, 257).

2. THE TRUSTWORTHINESS OF THE ACTS. The value of the *Acts* as a trustworthy source of our knowledge is being subjected, at the present time, to minute investigation. It is not necessary here to deal with the matter at length. Some writers who have upheld the historical value of the book have tended to weaken their case by over-stating it. The historical value, especially of the

portion dealing with St Paul, is undoubtedly high; but probably all will agree that however careful the author may have been to write with accuracy, his work—written several years after the events—cannot command quite the same confidence as the apostle's own statements about himself in his letters. Where *Acts* and epistles agree, our confidence can be complete; where they differ, the latter must be allowed full weight, while the former is used with the recognition that it is a secondary authority. And that recognition must include the speeches and addresses attributed to St Paul in the *Acts*. They may rest, to a considerable extent, upon traditions of his actual words, or at least of the substance of what he said But there is little doubt that St Luke, whom we may assume to have been the author, followed a well recognised literary method of ancient authors in writing the speeches which he attributed to St Paul and others, as a means of representing his own views of the several situations, and of the character, aims, and circumstances of the speakers.

3. THE 'WE'-SECTIONS. The passages generally known as the 'We'-sections, because in them the narrative falls into the first person plural, are, according to the ordinary text, (*a*) Acts xvi. 10–17, (*b*) xx 5–15, (*c*) xxi 1–8, (*d*) xxvii. 1–xxviii. 16. These cover St Paul's movements (*a*) from Troas to Philippi on the second missionary tour, (*b*) from Philippi to Miletus on the third tour, (*c*) from Miletus to Jerusalem at the end of the same tour, (*d*) from Caesarea to Rome[1].

To what extent the book of the *Acts* as a whole was

---

[1] The first person occurs also in D and Augustine at xi. 27 (see p 23) and in D and the Sahidic version at xvi 10 (see p. 55).

compiled from written documents or from tradition, or both, is a difficult problem which is still a subject of much discussion. But it seems clear that in the 'We'-sections a written document supplied St Luke with at least the main facts. With regard to the extent, and the authorship, of this document opinions differ. It is generally recognised that the style and vocabulary of these sections cannot be distinguished from those of the rest of the book, and that the whole book *in its present form* was the work of one writer. Many have therefore concluded that these sections formed part of a diary or travel-document written by St Luke himself in the actual course of his journeys with St Paul, and that at a later time he introduced some parts of the diary, just as they stood, into his narrative But the 'We'-sections are not quite as free from difficulties and obscurities as we should expect such a diary to be. And since the narrative in the first person passes in every case without a break into a narrative in the third, the original extent of the 'We'-sections is difficult to determine. The style and vocabulary are not necessarily decisive of St Luke's original authorship of the sections. He was quite capable, as we know from his Gospel, of taking a written document and largely re-writing it, colouring it with his own style and vocabulary. And in doing this he might still preserve the first person plural which he found in his document, much in the same way as the compiler of Ezra Nehemiah preserved in certain passages the first person singular. The original diary might, therefore, have been made by some unnamed companion of St Paul, and have been either a fairly full narrative or the briefest travel notes. But on this supposition it is a real difficulty that there is not the slightest indication in the *Acts* or the Epistles as to who this unnamed companion could have been. The facts can best be accounted for by supposing that the original notes, mostly quite brief records of St Paul's movements, but with an occasional anecdote added, were the work of St Luke, and that many years later he made them the basis of the narrative in its present form.

4. THE TEXT OF THE ACTS. For some years after its composition the *Acts* was not considered a sacred writing, and scribes therefore felt at liberty to treat its text very freely. In the manuscripts D, E, and some others, in one or two Old Latin versions, some early Latin writers, and in the margin of the Harclean Syriac, a number of more or less interesting variants appear, which are often referred to by the general description of the 'δ' text. Various suggestions have been made as to their origin, among them that of Blass[1] who conjectured that they represent the first edition of the book, made by St Luke for Roman readers, while the ordinary text, which is often slightly shorter, was a revised edition which he made for Theophilus. Few writers have accepted this solution. But several have treated these variants very seriously as being, in many cases, nearer to the original than the readings in the ordinary text. Of recent years, however, it has been thought more probable that they were made gradually by a succession of scribes or editors. They would not call for special mention were it not that they are more numerous and striking in the *Acts* than elsewhere, and that they occasionally add what is very possibly reliable information. The more noteworthy readings are recorded in the footnotes.

Philology of the Gospels, p. 101.

INTRODUCTION xiii

5. CHRONOLOGY. The reader will not find dates scattered throughout this volume; *relative* dates and the succession of events are all that is required in the chronology of St Paul's life. But a short discussion of the subject must be made here. The exact dates cannot yet be determined, because no quite certain date has been discovered in non-Biblical sources which coincides with an event in his life. But fortunately, with regard to the dates during the period of his missionary activity the margin of uncertainty has been reduced to a single year. A large number of the variations in the schemes supported by different writers are noted by Moffatt, *Introd. to the Literature of the N.T.* p. 62 f. Most of the material is collected by Turner in his useful article in Hastings' *Dict of the Bible*, i. 403–425. He bases his dates on ten considerations, of which the following may be mentioned: (1) Aretas was probably not in possession of Damascus (cf. 2 Cor. xi. 32) before 37 A.D. (2) The famine under Claudius (Acts xi. 28) was not before 46. (3) The expulsion of Jews from Rome under Claudius (xviii. 2) was perhaps in 49 or 50. (4) Felix married Drusilla (cf. xxiv. 24) not before 54. (5) Felix was succeeded by Festus (xxv. 1) in one of the years 57–59, probably in 58. Turner's scheme, accordingly, is as follows:

	A.D.
The Crucifixion	29
St Paul's Conversion	35–6
1st visit to Jerusalem	38
2nd visit to Jerusalem	46
1st missionary journey	47
Council at Jerusalem, 2nd journey	49
Corinth reached late in	50
4th visit to Jerusalem, 3rd journey	52
Ephesus left	55

	A.D.
5th visit to Jerusalem, arrest at Pentecost	56
Rome reached early in	59
Acts closes early in	61
Martyrdom of St Peter and St Paul .	64–5

The date of the Crucifixion need not here be discussed. But Turner's second and third dates are open to serious doubt, because he identifies the second visit to Jerusalem (of Gal. ii. 1–10) with the visit for the Council (49), not with the visit to take relief for the famine (Acts xi. 29 f.) which is much the more probable (see pp. 23–8). St Paul says (Gal. ii. 1) that he went up to Jerusalem 'after fourteen years,' which Turner feels compelled to understand, against the natural meaning of the words, to be fourteen years after his conversion; hence reckoning back from 49 he dates the conversion in 35–6. It is true that to take the words in their natural meaning of fourteen years since his previous visit causes difficulty. It throws that previous visit back to 35, which is impossible if Aretas was not in possession of Damascus till 37. Conversely, if on this account the first visit is dated in 37, fourteen years later brings the second visit down to 51, which throws St Paul's missionary life altogether too late. Thus it will be seen that to give the words 'after fourteen years' their natural meaning, and at the same time to identify the Jerusalem visit of Gal. ii. 1–10 with the famine visit of Acts xi. 29 f. lands us in a dilemma. But an escape from it is offered by a conjecture revived by Kirsopp Lake[1] which deserves serious consideration, that St Paul originally wrote 'after *four* years[2].' If the two Jerusalem visits were

[1] *Expositor*, Nov. 1912.
[2] ΔΙΑ$\overline{\Delta}$ΕΤΩΝ, which an early scribe wrote as ΔΙΑ$\overline{\text{ΙΔ}}$ΕΤΩΝ.

INTRODUCTION xv

separated by only four years[1], and the second is identified with the famine visit, the first visit (reckoning back from Turner's date 46) was in 42, and the conversion three years previously (Gal. 1. 18) was in 39.

Turner's last date is uncertain. St Paul's martyrdom may have occurred at any time after the 'two whole years' of Acts xxviii. 30 until the Neronian persecution which broke out in 64 (see p. 257 f.). If St Peter's martyrdom at Rome is historical, which there is no good reason for doubting, it cannot have been earlier than the persecution.

For the intervening events (from the second Jerusalem visit to the close of the *Acts*) one piece of evidence has been discovered since Turner wrote which enables us to fix the dates with the uncertainty of only one year throughout. In 1905 Bourguet[2] published four fragments of an inscription found at Delphi, which is thought to have stood originally on an outer wall on the South side of the temple of Apollo. It appears to contain the words of a friendly letter from the emperor Claudius to the city of Delphi, in which Gallio is mentioned as the proconsul of the country, i.e. Achaia. Many similar letters from emperors have been preserved, by comparison with which some of the lost portions can be

---

[1] It should be noticed that if there were ten years between them nearly nine of them must have been spent at Tarsus, for only 'a whole year' was spent at Antioch (Acts xi 26) before the famine visit. A man of St Paul's temperament, filled with his new Christian zeal, is very unlikely to have passed nine years in quiet retirement at home; and if he preached during that time, St Luke would probably have given some account of it, since he is so careful to relate the one year's work at Antioch

[2] *De rebus Delphicis imperatoriae aetatis capita duo*

restored with some probability. It is much mutilated, as will be seen from the following transcription[1]:

ΤΙΒΕΡ	ΑΙΣ	ΟΣ Γ
ΣΙΑΣ	Ο·ΚCΙΠ	ΑΤΡΙ
ΠΑΛ ΤΗΙΠ	ΤΩΝΔΕΛΦ	ΥΜΟ
ΧΗΣΑΕΠΕΤΗΡΗ	ΝΘΡΗΣΚΕΙ	ΟΥΑΠΟ
ΝΥΝΛΕΓΕΤΑΙΚΑΙ	ΕΙΤΩΝΕΡΙ	ΚΕΙΝΑΙΩ
ΝΙΟΣΓΑΛΛΙΩΝΟΦ	ΜΟΥΚΑ	ΠΑΤΟΣ
ΕΤΙΕΞΕΙΝΤΟΝΠΡΟ	Ο	Ε
ΛΩΝΠΟΛΕΩΝΚΑ		
ΑΥΤΟΙΣΕΠΙΤΡΕ		
ΦΩΝΩΣΠΟΛΕ		
ΤΑΙΜΕΤΩΚΙ		
ΥΤΟΥ		

For our purpose only four lines are important, with regard to which there is fairly general agreement. Deissmann[2] restores them as follows:

1. Τιβεριος Κλαυδιος Καισαρ Σεβαστος Γερμανικος αρχιερευς μεγιστος δημαρχικης εξου
2. σιας το ·ιβ′ αυτοκρατωρ το ·κς′ πατηρ πατριδος υπατος το ·ε′ τιμητης Δελφων τηι πολει χαιρειν
5   Λουκιος Ιου
6. νιος Γαλλιων ο φιλος μου και ανθυπατος της Αχαιας

'Tiberius Claudius Caesar Augustus Germanicus Pontifex Maximus, in the twelfth year of his tribunician authority, saluted as Emperor *the twenty-sixth time*, Father of his country, Consul the fifth time, Censor, to the city of Delphi greeting...Lucius Junius *Gallio my friend and proconsul* of Achaia....'

The words in italics are certain, and provide the necessary clue. The emperor's tribunician authority was reckoned each year from Jan. 25th. The number of the year originally given in the inscription is lost; but other

[1] It is printed thus for convenience of space, but the lines in the original inscription were at least twice as long as line 1.
[2] *St Paul*, Appendix 1.

inscriptions enable us to say with certainty that it was either 11 or 12, i.e. A.D. 51 or 52. The 26th and 27th imperial salutations of Claudius are known to belong to the 12th tribunician year, and the 22nd, [23rd], and 24th to the 11th. The 25th also probably fell in the 11th, and just possibly the 26th also. The emperor's letter to Delphi was therefore written in 52, after (or possibly just before) Jan. 25th. And Gallio's year of office consequently included part of A.D. 52.

The inscription, however, does not help in determining the exact date of his *entry* upon office, to which there is little doubt that St Luke refers in Acts xviii. 12. The proconsulate normally lasted a year. In A.D. 43 Claudius made a rule that every proconsul must leave Rome not later than the middle of April to take up his office[1] Deissmann therefore places Gallio's arrival at Corinth at about the beginning of July. We may roughly call it midsummer. But the question which cannot at present be solved is whether it was the midsummer of 52 or 51, since we do not know on what day in the year 52 Claudius received his next (27th) salutation; it may have been either shortly after Gallio entered upon office or after he had vacated it

We can now, in the light of the narrative of Acts xviii., date forwards and backwards from the midsummer of 52 or 51. The trial took place soon after Gallio's arrival, some time say in July—September. St Paul 'tarried after this yet many days' (*v.* 18), i.e. probably over the winter, before he started, as soon as the sailing season began, to journey hurriedly *via* Ephesus to Jerusalem (perhaps for the Passover) in the spring of 53 or 52. Before Gallio's arrival he had spent 18

[1] Dio Cassius ix. 17, 3.

months in Corinth (*v.* 11) since his vision (*vv.* 9, 10); so that the vision occurred at the beginning of 51 or 50. And he had been for a little time in Corinth before that (*vv* 1-7); he therefore arrived in Corinth in the late autumn of 50 or 49 (or possibly at the beginning of 51 or 50 if the 18 months is intended to include his whole time in Corinth before the trial) This was soon after the arrival of Priscilla and Aquila from Rome owing to the edict of banishment (*v.* 2). Assuming that they travelled without delay from Rome to Corinth this might seem to give a fixed date, for Orosius[1], quoting a certain Josephus[2], dates the edict in the 9th year of the reign of Claudius This should be A D. 49; but Ramsay claims that Orosius is always a year behind in his dates[3], while Deissmann thinks that the very fact of his giving 'Josephus' as his authority shews that he was not reckoning the date for himself. The matter cannot at present be settled, so that we are still left in uncertainty to the extent of one year.

St Paul, then, was in Corinth from the late autumn of 50 or 49 till the early spring of 53 or 52; and the principal dates of his life till his arrival at Rome may be calculated as follows, with the alternative of one year earlier throughout:

	A.D.
The Conversion	39
1st visit to Jerusalem	42
2nd visit to Jerusalem	46
1st missionary tour	47

[1] vii. 6, 15.
[2] The passage does not occur in the histories of Josephus that we possess.
[3] Taking 50 as the year of the edict Ramsay unnecessarily delays the arrival of Priscilla and Aquila at Corinth till the spring of 51.

INTRODUCTION

	A.D.
Council at Jerusalem, 2nd tour	49
Corinth reached late in	50
4th visit to Jerusalem, 3rd tour	53
Ephesus left	56
5th visit to Jerusalem, arrest at Pentecost	57
Rome reached early in	60

On this basis the epistles, apart from the Pastorals, can be dated as follows:

	A.D.
1 and 2 Thessalonians	51
1 Corinthians	55 or 56
2 Corinthians	56
Galatians	56 (?49)
Romans	57
Colossians, Philemon, Ephesians	c. 61
Philippians	c. 62 (?54–56)

PART I

THE LIFE OF ST PAUL

CHAPTER I

ST PAUL'S CHARACTER AND PERSON

1. PHYSICAL CHARACTERISTICS. No attempt is made in the *Acts* to *describe* the apostle[1]. But his letters help us, to a wonderful extent, to see him as he really was. His was a great soul which won a life-long triumph over his body. His physical disabilities were made the most of by his opponents (2 Cor. x. 10), but they were, in fact, an acute trial to him. On one occasion his ill health forced him to stay in Galatia, when he would otherwise have travelled further (Gal. iv. 13). The exact form of his complaint is unknown, but he describes it as 'a stake in the flesh, a messenger of Satan to buffet me' (2 Cor. xii. 7). It seems to have attacked him at intervals, and to have begun after he became a Christian. On the occasion of the first three attacks he 'besought the Lord that it might stay away from him,' but God helped him to realise that it was His will, and that His strength would support him (*vv* 8, 9). It was of so distressing a nature that it was very trying to those who saw him. But he thankfully acknowledges that the Galatians did not on that account despise or reject him in disgust (Gal. iv. 14). 'Luke the beloved physician' (Col iv. 14) during the periods of his ministry when he accompanied him no

---

[1] In the *Acts of Paul and Thekla* he is described as 'short, bald, bandy-legged, strongly built, with meeting eyebrows, with a rather large nose, full of grace, for at times he looked like a man, and at times he had the face of an angel.'

doubt did all that he could to give him relief when the attacks came on. Some have suggested that it was a weakness of eyesight, and that this would explain his need of an amanuensis to write his letters, and the 'large characters' in which he wrote with his own hand his closing words to the Galatians (vi 11); also the account in Acts xxiii. 1–9 of his trial before the Sanhedrin, at which he 'looked intently' at the council (*v*. 1), and did not realise that one of his judges who commanded him to be struck on the mouth was the high priest (*v*. 5) But even if these are to be explained as due to weakness of eyesight, that alone would not be enough to force him to postpone a journey and stay with the Galatians, or account for his language about their welcome treatment of him. Ramsay suggests malarial fever. A more probable conjecture is that it was some form of epilepsy. The weakness which occasioned the attacks may possibly also have affected his eyes. It seems also at times to have caused him to suffer from depression.

2. TEMPERAMENT. But nothing could subdue his unconquerable courage, which carried him through physical hardships under which many men would have succumbed. His letters contain many indications that he had a tensely strung nervous temperament, which though often a personal trial to him contributed to his extraordinary force of character. It was as though he were charged with a spiritual electricity which drew men like a magnet, but which also repelled. It gave him an eager, fiery energy—he calls it 'zeal'—which made him persecute Christians (Phil. iii. 6) before his conversion, but love them and yearn for them afterwards (2 Cor. xi. 2) He felt tortured when his converts lapsed into sin or mistakes, and was flooded with thankful joy

when they repented, or took his advice, or did him a kindness. And this same zeal kept him moving restlessly in his missionary work over Palestine, a large part of Asia Minor, Macedonia, and Greece; it made him anxious to visit Rome (Acts xix. 21, Rom. i. 15), and even Spain (see p. 256 f.).

And beside fitting him to work for others, his temperament enabled him to see visions, and to fall into mystic raptures. Instances of the former are related in the *Acts* (ix 3–6, xvi. 9, xviii 9 f., xxiii. 11, xxvii 23, and cf xvi 6 f., xx. 22 f.). The latter he describes himself in 2 Cor xii. 1–4, adding that the 'stake in the flesh' was sent to him to prevent him from being over-elated by the greatness of the revelation. He also claims in an unusual degree the power, possessed by many of the early Christians, of speaking with 'tongues' (1 Cor. xiv 18); and, though he does not actually say so, he no doubt possessed the gift, which he ranked higher than tongues, of ecstatic 'prophecy' (see 1 Cor. xiii. 2, Acts xiii. 1). Apart from these particular instances, his 'zeal' can be felt in his letters, notably in 1, 2 *Corinthians* and *Galatians*, and seen in his literary style,—rebuke, tender or stern, white-hot indignation, irony, pathos, a love which he compares with that of a father, a mother, a nurse, a tact which shrinks from wounding, and yet a strength which is willing, when need be, to wound in order to heal.

Such was the tumultuous complexity of the man whose life-work we are to study. It was the Spirit of God that made him what he became; but as always, He used the man's natural human temperament for His divine purposes; His strength was perfected in what might otherwise have been weakness.

3. TRAINING AND ENVIRONMENT. But St Paul was complex not only on the emotional but also on the intellectual side of his nature. Circumstances printed their mark upon him 'in letters of Hebrew and Greek and Latin.' Each of these must be noted.

(a) *Hebrew.* He was first and foremost 'a Hebrew sprung from Hebrews' (Phil. iii. 5); he was glad to claim descent from Abraham, through Israel (i.e. Jacob), and through the tribe of Benjamin in particular (*ib.*, 2 Cor. xi. 22). Possibly his name Saul (*Shā'ūl*) was given him by his parents in memory of the first king of Israel, the Benjamite warrior chief. Although he was a Jew of the Dispersion, having been born at Tarsus in Cilicia, and spoke Greek, he was not immersed in non-Jewish thoughts and interests. He preserved, until his conversion, the strictly orthodox, intolerant attitude of a Pharisee (Phil. iii. 5; cf. Acts xxiii. 6, xxvi. 5); he writes 'I advanced in Judaism [i e. the Jewish religion and rules of life] beyond many of mine own age in my race, being an exceedingly zealous follower of my ancestral traditions' (Gal. i 14). Further facts, on which his letters are silent, are reported in the *Acts*. He declared to the angry mob in Jerusalem, speaking to them in 'Hebrew,' i e. their native Aramaic, that he had been 'brought up in this city at the feet[1] of Gamaliel' (Acts xxii. 3). How long he was under the instruction of this well-known rabbi is not stated; 'brought up' implies that he spent most of his youth, perhaps since his 13th year, in Jerusalem. But whether his stay in the capital was long or short, it only carried on and deepened the

[1] The scene recalls Lk. ii. 46. Cf. Taylor, *Sayings of the Jewish Fathers*, p. 14, on Aboth i 4, 'Let thy house be a meeting-house for the wise, and powder thyself in the dust of their feet.'

impressions which he must have received from his home training; from infancy he must have breathed a Jewish atmosphere, first in his father's house, and then in the synagogue at Tarsus where he received the more systematic instruction in the Scriptures, especially the Law, which was given to every Jewish child[1]. And he declared to the same mob (Acts xxii. 4 f.) and to Agrippa (xxvi. 10–12) that his persecutions of the Christians were waged from Jerusalem with the authority of the Sanhedrin.

Thus his Jewish training, acting upon his highly strung temperament, produced in him instincts and a cast of mind that were Jewish with a peculiar intensity. And these could not suddenly disappear when he became a follower of Jesus. His energies were turned in a new direction by the driving power of a new motive, but the inborn Jewish elements were never obliterated or swamped[2]. This can be seen in his continued love for, and pride in, his race (Rom ix. 1–5, x. 1 f., xi. 1 f., 12, 15, 24, 28, 2 Cor. xi. 22, Phil. iii 5), in his use of Jewish *haggada*, i e. imaginative or legendary stories about Old Testament characters and events[3], and in certain aspects of his beliefs and doctrines (see pp. 268–275).

(*b*) *Greek* But born where he was he could not entirely escape the influence of Greek thought, literature, and life given to Cilicia by the victories of Alexander and the rule of his successors the Seleucids[4]. Long before

---

[1] See art 'Synagogue' in Hastings' *DB* iv. 642. Schurer, *Hist. of the Jewish People*, II ii 44–89

[2] See Sanday and Headlam, *Romans*, Preface, pp. vi, vii.

[3] See Thackeray, *The Relation of St Paul to Contemporary Jewish Thought*

[4] The dynasty of the family of Seleucus, one of Alexander's three great generals.

the age of 13 his pagan surroundings must have exercised some effect upon his child-consciousness, however strict and careful his home training might be Tarsus, the capital of Cilicia, was an important centre of commerce, and the seat of a celebrated university, hardly inferior to those of Athens and Alexandria. In Acts xxi. 39 it is related that in speaking (in Greek) to the chiliarch who rescued him from the mob he claimed to be 'a Jew, a Tarsian of Cilicia, a citizen of a distinguished city[1].' Ramsay takes this to mean that he had received the honour of full citizenship, and no doubt his father and perhaps his grandfather before him, they were more than merely inhabitants of Tarsus. If this is the meaning of the expression, they may have received this distinction from one of the Seleucid rulers who shewed considerable favour to the Jewish colonists[2]. The Greek which he wrote was such as a Hellenist could learn by hearing the language spoken around him, and by constant study of the Greek Old Testament. That he was a student at the Tarsus university is quite improbable; not only would his strict Jewish parents be very unlikely to allow it, but his Greek style would have been less Hebraic if he had attended lectures on Greek rhetoric and composition, though some think that the style and complexion of his exposition and arguments shew traces of Greek method[3]. But if he did not formally receive a Greek education, he could not escape the more subtle, but none the less penetrating, influence of Greek atmosphere, and that not only in Cilicia but

[1] R V 'A Jew of Tarsus' is not a strict rendering
[2] See Schurer, *op cit* II 11. 270–6
[3] See Canon E. L. Hicks (now Bishop of Lincoln), *Studia Biblica*, iv. 1–14.

even in Judaea[1] His knowledge of Greek thought was gained 'partly by assimilation of the knowledge which floated on the surface of a more or less educated society and became insensibly the property of all its members[2].' He made use in his metaphors of the life of Greek cities, the stadium, the market-place, the temples. He was probably acquainted with Alexandrian Jewish thought in Philo and the book of *Wisdom*. He knew how fascinating, and yet how unsatisfying, Greek 'wisdom' was (1 Cor 1. 21–25, ii. 1–8, iii. 18 f., 2 Cor. i. 12, Col. ii. 23) He knew something of the angel-worshipping asceticism affected by Jews in Colossae and the neighbourhood (see p 206); and he had seen with his own eyes the terrible sins of paganism and the degradations of idolatry (Rom i. 18–32) Lastly he was acquainted with the aspirations and methods of the Mysteries, some of the vocabulary of which he adopted, and adapted to Christian use (see pp 305–7).

(c) *Roman* The rule of Alexander and the Seleucids was followed by the rule of Rome, with its great provincial system controlled by the central authority in Rome itself. A Jew by birth and training, and a Hellenist by environment, St Paul was also a Roman citizen (Acts xvi. 37, xxii 25, 28). In *v.* 28 he declares that he was 'born' with this privilege, which implies that his father had already received it. He bore the Roman name Paulus, as well as the Hebrew name Saul. It was in virtue of this coveted distinction, which the chiliarch in Jerusalem had gained only by a large payment (*v* 27), that he could appeal to Caesar (xxv. 11). It gave him a standing and prestige wherever he went, so that when

---

1 Conybeare in Hastings' *DB*. ii. 262.
2 Ramsay in Hastings' *DB*. Extra Vol. 150.

he came into contact with Roman officials—occasions which seem to be noticed with special attention by St Luke—he usually received friendly treatment. And it may well have exercised, together with his Tarsian citizenship, an influence upon his mind, which, in spite of his zealous Pharisaism, was moulding his ideas, and making it easier for him, when the crisis of his conversion came, to open his arms to Gentiles, and to fight with all his energy for their inclusion in the Christian Church Further, his conception of the Church must have owed something to his citizenship (Phil. iii. 20); the splendid unity of the Empire under the sway of Caesar doubtless contributed to his picture of the one Church, united under Christ its Head, each member of the Body performing its functions for the good of the whole (Rom. xii. 4 f., 1 Cor xii. 12–27, Col. i. 18, ii. 19, Eph. i. 22 f , iv. 12, 15, v 30)

St Paul thus combining in one person Jew, Greek, and Roman, was fitted by natural endowment to be the champion of the religion which, born in Palestine, was destined to conquer the Roman empire.

CHAPTER II

CLASSES OF CHRISTIAN CONVERTS

St Paul's conversion and missionary activity cannot be rightly understood without a reference to the various classes of people to whom Christianity came. Six classes can be distinguished, three of them Jewish and three Gentile.

1. ORTHODOX HEBREWS. These would mostly be found in Palestine, especially in and near Jerusalem

They were Aramaic-speaking Jews who had never settled abroad, and in most cases had never travelled to a foreign country. They were under the ecclesiastical control of the priests, and the moral influence of the Scribes and Pharisees.

2. ORTHODOX HELLENISTS. These were Jews who had settled abroad—in many cases their families had lived in foreign countries for generations—and spoke Greek. They were often loyal and patriotic citizens of the country of their adoption, much as a modern Jew can be a loyal Englishman or American. But in religious matters they kept themselves, as for example the youthful Saul and his parents, strictly separate from the surrounding paganism. Continuous opposition and protest tended to create in them a spirit of narrowness, sometimes of moody bigotry. It was when they returned, as they often did, to Jerusalem, that they felt themselves to be in their true atmosphere, and all the more zealous for their religion for having seen what they felt to be the degrading influences of paganism.

3 LIBERAL HELLENISTS. Many foreign Jews did not preserve this spirit of protest. They opened their minds freely to much that was good in Greek life, its art and literature and philosophy. They did not renounce their loyalty to the God of their fathers, but they sat loosely to the rules and ordinances of the Jewish law and scribal tradition. Some of them, especially in Alexandria, went so far as to interpret the Old Testament entirely in an allegorical and spiritual sense, so that they renounced the practice of circumcision and the observance of the Jewish festivals[1].

[1] Josephus, *Ant.* xx. 11 4. Philo, *De Migr. Abrah*, ed. Cohn-Wendl. 11. 285 ff.

4. PROSELYTES These were Gentiles who were converted to Judaism, and entered into membership of the Jewish Church by circumcision. They came to Jerusalem for the festivals, and were allowed to worship in the Court of the Gentiles.

5. GENTILES MORE OR LESS FAVOURABLE TO JUDAISM. In the welter of idolatry, mysteries, magic, superstitions, and philosophies of the pagan world many high-minded Gentiles were strongly attracted by the pure monotheism and moral life of the little colonies of Jews in their midst The latter looked upon them with sympathy, and hoped to convert them into proselytes. Of late years the term 'God-fearers[1],' which occurs in Acts x. 2, 22, 35, xiii 16, 26, has been employed to designate them. But it must not be taken to imply that they formed in any sense a recognised body Their appreciation of Judaism, either liberal or orthodox, must have varied greatly, from mere interest and enquiry to the state of mind which would lead them to become actual proselytes.

6. GENTILES WITH NO LEANINGS TO JUDAISM, many of whom 'worked all uncleanness with eagerness' (Eph. iv. 19, cf Rom. i. 21–32, 1 Cor. vi. 9–11, Col iii. 5–7), and worshipped 'gods many and lords many' (1 Cor. viii. 5), or none at all.

To all these six classes came the Gospel of Jesus Christ, with its message that Jesus the Galilean, who had been crucified, had risen from the dead, and was the Messiah—the Christ—expected by the Jews, and would very soon come from heaven to inaugurate the

---

[1] φοβούμενοι τὸν θεόν Other expressions occur σεβόμενος τὸν θεόν (xvi. 14, xviii. 7), σεβόμενοι (xiii 50, xvii. 4, 17), σεβόμενοι προσήλυτοι (xiii. 43).

divine Kingdom and to judge the world. It was natural that the last four classes should be the most ready to open their hearts to the new influence, but many converts were found also in the first two. Apart from the original apostles chosen by Jesus the most notable convert in the first class was James the Lord's brother, who became the head of the Church in Jerusalem. To the second class belonged St Paul himself, and Barnabas a Levite of Cyprus. The chief representatives of the third class were Stephen and Philip, who with four other Hellenists and one Gentile proselyte[1] were appointed to look after the provision of food for the poor widows of Hellenists in Jerusalem (Acts vi 1–6). Stephen receives special notice in the *Acts* because his martyrdom is the occasion of the introduction of Saul upon the scene.

The significance of this variety of classes will appear later. We must now study the wonderful phenomenon of Saul's transformation from an orthodox Hellenistic Jew to a liberal Hellenistic Christian.

CHAPTER III

ST PAUL'S CONVERSION

1 THE PREPARATION. In none of his letters does St Paul mention the martyrdom of Stephen[2]. But in Acts vii 58 it is related that the witnesses who stoned him[3]

1 St Luke nowhere calls them 'deacons,' a word which does not appear as a designation of a class till Phil 1. 1. Stephen and Philip soon took part in the apostles' 'ministry of the word' instead of the 'ministry of tables,' becoming energetic and successful Christian preachers.

2 In Acts xxii 20 St Luke introduces a mention of it in the apostle's speech to the mob.

3 It should be noticed that the Jews could execute in this case, although in the case of our Lord they were obliged to

'laid aside their cloaks at the feet of a young man called Saul.' It is not clear whether this means that Saul in some sense superintended the execution, or whether, more probably, it merely resulted from his youthful zeal in urging them on[1]. We can only guess what effect the martyr's death may have had on his thoughts. It is not at all impossible that his mind had already begun to be torn in two by inward debates as to whether his strict Pharisaism were after all the highest idea of life. Such a passage as Rom vii. 7–25 may reveal struggles against his lower nature which had already begun to trouble him before he became a Christian. The Mosaic Law did not, as a fact, lead him to the 'righteousness' for which he yearned; on the contrary, it only made it more difficult to attain. And the heroic martyrdom might well add a twinge of conscience, though as a rising young man, and a zealous Pharisee with a reputation to keep up, he had of course been in favour of the extreme penalty. 'Saul was consenting to his murder[2]' (Acts vii. 60). But if he felt compunction he tried to drown it in

hand the Accused over to the Roman procurator The event may have occurred when the procurator was absent, or when the office was momentarily vacant. Pilate was sent to Rome by Vitellius to answer to Tiberius for his conduct. Caius Caligula on his accession appointed Marullus procurator of Judaea. Meanwhile 'Vitellius sent Marcellus, a friend of his, to take care of the affairs of Judaea' (Joseph. *Ant.* XVIII. iv 2). He is not called 'procurator,' and until the arrival of Marullus the government of Judaea may have been in an unsettled state. If the date suggested (on p xviii) for Saul's conversion is correct, his persecution of the Christians continued for some two years after Stephen's death

[1] It need not imply 'that he was the principal witness against the accused' (McGiffert). The principal witness would have taken part in the act of stoning.

[2] St Luke's frequent word for the infliction of violent death upon innocent persons.

strenuous efforts against the Christians 'Beyond measure I persecuted the Church of God, and made havoc of it' (Gal. i. 13). A more detailed account is given in Acts ix. 1 f , xxii. 4 f., xxvi. 9–12: he begged warrants from the high priest that he might go with official authority to Damascus and other towns to require the synagogue authorities to hand over to him all who had embraced the new 'Way[1],' that he might bring them bound to Jerusalem.

It is important to remember that every Christian whom he arrested would be asked questions; some would make a formal defence before the local synagogue courts in Saul's hearing, or, like Stephen, before the great Sanhedrin at Jerusalem. In this way Saul was gaining a pretty accurate knowledge of what their beliefs were, and he was learning that an orthodox Jew was not the only person who could be filled with a flaming enthusiasm for what he believed to be right. These Christians were 'filled with the Spirit,' and he found it increasingly hard to resist the effects which they produced on him. He 'kicked against the goad-pricks' (Acts xxvi. 14) like a refractory ox, but that only hurt him more. And at last he 'could no longer resist the spiritual powers which were urging him into the furrows of the Christian mission-field[2].'

2. THE CRISIS which precipitated into a settled conviction the mixture of ideas floating in his mind is not described in any of his letters. A humble reticence seems to have kept him from putting on paper the experience

---

[1] This use of 'the Way,' as a distinctive term for Christianity, is confined to the *Acts* (ix. 2, xix. 9, 23, xxii. 4, xxiv. 14, 22; cf. xviii. 25).

[2] Gardner, *The Religious Experience of St Paul*, p. 28.

Acts ix.	Ch. xxii.	Ch. xxvi.
And while he was going it came to pass that he drew near to Damascus;	And it came to pass while I was going, and drawing near to Damascus,	As I was going to Damascus,
and suddenly there shone round him a light out of heaven,	about noon suddenly out of heaven there shone a great light round me,	at midday on the way I saw from heaven above the brightness of the sun a light shining round me *and them that were going with me, and when we had all fallen to the earth*
and having fallen upon the earth he heard a voice saying to him,	and I fell to the ground, and I heard a voice saying to me,	I heard a voice saying to me *in the Hebrew dialect*,
Saul, Saul, why persecutest thou Me?	Saul, Saul, why persecutest thou Me?	Saul, Saul, why persecutest thou Me? *it is hard for thee to kick against the goad-pricks*[1].
And he said, Who art Thou, Lord? and He [said], I am Jesus whom thou persecutest	And I answered, Who art Thou, Lord? and the Lord said to me, I am Jesus *the Nazarene* whom thou persecutest.	And I said, Who art Thou, Lord? and the Lord said, I am Jesus whom thou persecutest.

HIS CONVERSION

	Arise	But arise and stand upon thy feet.
But arise		
and enter the city	and go to Damascus,	
and it shall be told thee what thou must do.	and there it shall be told thee concerning all things that have been appointed for thee to do.	
And the men that journeyed with him stood dumb, hearing the voice but beholding none	And they who were with me beheld the light but heard not the voice of Him that was speaking to me	
And Saul arose from the earth, and when his eyes were opened he saw nothing; but leading him by the hand	And when I saw not from the glory of that light, being led by the hand of those who were with me	
they led him into Damascus.	I came to Damascus.	
[Here follows the account of Ananas]	[Here follows the account of Ananas]	[No account of Ananas follows; but God's commission to Saul to preach to the Gentiles agrees in substance, though not in language, with His words to Ananas about him in ch. ix. and in a brief form in ch. xxii]

[1] A common Greek proverbial expression

of the tempestuous moment when he stepped from bondage into liberty. In a single sentence he speaks of it as an act of God performed for His high purposes: 'It was God's pleasure, who set me apart since my mother's womb, and called me through His grace, to reveal His Son in me that I might proclaim the tidings of Him among the Gentiles' (Gal. i. 15 f). Ever since his birth he had been destined for his high office; then came the moment of his 'call,' followed by the lifetime in which it was not he that lived but Christ lived in him (ii. 20). He does not here explicitly refer to the crisis on the Damascus road; but that is probably his meaning, because the words stand in an account of himself which is intended to be chronological. The circumstances at the moment of the crisis are described in narrative (Acts ix. 3–19), and in two speeches attributed to him, delivered before the Jerusalem mob (xxii. 3–21) and before Agrippa, Bernice, and Festus (xxvi 2–23) as on pp 14, 15.

In the essential facts the three accounts agree, i e that Saul on the road to Damascus saw a light and heard a voice which made him fall to the ground St Luke's traditions also related that those who were with Saul heard, or saw, something, but he was not concerned to make the accounts agree in detail, 'hearing the voice' (ch. ix) and 'heard not the voice' (ch. xxii) are mutually contradictory. It is not the details that matter, but only the fact that Saul rose to his feet ready to obey and not to oppose Jesus the Messiah. The remainder of the story is omitted in ch. xxvi , but the other accounts relate, again with many differences of detail, that Ananias, a Christian in Damascus, visited him, restored his sight, and baptized him. In ch. ix. only, he is related to have gone to him in obedience to a vision in which he was told that Saul had been prepared by a vision for his coming. During the period of his blindness, three days (ix 9), Saul must have pondered quietly and deeply about the meaning of it all; and the restoration of his eyesight was the physical counterpart of the spiritual illumination which flooded his soul. Whereas he was blind, now he saw.

CHAPTER IV

ST PAUL'S MOVEMENTS AFTER HIS CONVERSION

1. ARABIA AND DAMASCUS. The accounts given by the apostle and by St Luke are as follows.

Gal 1. 16 b, 17	Acts ix 19 b, 20
Immediately I conferred not with flesh and blood; neither went I up to Jerusalem to them who were apostles before me But I went away into Arabia, and again I returned to Damascus.	And he was certain days with the disciples who were at Damascus. And immediately in the synagogues he proclaimed Jesus that He is the Son of God.

Wishing to vindicate his claim to a divinely given apostleship, St Paul assures the Galatians that he made no attempt to gain from the apostles at Jerusalem any authorisation, guidance, or teaching; and his movements prove it. Whether the stay in Arabia was long or short, St Luke does not allow for it. But a marked characteristic of his writings is his habit of compressing a series of events in order to bring a particular fact or consideration into prominence. He is concerned only to shew the radical effects of Saul's conversion: he preached Jesus in the very town whither he had gone to arrest the Christians. Anyone who wishes to harmonize the two accounts must suppose that the visit to Arabia occurred after the 'certain days' spent with the disciples, and before his preaching 'immediately' began.

What St Paul means by Arabia has received different explanations. (*a*) Lightfoot[1] and others have thought that he means that part of Arabia in which Mt Sinai stands, because the name occurs with that meaning in Gal. iv. 25 He went for a solemn season of communing with God in the place where the Law was given, before emerging to preach that men have been released from that Law by Christ. (*b*) But the meaning, and text, of Gal. iv. 25 are both doubtful, and even if that verse refers to the Sinaitic part of Arabia, there was nothing to prevent the apostle from mentioning, in an earlier passage, a brief move to another part. It is probable that the stay in Arabia was a minor episode in his life. For his special purpose it was necessary to record to the Galatians his every movement, but to St Luke it was unimportant if not unknown. Damascus was at the time subject to Aretas the king of Arabia Petraea; 'and the natural interpretation is that a person describing incidents in Damascus means by Arabia the adjacent country on the East[2].'

2. HIS ESCAPE. Returning to Damascus he stayed there until three years had elapsed from his conversion (Gal. i. 18); these are the 'many days' of Acts ix. 23. His preaching roused to fury the Jews in the town, and they plotted to murder him, guarding the gates day and night. In 2 Cor. xi. 32 St Paul says that 'the ethnarch of Aretas the king was guarding the city of the Damas-

---

[1] *Galatians*, p 88 f.
[2] Ramsay, *St Paul the Traveller and the Roman Citizen*, p. 380.

AFTER HIS CONVERSION

cenes to seize me.' The Jews had managed to persuade him to take their side against the troublesome preacher. But the troublesome preacher had won some staunch converts by that time, and they let him down by night through a window in the wall, hidden in a large basket. To such humiliating straits was the honoured young Pharisee of three years ago reduced! It was one of 'the things concerning his weakness' of which he boasted (2 Cor. xi 30).

3. HIS FIRST VISIT TO JERUSALEM, AND DEPARTURE TO TARSUS. The following accounts are to be compared:

Gal 1 18–24	Acts ix. 26–30
I went up to Jerusalem to make the acquaintance of Kephas, and abode with him fifteen days. But none other of the apostles did I see, except James the brother of the Lord (What I write unto you behold before God I lie not!) Then I came to the regions of Syria and Cilicia But I remained unknown by face to the churches of Judaea which were in Christ, only they heard that 'he who at one time persecuted us, now proclaims the faith of which he at one time made havoc,' and they glorified God in me.	And having arrived at Jerusalem he tried to join himself to the disciples And all feared him, not believing that he was a disciple But Barnabas took him, and brought him to the apostles, and related to them how on the road he had seen the Lord, and that He had spoken to him, and how in Damascus he had preached boldly in the name of Jesus. And he was with them going in and out at Jerusalem, preaching boldly in the name of the Lord, and he spake and disputed with the Hellenists, but they purposed to murder him. But when the brethren were aware of it, they brought him down to Caesarea, and sent him away to Tarsus

The difficulty of harmonizing the two accounts is here greater than before. St Luke's does not simply differ from the other in details; it conveys quite a different impression of the nature of the visit. It was not merely the spending of a fortnight in making the acquaintance of Kephas, but a definite attempt on Saul's part to get into touch with the Christian community in Jerusalem. St Luke simply desired to shew, as in the story of Damascus, the effects of Saul's conversion; he attached himself to the Christians, and preached, in the very Jewish capital where he had formerly been an arch-persecutor[1]. And from Jerusalem as from Damascus he was obliged to flee, his fellow Christians getting wind of the plot and hurrying him away[2].

Three of St Paul's statements should be noticed.

(a) 'None other of the apostles did I see, except James'; or it can be rendered '...did I see; I only saw James.' In the former case 'the apostles' include not only the Twelve but also other leading Christians in Jerusalem; in the latter the word seems to be confined to the Twelve. St Luke also may use the term in either sense[3], but his account does not tally with St Paul's. The latter says that he saw either one apostle or two, but no more; St Luke certainly gives the impression that he saw more than two[4].

(b) 'I remained unknown by face to the churches of Judaea.' St Luke's account so far agrees with this that it does not relate any preaching by St Paul in Judaea,

[1] Cf Acts xxii. 19, 20, where the same thought occurs.
[2] In Acts xxii 17, 18 it is related that the Lord warned him to escape while he was in a trance in the temple Ramsay (*St Paul the Traveller*, etc , pp. 60–63) needlessly places this vision in the *second* visit to Jerusalem.
[3] Though the narrower sense seems to be implied in viii 1.
[4] Ramsay, *op. cit.* p 381, explains that St Luke 'speaks loosely of "the apostles," meaning the governing body of the Church, without implying that they were all present in Jerusalem ' But this does not overcome the difficulty that, according to St Paul, there were only two present.

in the sense of the surrounding country as distinct from Jerusalem: 'going in and out at Jerusalem' seems to mean simply that he moved freely about within the city.

(c) 'I came to the regions of Syria and Cilicia.' The expression is probably intended to couple these into one district[1], and they were in fact united into one Roman province. Syria is probably mentioned the first as the more important[2]. Treating them as distinct, some have felt it a difficulty that St Paul names Syria first, since his work, in Antioch, the capital of Syria, followed his retirement to Tarsus, the capital of Cilicia. If by naming Syria first he implies that he travelled *via* Syria to Cilicia, i e that he went round by land (cf Acts xv. 41), he does not necessarily differ from St Luke, who relates that the brethren 'brought him *down* to Caesarea.' This might indeed mean 'brought him down to the coast' so that he could cross to Cilicia by boat; but 'down' can mean simply 'away from Jerusalem,' a journey to which was always thought of as a going *up*.

How long Saul remained at Tarsus depends upon the view taken of the chronology (see p. xiv f.)

CHAPTER V

ST PAUL AT ANTIOCH WITH BARNABAS

Acts xi 19–26

The martyrdom of Stephen was the beginning of a severe persecution which scattered the Jerusalem Christians, with the exception of the apostles (Acts viii. 1). But the wrath of man turned to God's praise, because

[1] τῆς Συρίας καὶ τῆς Κιλικίας. In ℵ and three minuscules the omission of the second article unites them more distinctly.
[2] So Lightfoot.

the Christian teaching was thus spread over a considerable area (v 4). Through Philip the Gospel reached Samaria (vv. 5–25), an Ethiopian eunuch near Gaza (vv. 26–39), and cities along the coast from Azotus to Caesarea (v 40). St Peter is related to have worked in Lydda (ix. 32–35), and Joppa (vv. 36–43), and above all he received into the Church a God-fearing Gentile, the centurion Cornelius (x. 1–xi. 18) Others had preached to Jews as far as Phoenicia, Cyprus, and Antioch (xi. 19). In the last town some Hellenist Christians had been preaching also to Gentiles[1] (v 20). The preaching would be, as usual, in the synagogues, to which Gentiles would be attracted to hear them. The number of converts increased rapidly, so that Antioch was becoming an important Christian centre (v. 21). Barnabas was sent from Jerusalem to see whether the movement was satisfactory and ought to be encouraged (v. 22) What he saw there delighted him (vv. 23 f.) He felt it to be of supreme importance to further it with all his power: so he determined to get the help of the strongest man he knew, and the best fitted for work in the great pagan city. Accordingly he went to Tarsus, and fetched Saul back (v 25) How he knew that he was at Tarsus is not told us· but he was probably one of the brethren who sent him off thither to escape the plot in Jerusalem[2]. For a full year they carried on a splendid work together in the corrupt and beautiful Syrian capital Their con-

[1] There is little doubt that Ἕλληνας ('Gentiles,' R V. 'Greeks') in ℵ^cAD* arm is the true reading, not Ἑλληνιστάς ('Hellenists') as in BD²EHLP St Luke evidently relates it as a new stage in the Church's development

[2] D has 'And hearing that Saul was at Tarsus he went forth seeking him; and when he fell in with him he exhorted him to come to Antioch.'

verts became popularly known as a sect or party by the nickname 'Christians[1],' the followers of Christos of whom they so often spoke (*v* 26)

The chief importance of the Antioch community lay in the fact that it was predominantly Gentile Many of the converts were no doubt circumcised proselytes: but as time went on an increasing number entered the Christian Church *without circumcision*.

CHAPTER VI

ST PAUL'S SECOND VISIT TO JERUSALEM

1. The following passages probably deal with the same visit:

Gal II 1–10	Acts xi. 27–30
Then after fourteen years I again went up to Jerusalem with Barnabas, taking with me also Titus And I went up according to a revelation And I communicated to them the gospel which I preach among the Gentiles, but privately to those who were recognised as important, lest perchance I was	And in those days there came down from Jerusalem prophets to Antioch[2] And one of them, by name Agabus, arose and signified through the Spirit that a great famine was about to take place over the whole [civilized] world, which took place under Claudius[3] And the disciples, in proportion to the prosperity

---

1 ℵ has Χρηστιανούς ('Chrēstians') from the adj. *chrēstos*, which was a not uncommon proper name Cf Suetonius, *Claud.* 25 'Judaeos impulsore Chresto assidue tumultuantes Roma expulit'

2 The next words in D are 'And there was great exultation And when *we* were gathered together [d has 'returned'] one of them, by name Agabus, spake signifying etc' (see p x) The writer of the sentence in this form may have known a tradition, or may simply have conjectured, that St Luke was already a Christian, and present at the scene.

3 This is supported by Josephus, *Ant* xx 11. 5, v. 2, and Orosius vii 6.

Gal ii 1–10	Acts xi 27–30
running or had run in vain ...For to me those who were recognised as important added nothing; but on the contrary.. James and Kephas and John who were recognised as pillars [of the Church] gave to me and Barnabas pledges of fellowship [in work], that we should go to the Gentiles, and they to those who were circumcised, only that we were to remember the poor, —which was the very thing that I was eager to do.	of each of them, determined to send [money] for ministration to the brethren which dwelt in Judaea, which also they did, sending it to the elders by the hand of Barnabas and Saul

St Paul, still continuing his line of argument to the Galatians (see p 17 f) to prove that his apostleship received no official authorisation from the leaders of the Church, is relating his *every movement* until the time that they fully and freely acknowledged the validity of his teaching to the Gentiles He therefore relates his next visit to Jerusalem, in the course of which he held, not a public or official consultation, but merely some private conversations with the leading spirits, to find out whether they were in sympathy with the aims and methods of his work at Antioch. That they were, is proved by the joint scheme of work on which they agreed with him, so as to reach both Jews and Gentiles[1]. All that they asked of him was that he would remember the needs of the poor Jews. He was not only willing but anxious to do that, because he must already have realised that alms from Gentile churches would form a strong bond of

[1] Notice that this was intended to include *uncircumcised* Gentiles Circumcised proselytes had been among their converts from the first (Acts ii. 10), and one of them had actually been given a public office in the Church at Jerusalem (vi. 5).

union with the Jewish Christians, and would lessen the danger of the division of the Church into two parties.

St Luke's narrative gives the occasion which suggested this reference to almsgiving. St Paul's words 'I went up according to a revelation' can perhaps be explained as referring to the inspired prediction of Agabus. At any rate it was not owing to any command or request of the apostles.

How long Barnabas and Saul stayed in Jerusalem is not stated. Ramsay thinks that they were there some time, superintending the actual distribution of food. But this is hardly probable. The 'presbyters' to whom the money was taken were the proper officials for the purpose. It is not at least *required* by the statement in Acts xii. 25: 'Barnabas and Saul returned from Jerusalem when they had completed the ministration'

2. TITUS. One statement made by St Paul is omitted in the passage printed above: 'But not even Titus who was with me though he was a Gentile was compelled to be circumcised. But on account of false brethren brought in secretly, who came in secretly to spy out our liberty which we have in Christ Jesus, that they might enslave us—to whom not even for an hour did we yield in obedience, that the truth of the Gospel might abide with you ' In the last part ('But on account of etc.') St Paul in his indignant excitement breaks off in the middle of a sentence, and starts a fresh one ('to whom etc'), so that it is impossible to determine what he originally intended to say. But it is probable that knowing the true character of the opposition of the Judaizers who had come to Antioch ('on account of the false brethren') he resolutely opposed a suggestion made in Jerusalem that, whatever he might teach in Gentile countries, he should

26   THE LIFE OF ST PAUL   [CH.

at least circumcise his Gentile companion Titus if he wished to take him about with him in Palestine. To lay the emphasis on 'compelled,' as though Titus was circumcised voluntarily, but not by compulsion, is possible but unnecessary[1].

3. ANOTHER VIEW OF GAL. II 1–10. Many writers, notably Lightfoot, think that the Jerusalem visit of Gal. ii. 1–10 was not the famine visit, but the visit to attend the Apostolic Council (Acts xv. 6–29)[2], which occurred later than St Paul's first evangelizing journey to the churches of Galatia. (1) It is thought that his private consultation with the leading Christians was a preliminary to the public conference. But for this there is no sort of evidence. (2) St Luke, it is said, does not mention that St Peter and James the Lord's brother were present at Jerusalem on the occasion of the famine. But neither does he say anything to make it clear that they were absent. He expressly states that the apostles did not flee from the city when persecution scattered the rest of the Christians (viii. 1); that St Peter and St John, after their brief visit to Samaria, returned to Jerusalem (viii. 25); and that St Peter returned to Jerusalem after his visit to Cornelius (xi. 2) 'James and the brethren' were still in Jerusalem when St Peter escaped from prison· and he, after appearing at the house of Mary the mother of Mark, 'went to another place' (xii. 17), which, according to the natural interpretation of the words, means 'another place, or house,

---

1 It becomes, indeed, necessary if οἷς οὐδέ ('to whom not even') be omitted with D d c Tert, and one or two other Latin authorities. But the reading is improbable.

2 McGiffert, *History of Christianity in the Apostolic Age*, p. 171, attempts a solution of the problem by assuming that Acts xi. and xv. both refer to the same event.

in the city.' Cf iv. 31, where 'place' seems to mean 'house.' But even if it means another city, the length of his absence is not stated, nor the time at which Agrippa's persecution occurred No other movements of the apostles are related (3) Barnabas and Saul, it is pointed out, brought the famine contribution not to the apostles but to the elders. But this need not imply that the apostles were absent If 'elders' is not used loosely for all the leading Christians, including the apostles, it must be remembered that the latter had expressly refused to spend their time in 'serving tables' (vi. 2), and had appointed others for the purpose· and the 'elders,' as the local officials, would naturally carry out the distribution.

An important consideration in favour of the famine visit may be added St Paul, as already said, is relating to the Galatians his *every movement* till the time when the leading Christians in Jerusalem fully and freely recognised his claim for the Gentiles If he took the trouble to mention an incidental visit to Arabia, where he could not have met any apostles, it would be extraordinary if he had omitted a visit to Jerusalem, and scarcely less strange if he had passed over the whole of his first missionary tour.

There is really nothing to connect the visit of Gal. ii. 1-10 with the Council[1]. When Barnabas and Saul brought the alms to the city, they had already been

[1] Gal. ii 5, 'that the truth of the Gospel might continue with *you*' need not mean that the Gospel had by that time been preached in Galatia St Paul is thinking of the blessings which had, by the time that he wrote, accrued to the Galatians from the firmness which he shewed at this juncture. He could have written the same words to any of his Gentile converts at any period of his life.

converting and receiving into the Church uncircumcised Gentiles[1]. And St Peter's account of his own action with regard to Cornelius had already gone far in convincing the leading Jerusalem Christians that an uncircumcised Christian was not quite impossible (Acts xi. 1–18) When Barnabas and Saul came, therefore, James, Kephas, and John expressed, in a private conversation, their willingness to agree with their methods, and to recognise them as missionaries[2] to the Gentiles,— i.e. all Gentiles, not only circumcised proselytes. Accordingly on their first missionary tour, which now follows, they preached to and converted Gentiles in large numbers, to the indignation of the Jews.

CHAPTER VII

THE DEDICATION OF BARNABAS AND SAUL TO WIDER WORK

Acts xiii 1–3

His right to preach to, and receive into the Church, uncircumcised Gentiles having now been privately acknowledged by the leading Christians in Jerusalem, St Paul's restless energy could not long be content to remain at Antioch: he must strike further afield. And Barnabas was of one mind with him. St Luke, looking back at it, realised that it was the work to which the Holy Spirit had called them. He relates that while some of the Christian prophets and teachers in Antioch (among

[1] Titus for example, whether he was circumcised or not after his reception into the Christian Church, was certainly not circumcised before it

[2] It is not said that they recognised St Paul as an 'apostle'; he claimed that authority himself as having been given him 'through Jesus Christ, and God the Father' (Gal. 1 1).

whom he reckons Barnabas and Saul) were engaged in fasting and religious devotions, perhaps at some special season, one of the prophets, under the influence of spiritual ecstasy, declared ('the Holy Spirit said') that the two missionaries were to be set apart for their special work. Accordingly after another interval 'when they had fasted and prayed, and laid their hands on them, they sent them away.' The subject of the verbs may be the particular prophets and teachers named (Symeon called Niger, Lucius the Cyrenaean, and Manaen who had been brought up with Herod the tetrarch), or the Christians in general. This is not equivalent to what we now call ordination. Saul and Barnabas had been filled with the divine Spirit long before, and had already done important missionary work. But they were formally committed by the laying on of hands to be the Church's representatives in the larger work which lay before them. In *v.* 4 St Luke goes on to say, with solemn emphasis, that they were 'sent forth by the Holy Spirit.'

CHAPTER VIII

ST PAUL'S FIRST MISSIONARY TOUR

Acts xiii 4–xiv 28

1. It is customary to speak of the three missionary 'journeys', but 'tours' is a more suitable word. St Paul had already, according to the *Acts*, made two journeys to places where he preached, to Jerusalem from Damascus, and to Antioch from Tarsus. And in the course of the travels which he now undertook, he sometimes stayed in a place for a considerable time. St Luke does not seem to have thought of dividing his work formally

into three tours: notice the rapidity with which he passes from the second to the third (xviii. 22, 23). This was because he wished, not to construct a biography but to trace progress. Nor is there any indication that the apostle was officially sent in any given direction, or mapped out his route beforehand; he followed the divine impulse of the moment, and the divine guidance of circumstances. Hence some recent writers are inclined to discard the usual scheme of three tours, and prefer to divide the apostle's activity into two periods, before and after the Council at Jerusalem, in which he worked in two main mission spheres: (1) the 'regions of Syria and Cilicia' (Gal. 1 21) with Antioch and Tarsus as the centres, and with Barnabas as his principal companion, (2) the larger area of Asia Minor, Macedonia, and Achaia, accompanied chiefly by Silas and Timotheus. Three tours, however, are distinguished in this volume as a matter of convenience, though they must not be regarded as of importance for the understanding of St Paul's work.

2. CYPRUS. xiii. 4–12. Attended by their young companion John Mark, a relation[1] of Barnabas (Col. iv. 10) whom they had brought back from Jerusalem (Acts xii. 25), they went from Antioch westward some dozen miles to the coast, to the harbour **Seleucia**,—probably in the spring when the sailing season began. Thence they took ship to **Salamis**, on the east of the island of Cyprus. The reason for this move no doubt was that Cyprus was Barnabas' native place (iv. 36).

[1] Probably not 'sister's son' (A V) but 'cousin.' How close the relationship was is not known. He seems to have acted simply as their attendant. It is not stated that he was filled with the Spirit, or that he was commissioned by the laying on of hands.

VIII] THE FIRST MISSIONARY TOUR 31

Although St Paul was the apostle to the Gentiles, yet he loved his own nation, and made a regular practice of preaching, as far as possible, to Jews first. To ignore them, and to speak exclusively to Gentiles would have been to cut himself off from the possibility of influencing Jews, and to a large extent those Gentiles who were favourable to Judaism and offered the most promising material for his work. There were probably several Jewish communities in the island: and they preached in the synagogues, where, however, Gentiles must frequently have been present. In this way they moved through the island about 50 miles to **Paphos** on the S.W. coast. Here St Luke relates an incident which he probably felt to be of importance. The Roman governor of the island was in the town, a proconsul named Sergius Paulus[1], whom St Luke describes as 'a sensible man,' because of his readiness to listen to the missionaries They had no doubt preached, as usual, in the synagogue. and the proconsul, hearing of them, may have taken them to be teachers of rhetoric or philosophy such as used to travel about to lecture in the important towns of the Empire At any rate he commanded them to come and speak to him about the word of God. But a certain man who was present with him disputed what they said, and tried hard to prevent him from being convinced[2]. [Who this opponent was is very uncertain. In *v.* 6 he is described as 'a certain magian, a Jewish false prophet, whose name was Barjesus.' But in *v* 8 it is said 'But Elymas the magian (for so is his name inter-

[1] Perhaps the same as 'the proconsul Paulus' named, unfortunately without a date, in an inscription found at Soloi in the north of the island

[2] DE syr[hcl] add 'because he was listening to them with pleasure.'

preted) withstood them.' Other forms of both names occur in some MSS and early writers[1]. Some think that the accounts of two different magians have been confused. The whole passage is obscure, especially the name Elymas and the parenthesis attached to it.] But 'Saul who is also called Paul,' filled with the Spirit, gazed at him, and rebuked him vehemently, addressing him as 'son of the devil'—perhaps drawing a contrast with his name Bar-jesus ('son of Jesus')—and telling him that he would be blind for a time. This came to pass immediately, and he needed someone to lead him by the hand. Thus Saul's blindness on the Damascus road repeated itself in the case of his opponent. The proconsul was so much struck by the catastrophe that he was convinced of the truth of the Christian teaching.

It is interesting to notice that whereas till this point St Luke has always named Barnabas first, or pictured him as more important than Saul (Acts ix. 27, xi. 25, 30, xii. 25, xiii. 1, 2, 7), from now onwards their positions are reversed[2]. Marking this new departure, St Luke at this point introduces the Roman name for the first time: *Sha'ul* who is also called *Paulus*. Ramsay suggests that at this first preaching of the Gospel to a representative of the Roman government, Saul made the proconsul aware of his Roman citizenship, and took, instead of Barnabas, the leading position to which that dignity entitled him. That the apostle took his Roman name at this time from Sergius Paulus, as Jerome suggested,

---

[1] D Βαριησουάν (d—suam), syr[pesh] Barshūma, vulg[codd] Barieu, Hier. Berieu, Lucif Bariesuban, D 'Ετοιμᾶς, Lucif. Etoemus.

[2] With two exceptions, xiv. 14 and xv. 12; see pp. 38 and 43.

is very improbable. He had been a Roman citizen, and therefore probably had borne his Roman *cognomen*, all his life. Perhaps Paulus was the name of the official who had given the *civitas* to his family.

3. PASSAGE THROUGH PAMPHYLIA xiii. 13, 14 a. The length of time spent in Paphos is not stated. 'Paul's party,' as St Luke here calls them, next took ship for the mainland of Asia Minor. Having landed, no doubt at Attalia, though that is not stated, they reached **Perga** in the Roman province of Pamphylia. Here, for some unexplained reason, John Mark suddenly deserted them, and returned to Jerusalem. Ramsay ingeniously suggests that St Paul intended to stay and preach in and around Perga; but that in the enervating climate of Pamphylia, facing southward and sheltered by the high ground of the Taurus range, he suffered from a severe attack of his recurrent illness, and felt obliged to strike northward at once to reach higher ground and better air; and that John Mark did not approve of this change of plan, and so went home. St Luke's expression, however, that Mark 'went not with them to the work' (xv. 38) hardly supports the idea that the northward journey was for the purpose of convalescence. The absence of any account of preaching at Perga does not necessarily mean that they left the place at once. If St Paul contracted the disease in a malarial region near Perga, it may not have made its appearance till Pisidian Antioch was reached (McGiffert). This town lay in Phrygia within the Roman province of Galatia. If his illness forced him to stay there awhile, his words in Gal. iv. 13 receive a good explanation, 'Ye know that because of an infirmity of the flesh I preached the Gospel unto you formerly[1].'

[1] On the last word see p 169.

4. PISIDIAN ANTIOCH[1]. xiii. 14 b–52. According to his usual custom St Paul went with Barnabas to the synagogue on the Sabbath. After the reading of the two lessons for the day from the Law and the Prophets, the rulers of the synagogue noticing some strangers in the congregation asked them to speak. St Luke gives *St Paul's sermon*. He sketches (as Stephen had done, vii. 2–50) the history of Israel, but he begins with the Exodus. God 'brought up[2]' (R.V. exalted) the people, i.e. nourished them when they were in Egypt, and 'bore them as a nursing father[2]' in the wilderness, and gave them the land of Canaan[3]. He gave them judges till

[1] The best MSS (אABC) at v. 14 have τὴν Πισιδίαν, an adjective DE etc. have τῆς Πισιδίας 'Gradually that part of Phrygia, which was included in the province of Galatia and separated from the great mass of Phrygia (which was part of the province of Asia), was merged in Pisidia' (Ramsay in Hastings' *DB* i 104) Hence the name Pisidian Antioch afterwards gave place to the name Antioch of Pisidia.

[2] The two verbs are interesting The former, ὕψωσεν, would not have this meaning in classical Greek, but it occurs four or five times in the LXX, including Is. i. 2 to which St Paul seems to refer. The latter, ἐτροφοφόρησεν, occurs only twice in the LXX, 2 Mac. vii 27 (of a mother), and Deut 1 31 (of God as a Father) to which, again, St Paul seems to refer. This is the reading in AC*E and several minuscules, d e syr^pesh memph. sah arm aeth But in אBC²DHLP and the mass of minuscules, vulg. syr^hcl marg (which is strong evidence) it is ἐτροποφόρησεν, a commoner word meaning 'bore with their behaviour' which occurs nowhere in the LXX, except as a variant in B* for τροφοφορήσει in Deut. 1. 31. But though the weight of the MS evidence is against it, the reading ἐτροφοφόρησεν can claim a possible support of a different kind In later times, and very possibly in St Paul's day, Deut. i. and Is. 1 were lections appointed for the same day in the synagogue services, and St Paul is perhaps referring to the two lections which had just been read.

[3] The best MSS have 'He gave them their land about 450 years And after this etc.' DE and others place 'And after this' before 'He gave them etc ,' which is more in accordance with the history as given in the Old Testament.

VIII] THE FIRST MISSIONARY TOUR 35

Samuel, then Saul the first king, and then David. At the mention of David he passes suddenly to the Son of David, the Saviour Jesus heralded by John the Baptist. At this point he indicates (*v.* 26) the mixed audience whom he was addressing in the synagogue: (1) Children of the stock of Abraham, i.e. Jews, (2) those among you that are fearers of God, i.e. devout Gentiles. He goes on to say that the Jews in Jerusalem, not understanding their own Scriptures, demanded from Pilate[1] the death of Jesus. They took Him down from the tree, and laid Him in a tomb[2]. But God raised Him from the dead, and He was seen by many who are now witnessing to the fact. The Resurrection is the fulfilment of promises made in the Old Testament to David, but which could not find their true fulfilment in David himself[3]. Through this Jesus can be gained remission of sins, and that justification from sin[4] which the Mosaic Law cannot give. He ended with a warning to them, drawn from Habak. i. 5, not to despise the divine work which had been done.

On the conclusion of the sermon, as they went out, the congregation begged to hear the same wonderful message on the next Sabbath, and Jews and proselytes in considerable numbers followed the two missionaries to hear some more of their teaching. During the week rumours of the sermon got about; and on the next Sabbath the synagogue was crowded with a congregation

[1] This suggests that they are not St Paul's actual words, since the majority of a Galatian audience would probably have no idea who Pilate was.
[2] In the Gospels it was not the hostile Jews who took Him down and buried Him, but the Lord's disciple Joseph of Arimathea.
[3] Cf the similar argument in St Peter's sermon, ii. 22–35.
[4] The construction 'to be justified from ($\dot{a}\pi\acute{o}$)' recurs only in Rom. vi. 7.

of which the large majority must have been Gentiles, 'almost the whole city.' This made the Jews jealous of St Paul's popularity, and they opposed him angrily in public. St Paul and Barnabas were roused to an outburst of indignation, and they declared that they would now, for the first time, confine their preaching to the Gentiles in the city, i.e. they would preach elsewhere than in the synagogue[1]. Cf. St Paul's similar action at Corinth (xviii. 6) and Ephesus (xix. 9). The Gentiles were delighted, and many throughout the whole region became believers. But the Jews stirred up the wealthy ladies (who took a more prominent part in Greek and Roman than in Jewish life, cf. xvii. 4, 12), and the local officials, to persecute the apostles, and drove them out of the place[2]. They 'shook off the dust of their feet against them,' and went away 50 miles S.E. to **Iconium**.

5. ICONIUM. xiv. 1–7. The apostles' indignant action at Antioch did not mean a cessation of their regular habit of preaching to Jews first; they at once taught in the synagogue at Iconium, gaining both Jews and Gentiles to the Christian faith. But there were also Jews who remained unconvinced, and these stirred up the Gentiles against them. (In *v.* 3 it is stated parenthetically that the apostles made a long stay there, preaching and working miracles[3].) Opinion in the town was sharply

---

[1] This does not mean that the apostle now preached for the first time to Gentiles; see p. 22 f.

[2] It is possible that this persecution included a beating with rods by the magistrates' lictors, which would be the first of the three beatings recorded by St Paul in 2 Cor xi. 25.

[3] The verse stands somewhat awkwardly in the middle of the description of Jewish hostility. Some think it is a later addition to the narrative, perhaps due to a marginal note. An early attempt was made to form a link after *v.* 2; D syr[hcl marg] add 'but the Lord quickly gave peace,' E 'but

VIII] THE FIRST MISSIONARY TOUR 37

divided; 'part held with the Jews and part with the apostles.' The former, at last, with the authorisation of the magistrates, made preparations to assault and stone them; but the plot leaked out, and they fled 'unto the cities of Lycaonia, **Lystra**, **Derbe**, and the neighbourhood; and there they were preaching[1].'

St Luke here follows local native usage in implying that Iconium was not in Lycaonia. *Officially* it had been united by the Romans with Lycaonia for administrative purposes. But since the days of Persian dominion it had been the frontier city of Phrygia, and the local native officials were different from those in the towns of Lycaonia proper. Thus the district in which Iconium stood was *popularly* called Phrygia, or Galatic Phrygia, because it was that part of Phrygia which was included in the Roman province of Galatia. The apostles now fled into Galatic Lycaonia (as distinct from Antiochian Lycaonia further East, governed by king Antiochus). Thus, although Lystra was only 18 miles distant, they came under a different jurisdiction, and entered upon a new sphere of work[2].

6. LYSTRA AND DERBE. xiv. 6–21 a. In *vv.* 6, 7 their work in the district generally is stated. Two incidents in Lystra are now described.

A man crippled from birth was healed by St Paul; and the native population thought that he and Barnabas were gods come down from heaven. St Paul took the

---

the Lord made peace,' thus dividing the time into two distinct periods of disturbance with an intervening period of peaceful and successful work
[1] D adds 'And the whole multitude was disturbed at the teaching; but Paul and Barnabas remained at Lystra'; and E similarly.
[2] Ramsay, *op. cit.* pp. 109–113.

lead, as always, in preaching, so they called him Hermes, the messenger of the Gods. Barnabas, who remained more passive, was for that very reason, according to oriental ideas, taken to be the superior, great Zeus himself[1]. The priest[2] of the local temple of Zeus was actually about to offer sacrifice in their honour; but the apostles[3] ran to the crowd, tearing their clothes at the thought of the blasphemy, and with difficulty persuaded them that they were ordinary mortals. St Luke relates that they exhorted them to turn from these pagan ideas and practices to the living God, 'who made heaven and earth and sea and all that is in them' (cf. Exod. xx. 11), who even though He allowed Gentiles in the past to make these mistakes, yet revealed something of what He was by His work in nature[4].

But the Jews in Antioch and Iconium, from whom they had fled, followed them over the Lycaonian border, stirred up the populace, and stoned St Paul (cf. 2 Cor. xi. 25, 'Once was I stoned'). They dragged him out of the city, and left him there, supposing him to be dead. But while his sorrowing Christian companions stood round him he revived enough to go back into the town, and next day moved on more than 20 miles to **Derbe**.

1 These gods in their Latin forms, Mercurius and Jupiter, were said to have wandered in Phrygia in human shape, and to have been given hospitality by Baucis and Philemon (Ovid, *Metam.* viii. 631 ff.)

2 D has 'priests'

3 St Luke's order of the names 'Barnabas and Paul' (v. 14) may have been due to the greater honour given by the priest to Barnabas (see p 32).

4 St Paul would not have spoken so to a Jewish synagogue audience, but as St Luke represents his words they are not unsuitable for simple-minded Gentiles. Somewhat similar language occurs in the speech at Athens (xvii. 24); and cf. Rom. i. 19 f., iii. 25.

What that walk must have been to him in his pain and weakness it is difficult to imagine. At Derbe he stayed long enough to convert many to Christianity.

7. THE RETURN JOURNEY. XIV. 21 b–28. They did not go further East and return to Antioch by the land route through the Cilician Gates and Tarsus, but, regardless of the perils through which they had passed, deliberately returned through **Lystra, Iconium,** and **Pisidian Antioch,** preaching in each city[1] and encouraging their recent converts to endure persecution. For the care of these Galatian churches 'having appointed [*or* elected] for them elders in each church praying with fastings they committed them to the Lord on whom they had believed.' Then they went down, through the Taurus range, to **Perga** in Pamphylia, where they delivered the Christian message which St Paul is not related to have preached there before (see p. 33). Lastly, having reached the port of **Attalia,** now mentioned for the first time, they took ship back to **Antioch** in Syria from which they had started on their tour. There they gave an account of all that they had done, or as St Luke truly puts it 'all that God had done with (i.e. in company with) them' (cf. xv. 4), 'and that He had opened to the Gentiles a door of faith.' At Antioch they stayed some time[2], resuming their previous pastoral work.

1 They perhaps avoided causing disturbance by confining themselves to private Christian assemblies.
2 As to the length of time see p. xviii f.

CHAPTER IX

THE APOSTOLIC COUNCIL AT JERUSALEM

1 THE EVENTS LEADING TO IT. (*a*) Acts xv. 1, 2 a. Their pastoral work at Antioch suffered an important interruption. The student should, at this point, read again what was said in ch II about the different classes of Christian converts Many of those who had been orthodox Hebrews or orthodox Hellenists still clung tenaciously to a Judaistic form of Christianity. That is to say they remained, in all outward respects, strict Jews, practising circumcision, and observing the festivals and other regulations of the Law. They differed from the Jew pure and simple, in believing that the Messiah expected by their nation was Jesus, who had died and risen, and would soon come to inaugurate the divine Kingdom and to judge the world. In a word, they were a Jewish sect marked by some new and peculiar beliefs; and they were admitted to membership in the sect by baptism in the name of Jesus. The sect was kept in existence by the addition, from time to time, of fresh converts—Jews and circumcised proselytes. Thus their conception of true religion was the Jewish religion (in which, of course, circumcision was a necessity) with some Christian beliefs and baptism superadded. On the other hand, in Antioch and elsewhere, largely owing to the activity of St Paul, many Gentiles had been received into the Christian Church by baptism *without circumcision*. Some of these Gentiles had been God-fearing sympathizers with Jewish monotheism and morals[1], but

[1] A notable instance of the God-fearing Gentile was the centurion Cornelius, whom St Peter, some time before, had

some had not, and were sheer pagans when they were converted to Christianity. This conflict of opinion between Jewish and non-Jewish Christians at last came to a head by the action of some of the former, who came from Jerusalem to Antioch and opposed the line taken by the apostles of the Gentiles[1] (xv. 1, 2 a).

(b) Gal. ii. 11–14[2]. But a further problem was beginning to make itself felt. The private agreement between St Paul and Barnabas on the one hand and Kephas and James on the other (vv. 7–9) involved the separation and mutual recognition of the two parties; and St Paul loyally observed his side of the agreement. (In Acts xxi 26 his action shewed that he repudiated the false charge brought against him of teaching Jews to abandon the Mosaic Law.) The difficult question now arose as to *social intercourse* If Jewish Christians were to eat meals with Gentile Christians, they might be given food which had been sacrificially offered in idol temples, from which they shrank as from dire pollution, while the Gentiles did not feel it to be pollution This matter, in turn, was brought to a head by the action of St Peter (Gal. ii. 11–14). He paid a visit to

received into the Church without previous circumcision (ch xi) But he had been treated as an exceptional case which had no bearing on the general principle It was exceptional because he and his family had visibly and undeniably received an outpouring of the Spirit *before baptism.*

[1] According to the view which places the writing of *Galatians* at this time (see pp 171–3) they extended their activities beyond Antioch, and tried to subvert St Paul's converts in the Galatian churches.

[2] Some (e g. Zahn, *Galatians*, p. 110 f , and Turner, Hastings' *DB* 1. 423 f), who identify the visit of Gal ii 1–10 with the Council visit, nevertheless feel the necessity of dating ii 11–14 before it.

Antioch, perhaps before St Paul and Barnabas returned from their first tour. And interpreting his private agreement with them in its full natural sense, he waived Jewish scruples and ate meals with Gentile Christians. But after St Paul's return, some emissaries from James took the stricter attitude; and St Peter suddenly became afraid of his own wide-mindedness, and refused further intercourse with the Gentile Christians. Other Jewish Christians in the place were led astray by his example, among them Barnabas who had so long and eagerly worked with St Paul among the Gentiles. St Paul realised that it was a critical moment for the Church, and boldly rebuked St Peter in public, i e. probably in a Church assembly. He took the line that he afterwards took in his epistles, that charity must be the supreme principle. The recognition of Jewish and Gentile Christians must be mutual. Gentiles must, at meals with Jews, respect Jewish scruples in the matter of food, but, he declared to St Peter, Jews, on their part, must not force those scruples upon Gentiles. 'If you, a Jew, have been willing to join with Gentiles in meals, why do you *compel* them to Judaize?' Why, that is, do you compel them to respect your scruples by abstaining from all possibility of taint from idol foods before you consent to have meals with them? They are new converts in all the joyful enthusiasm of Christian liberty, which you have yourself conceded to them. You ought to have been the one to shew some Christian charity and forbearance.

Thus on both these aspects of the problem, *circumcision* and *foods*, friction had reached a point when a definite public settlement was urgently needed. So the Church at Antioch, or perhaps the Judaizers from Jerusalem¹, 'determined that Paul and Barnabas and some others of them should go up to the apostles and elders to Jerusalem.' Escorted a little way by the Christians they travelled *via* Phoenicia and Samaria, spreading *en route* the good news of the conversion of Gentiles (Acts xv. 2 b, 3).

2. THE DEBATE. Acts xv. 4–18. The apostles and elders received them, and heard their report of 'all things that God had done (in company) with them' (cf. xiv. 27). But some Jewish Christians, Pharisees who had joined the Church, insisted on circumcision and obedience to the Law for all Gentile converts; and a keen debate was soon in progress.

St Luke relates the three points in the discussion which turned the scale in favour of Gentile freedom: (*a*) A speech by St Peter (*vv.* 7–11) in which he referred to the Cornelius incident, and asked why the Gentiles, if they had (as was undeniable) received the outpouring of the Spirit, should be burdened with the yoke of Jewish observances which the Jewish nation itself had found too heavy. (*b*) An account (*v.* 12)² by 'Barnabas and Paul³' of the miracles which God had wrought through them among the Gentiles. (*c*) A speech by James the Lord's brother, the president of the conference (*vv.* 13–21). He pointed out that Symeon's (i.e. Simon Peter's) action with regard to Cornelius was, after

1 The subject of the verb is not clear. It is made so in D syr[hcl marg] which read 'for Paul said strongly that they ought to remain as they were when they became believers; and those who came from Jerusalem commanded Paul and Barnabas and certain others to go up etc.'

2 At the beginning of *v.* 12 D syr[hcl] insert 'And the elders agreeing with the things spoken by Peter.'

3 Before the Jerusalem audience Barnabas was still the more important of the two (see p. 32).

all, in keeping with the words of Amos ix. 11, 12. (St Luke represents him as quoting the passage in accordance with the LXX, 'that the residue of men may seek the Lord,' which was more suitable to his purpose than the Hebrew, 'that they may possess the residue of Edom.') And then he pronounced his own opinion.

3. THE OPINION OF ST JAMES. Acts xv. 19–21. This consists of two distinct parts, corresponding with the double problem of *circumcision* and *foods* which had made the conference necessary. (*a*) With regard to the former, which was the primary matter, he decided (*v.* 19) *against the Judaizers*; Gentile Christians were not to be 'troubled' with it. (*b*) But widely spread in Gentile countries, 'in every city,' the Mosaic Law had for generations past been 'read in the synagogues every Sabbath' (*v.* 21); in other words St Paul's mission to the Gentiles had not been the only one, for it had been anticipated by the far older Jewish missions What, then, was to be the relation of Jew to Gentile? The former learnt from the Mosaic Law that distinctions of food were important for the preservation of ceremonial purity. Therefore, *for the sake of the Jews* supplementary injunctions must be added, bidding the Gentiles to abstain from the four things mentioned in *v.* 20. Both parts of this decision are embodied in the decrees in *vv.* 28, 29.

4. THE OFFICIAL ACTION. *vv.* 22–35. This decision having been reached, the Church at Jerusalem acted promptly. They selected as official representatives two of the most prominent of their number, Judas called Barsabbas and Silas, to accompany St Paul and Barnabas back to Antioch, and to carry with them a letter to the Gentiles in Antioch and in the whole Roman

province of Syria-Cilicia¹. The letter stated that the Judaizers who had come from Jerusalem to Antioch and troubled the Gentile Christians (see $v.$ 1) had not come with the authority of the Church; but that Judas and Silas were fully authorised, and they would endorse the contents of the letter by word of mouth. Then followed the injunctions which St James had proposed.

Arrived at Antioch the bearers duly delivered the letter, which naturally caused great delight. Judas and Silas spent some time there, giving much spiritual help by their preaching, and then the former returned to Jerusalem, and St Paul and Barnabas resumed their interrupted pastoral work. (In $v.$ 33 St Luke says that Silas as well as Judas returned, and yet in $v.$ 40 Silas is evidently still at Antioch, with no statement that he came back again from Jerusalem. The account has undergone a slight confusion².)

Such is St Luke's account of the crisis. Of one thing we may feel sure: had the Council arrived, as regards circumcision, at the opposite result and upheld the Judaizers, it would not have moved St Paul a hair's-breadth from his purpose. He would have continued his successful work among the Gentiles on the lines that he felt sure had been drawn for him by God. But the Christian Church would have been split into two parties even

1 In Acts xvi. 4 St Luke says that St Paul and Silas delivered the decrees even in Galatia. This was going beyond those addressed in the apostolic letter, and it is possible that St Luke received an erroneous tradition.

2 In accordance with CD and many minuscules, vulg^{clem} sah. arm. aeth v 34 is added in the A V, 'Notwithstanding it pleased Silas to abide there still,' to which D vulg^{clem} arm. further add 'and Judas went alone' These are glosses which rightly correct $v.$ 33.

more sharply defined than they continued to be in fact
—circumcised Christians and uncircumcised Christians.
In the long run the latter was bound in any case to
prevail, but it would have taken much longer for
the Judaizing party to dwindle and die out. As it was,
although St Paul was opposed for a time by Judaizers,
it was in defiance of, and not in accordance with, the
carefully considered decision of the first heads of the
Church.

But what was St Paul's attitude to the second part
of the apostolic decision—the four prohibitions laid on
the Gentile Christians? To understand that, we must
examine a rather complicated problem.

5. THE NATURE OF THE APOSTOLIC PROHIBITIONS.
Acts xv. 20, 29, cf. xxi. 25. The ordinary text[1], followed
in the English versions, contains *four* prohibitions:
(1) Things sacrificed[2] to idols (in *v.* 20 'the pollutions
of idols'). (2) Blood. (3) Things strangled[2]. (4) Fornication.

The first three are usually explained as referring to
food[3]. If Jew and Gentile were to be Christians together
and join in meals, the latter must avoid eating things
from which the Jew shrank with a religious abhorrence.
The prohibitions were in that case of the nature of a
compromise.

But some have felt difficulties in the way of this interpretation: (*a*) The mention of fornication is thought to

---

[1] Uncials (except D), vulg[MSS], MSS known to Jerome, pesh. memph. sah. arm. aeth. Clem.-Al Orig. Cyr.-Jer. Didym. Epiph. Chrys. *al.*
[2] Singular in xxi. 25.
[3] Some earlier explanations which have now been discarded are not given here See Hort, *Judaistic Christianity*, pp. 68–73.

IX] APOSTLES' COUNCIL AT JERUSALEM 47

be strange and unexpected in conjunction with a compromise on the subject of foods. (*b*) 'Blood' is often explained to mean the eating of flesh from which the blood has not been drained. But this includes things strangled, which is only a particular instance of it, so that the third prohibition becomes superfluous[1].

With another reading there are not four but *three* clauses, the words 'and from things strangled' being omitted in several authorities[2].

Further, after the word 'fornication' a few authorities[3] add 'and whatsoever ye wish not that it should happen to yourselves, do not to another[4].' This addition cannot be original (it is not found e.g. in Tertullian), but it is useful as helping to make clear what was understood by scribes to be the nature of the three-clause prohibition, i.e. that it is a *moral* injunction; it forbids—not certain foods, or certain idolatrous practices, but—three great crimes against ordinary morality, idolatry, murder, and fornication.

But it is very difficult to suppose that the apostles took the trouble to press upon Christians elementary moral precautions such as would be entirely obvious to everyone. And 'abstain from blood' is a strange equivalent for 'thou shalt do no murder.' Even if the original

1 This difficulty would be removed if the true reading were that suggested by the strange rendering 'et sanguine suffocato' in the best MSS of the Vulgate, i e καὶ αἵματος πνικτοῦ (or πνικτῶν), and the adjective had the force of a substantive, 'and from the blood of a strangled beast (or beasts).'
2 D d gig. Iren[lat] Tert Cypr. Aug. Hier. Ambrst
3 D and some minuscules, syr[hcl] sah aeth. Iren[lat] Cypr.
4 This is a negative form, found variously in Jewish and Christian writings of the positive injunction, known as the Golden Rule, in Mat. vii. 12, Lk. vi. 31.

text in *v.* 29 omitted 'and from things strangled[1]' (and the singular in *v.* 20, and xxi 25), the three-clause prohibition need not be merely moral. It is probable that all the prohibitions, whether three or four, refer to heathen practices. The eating of idol-foods, the partaking of blood[2], and the ritual practice of fornication (in idol temples with women consecrated for the purpose), were all heathen customs by which the worshippers believed that they received into themselves the life of their gods or demons. And the eating of 'things strangled' (if it is part of the true text) probably had the same purpose though the exact meaning is doubtful. Gentile Christians in close contact with their heathen brethren were, according to the Jewish ideas at the time, in daily peril of pollution; and Jews felt it their sacred duty to keep themselves strictly free from contamination. Therefore the apostolic decrees laid down, not 'substitutes for circumcision' (Hort) but, as said above, supplementary injunctions that *for the sake of Jews living among Gentiles* the latter must abstain from these practices if they were to enjoy social intercourse with each other.

6. ST PAUL'S ATTITUDE TO THE PROHIBITIONS. The popular idea that there was a real pollution inherent in heathen food is contrary to what St Paul says in 1 Cor. viii. 4–6. The Christian 'strong' in his 'freedom' knows that an idol god is non-existent, and therefore idol-foods in no way differ from other foods. But for the 'weak,'

[1] It is possible that an early non-'Western' scribe with antiquarian interests, misunderstanding 'and from blood,' and remembering passages in the Old Testament which forbid 'eating with the blood,' may have added 'things strangled' as a marginal explanation, which afterwards crept into the text as a separate prohibition

[2] Tertullian, Clement of Alexandria, Origen and others say that this was avoided by Christians in their day.

who believe that in eating idol-foods they are partaking in the life of demons, they do constitute a source of pollution. A partaking of demons and a partaking of the Body and Blood of Christ are contrary to one another (1 Cor. x. 14–21; cf. 2 Cor. vi. 14–vii. 1). He therefore enjoins with great urgency upon Gentile converts that the 'strong' must bear with the 'weak' in this matter, and not put a stumbling-block in their way (1 Cor. viii., x. 23–33, Rom. xiv.). And that must have been his state of mind when he agreed to the apostolic decisions, and published them in Syria-Cilicia He had won the supreme point for which he had fought, i.e that Gentile Christians need not be circumcised and observe the ordinances of the Jewish Law. And therefore, after rebuking St Peter at Antioch for want of charity, in *compelling* Gentiles to observe Jewish scruples, he now accepted, in a spirit of charity, the corollary added by the Council for the sake of Jews[1].

With regard to fornication he must have agreed wholeheartedly. Marriage in his eyes was of the nature of a Christian sacrament, a reproduction in human life of Christ's union with His Church (Eph v. 22–33); and fornication meant union with a harlot, a ' Satanic sacrament.' Cf. 1 Cor. vi. 13 b–20, where the close conjunction of the passage with the words about 'foods' (*vv.* 12, 13 a) suggests that he had the decrees in mind. And in v. 9 he bids his converts keep themselves separate

[1] Sanday, *Theol Studien* for Zahn, p 331, writes 'I do not doubt that St James took the initiative in all this; St Peter and St Paul were just consenting parties It is probable enough that St Paul gave what was really a careless consent, he was indifferent to such matters, but at least he would not stand in the way of an agreement that made for peace ' But careless indifference is hardly to be expected in a champion of St Paul's character and temperament

from any Christian who is a fornicator, covetous, an idolater etc.,—'with such an one, no not to eat[1].'

CHAPTER X

ST PAUL'S SECOND MISSIONARY TOUR

Acts xv. 36–xviii. 22

1. THE QUARREL. xv. 36-41 St Luke, as often, does not state clearly the interval before the next phase of the history. He says only that 'after some days' (i.e. since St Paul and Barnabas returned from the Council) St Paul proposed to revisit the Christians in the towns where they had preached on their first tour. Barnabas wanted to take his cousin John Mark with them again; but St Paul had felt so keenly his desertion at Perga (see p. 33) that he refused. A sharp quarrel was the result. Their friendship, already strained by the incident at Antioch (Gal. ii 13; see p. 42), now gave way, and they parted, Barnabas taking his cousin to Cyprus[2],

---

[1] This discussion of the decrees owes much to an article by B. W. Bacon in the *Expositor*, Jan 1914, pp. 40-61. He draws, however, the unnecessary conclusion that since St Paul must have been hotly opposed to the decrees, he cannot have been present at the Council. The subject is variously treated by Hort, *Judaistic Christianity*, pp. 68-73, Bp. Chase, *The Credibility of the Acts of the Apostles*, pp 93-98, Sanday, *Expositor*, Oct. 1913, Kirsopp Lake, *The Earlier Epistles of St Paul*, pp. 48-60, McGiffert, *Apostolic Age*, pp. 208-216.

[2] There is no evidence that they ever met again, nor is Barnabas again mentioned in the Acts. He probably settled for a time at his own home in Cyprus with Mark 1 Cor. ix 6 suggests that the Corinthians, and therefore probably other churches, knew enough of him to be aware that he worked, like St Paul, for his living. Some think he was probably dead by the time that St Paul wrote to the Colossians, so that Mark was free to come to Rome (Col. iv 10; cf 2 Tim. iv. 11).

x] THE SECOND MISSIONARY TOUR 51

and St Paul taking Silas round by land through Syria-Cilicia, 'strengthening the churches[1].'

2. GALATIC LYCAONIA AND GALATIC PHRYGIA. xvi. 1–6. From the province of Syria-Cilicia St Paul and Silas went into the province of Galatia. They struck northward through the Taurus mountains by the famous narrow pass, the 'Cilician Gates,' through which the younger Cyrus, and Alexander, had marched towards the East. This brought them to the Galatian portion of Lycaonia, St Paul's eastern limit on his first tour; and they followed his former route in the converse direction, **Derbe**, **Lystra**, Iconium, and Pisidian Antioch. The last two are not named, but are implied according to the most probable explanation of *v.* 6. In that passage 'the region of Phrygia and Galatia' (R.V.), and still more 'Phrygia and the region of Galatia' (A.V.) fail to express the force of the Greek, in which both names are adjectival and agree with the one word 'region.' It was the **Galatic-Phrygian region**, as distinct from the larger portion of Phrygia, which lay in the province of Asia. The churches, then, according to this explanation, visited up to the point indicated in *v.* 6, were those of the first tour[2], and St Paul now visited them for the second time. They lay in the *southern* portion of the large Roman province of Galatia; and hence this is often called the 'South-Galatian' view of the apostle's movements. The 'North-Galatian' view, at one time widely held, in England notably by Lightfoot, but now given up by a growing number of scholars, is

---

[1] D (and similarly vulg[edd] syr[hcl marg]) adds 'delivering the commands of the presbyters' in accordance with *vv.* 23, 25

[2] In his account of the first tour St Luke does not use the name Galatia.

that St Paul at this point, and again in xviii. 23 (see p. 77 f.), visited a district further to the North, once the Kingdom of the Galatae (from which the large Roman province afterwards took its name), a Celtic people who had lived in the centre of Asia Minor, whose chief cities were Ancyra, Pessinus and Tavium; and that it was to the Christians in this district that he wrote the Epistle to the Galatians.

The problem is complicated by the question of the date of that epistle (see pp. 168–173); but independently of that, the following considerations against the North-Galatian view may be noted: (*a*) Apart from the geographical expressions in Acts xvi. 6, xviii. 23 which themselves require discussion, St Luke nowhere gives any hint of a journey into North Galatia (*b*) It would be very strange if, while St Luke gives a detailed account of work in Antioch, Iconium, Lystra and Derbe and none in North Galatia, St Paul should write with the deepest concern to dearly loved converts in the North, and in none of his epistles[1] make the slightest reference to his labours in the South. (*c*) St Paul first preached in Galatia 'because of an infirmity of the flesh' (Gal. iv. 13). This means either that he went thither because he fell ill, or that, having intended to go on elsewhere, he stayed because he was ill. But it is difficult to suppose either of these in the case of North Galatia. (*d*) Galatia took part in the collection for the poor at Jerusalem (1 Cor. xvi. 1). But among those named in Acts xx. 4, who accompanied St Paul with the money, North Galatia has no representative while South Galatia has two —Gaius and Timothy (*e*) Barnabas, who accompanied

[1] Except in 2 Tim. iii. 11, of which the Pauline authorship is disputable.

x]   THE SECOND MISSIONARY TOUR   53

St Paul on the first tour, but not later, is mentioned as though personally known to the Galatians (Gal. ii. 13).

(*f*) Ramsay[1] points out that as early as the latter half of the fourth century, Asterius of Amaseia in Pontus, in describing St Paul's third tour, makes 'Lycaonia' equivalent to 'the Galatic region' (see p 37).

3. TIMOTHY. A young Christian was at Lystra named Timotheus (Timothy), whose mother was a Jewish Christian, and his father a Gentile—whether Christian or not is not stated. His mother Lois, and his grandmother Eunikē (2 Tim i. 5) had probably been converted by St Paul on his first tour, two years before, having previously been pious Jews who had taught Timothy the Scriptures since his infancy (iii. 15). St Paul thought that the young man would be useful as an attendant in the place of John Mark[2]. He felt sure, also, that his usefulness would be increased if he were circumcised. He knew only too well, from his experience on the first tour, the bitterness of Jewish hostility; and in circumcising him[3] he was only carrying into practice the principle expressed in 1 Cor ix. 19–23, 'To the Jews I became as a Jew, that I might gain Jews.' He felt no incongruity in doing this to a half Jew for the sake of Jews, immediately after he had fought at Antioch and Jerusalem for the freedom of Gentiles from the necessity

1 *Expositor*, May 1895, p 391.
2 His confidence was justified, for Timothy remained one of his most faithful companions and supporters to the end; cf 1 Cor. iv. 17, xvi. 10, Rom xvi 21, Phil ii 19–22; and the first verse of 1, 2 Thes., 2 Cor , Col., Philem., Phil.
3 If *Galatians* was written later than this, he perhaps refers in the epistle to the insinuations of Judaizers, who may have held up his action against him, representing him as untrue to his own principles, chiefly intent on 'pleasing men' (i 10), 'building up again the things which he had destroyed' (ii. 18), 'still preaching circumcision' (v 11).

of circumcision. St Luke, indeed, relates (*v.* 4) that he was at that very time publishing the apostolic decrees[1].

4. THE ROUTE TO TROAS. xvi. 6–10. Having reached, or approached, Pisidian Antioch, St Paul had nearly completed the plan which he had proposed to Barnabas (xv. 36), and might, as on the first tour, have dropped down through Pamphylia to the port of Attalia, and taken ship back to Antioch in Syria. But longings stirred within him to go further afield. Where should he go? His first, and natural thought was, as we gather, to make westward for the great cities in the Roman province of Asia, such as Apameia, Laodicea, Hierapolis, Philadelphia, Ephesus and others. But he and his two companions were 'forbidden by the Holy Spirit to speak the Word in Asia.' An inward impulse, or a vision seen by one of them, or a message delivered in a state of spiritual ecstasy (cf. xiii. 2), made them turn in another direction. Exactly when this prohibition by the Spirit was given is uncertain. According to the best reading in *v.* 6[2] (followed in the R.V.) it was not after but before they had completed the journey through the Phrygian-Galatic region. This cannot mean that they went through that region *because* they had previously received the prohibition about Asia, but that they went through it with the prohibition—at some point or other *en route*—laid upon them, so that when they arrived at the borders of the province of Asia they did not preach in it. St Luke in summarising quickly a series of movements or

---

1 This, however, is possibly erroneous. See p. 45, n. 1.
2 διῆλθον ('They passed through') is read in all the best MSS. διελθόντες ('Having passed through') in HLP is an attempt to lessen the obscurity.

THE SECOND MISSIONARY TOUR

events is apt to be tantalizingly obscure as to their chronological sequence.

As they had come from the East, and were prevented from going West, and did not want to go South, the only remaining direction was North. So they travelled northward along a road part of which ran 'over against Mysia' (v. 7), i.e. parallel with the eastern boundary of the district of Mysia, which was also in the province of Asia. Then they 'tried to go into Bithynia,' no doubt with the important town of Nicomedia in view. But again 'the Spirit of Jesus suffered them not.' Thus they were debarred from preaching in Asia and Bithynia alike. But nothing daunted, they obeyed the divine guidance, and struck westward through Mysia[1]. But since this also was in the province of Asia 'they passed by **Mysia**' (v. 8), i.e. they passed through it without preaching, till they reached the coast at **Troas** (ib.).

What did all this mysterious but unmistakeable guidance mean? Further spiritual direction was at once given, in the dream in which St Paul saw a man of Macedonia who said 'Come over to Macedonia and help us[2].' As before, they accepted the guidance without hesitation (v. 10). In this verse the 1st person plural suddenly appears, as though the writer had joined St

[1] They perhaps turned westward at Kotiaion. But the words 'they tried to go into Bithynia' may imply that they approached nearer to the Bithynian border, in which case they may have reached Dorylaion, and then travelled westward In either case there was no great Roman road to Troas, and they must have travelled by smaller roads and paths In these unfrequented tracts there were rivers to ford, and probably brigands to encounter, the 'perils of rivers' and 'perils of robbers' mentioned in 2 Cor. xi. 26.

[2] For the first part of v. 10 D has 'Having arisen, therefore, [from sleep] he related the vision to *us*, and *we* considered that etc' Somewhat similarly the Sahidic version.

Paul immediately on the latter's arrival at Troas. But assuming that the 'We'-sections (see pp x–xii) are taken from, or based upon, a travel-document, it is difficult to suppose that it actually began with the words of *v.* 10, or with those in D in the preceding verse, and therefore it is impossible to feel sure that the writer of the document was not with St Paul prior to this point.

5. PHILIPPI. xvi. 11–40. It is difficult for us to judge whether St Luke, to whom Asia and Macedonia were two provinces within the same Roman empire, had the same feeling that we have, that it was an epoch-making step for St Paul to pass from the continent of Asia to the continent of Europe.

A helping S E wind brought them, apparently in one day's sail, half the distance across, i e. to the island of **Samothrace** It had no good harbour[1], but the ship probably anchored for the night at the town of the same name at the N. of the island. Next day they reached the port of **Neapolis** on the Macedonian coast, whence they went inland along the great Via Egnatia some 10 miles N W to **Philippi**, where St Luke, indefinite, as often, in his chronology, says that they stayed 'certain days'

Philippi is described (*v.* 12) in the words 'which is [the] first of the district [lit portion], a city of Macedonia, a colony.' It had recently been given the dignity of a Roman *colonia*, with the name 'Colonia Augusta Julia Philippensium,' and had received the 'jus Italicum[2].' The first part of the sentence is obscure. 'First'

---

1 Pliny speaks of it as 'importuosissima omnium'
2 Ramsay, who thinks that St Luke was a native of Philippi, finds in the words an indication of his pride in this Roman privilege.

x]   THE SECOND MISSIONARY TOUR   57

in the sense of 'chief[1]' was applied to Greek cities in Asia, but there is no evidence of its use elsewhere. Lightfoot (*Philippians*, p. 50) understands it to mean 'the first city in Macedonia at which St Paul arrived,' explaining why he did not stop at Neapolis, 'which was generally spoken of as a Thracian town[2].' The text is perhaps corrupt, and the true meaning yet to be discovered[3].

Even in a Macedonian town, where the population was mostly Greek, but possessing the Roman citizenship, St Paul did not desert his regular practice of seeking out the Jewish synagogue (v. 13). They 'supposed' or 'expected[4]' that there was one outside the city gate by the river side[5]. The narrative is not quite clear. The next words seem to imply that there was no synagogue

1 D has 'which is the head of Macedonia'. But both Thessalonica and Amphipolis were more important than Philippi.

2 By Pliny for example, but Strabo and Ptolemy connect it with Macedonia.

3 For $\pi\rho\omega\tau\eta$ $\tau\hat{\eta}s$ $\mu\epsilon\rho\iota\delta os$ Blass and others suggest $\pi\rho\omega\tau\eta s$ $\mu\epsilon\rho\iota\delta os$, 'a city of the first portion of Macedonia,' referring to the division of Macedonia into four political districts which the Romans had made long before. But Amphipolis was the chief city of this district, and $\mu\epsilon\rho\iota s$ nowhere else has this meaning. Hort conjectures $\Pi\iota\epsilon\rho\iota\delta os$ for $\mu\epsilon\rho\iota\delta os$, 'a chief city of Pierian Macedonia', but he admits that the name does not occur elsewhere, 'and would be more naturally applied to the more famous Pieria in the S.W. of Macedonia.'

4 A.V. 'where prayer was wont to be made' follows the reading $\dot{\epsilon}\nu o\mu\iota\zeta\epsilon\tau o$ $\pi\rho o\sigma\epsilon\nu\chi\dot{\eta}$ $\epsilon\hat{\iota}\nu a\iota$ in the lesser MSS EHLP and most minuscules. D has $\dot{\epsilon}\delta\acute{o}\kappa\epsilon\iota$ [e vulg videbatur] $\pi\rho o\sigma\epsilon\nu\chi\dot{\eta}$ $\epsilon\hat{\iota}\nu a\iota$. But the best MSS אABCE 13 40 61 memph, followed in the R.V., have $\dot{\epsilon}\nu o\mu\iota\zeta o\mu\epsilon\nu$ $\pi\rho o\sigma\epsilon\nu\chi\dot{\eta}\nu$ $\epsilon\hat{\iota}\nu a\iota$. The word $\pi\rho o\sigma\epsilon\nu\chi\dot{\eta}$ for 'synagogue' is found chiefly in Philo, but also in 3 Mac. vii. 20, Josephus, *Vita*, 54, and in inscriptions. It appears in Latin in Juv. *Sat.* iii. 296.

5 Lightfoot refers to the 'orationes littorales' mentioned by Tert. *adv Nat* i. 13, and other passages.

'we sat down and were speaking unto the women who were come together,' as though it were a favourite spot for strolling and gossip; this can hardly mean 'we sat down in the synagogue,' since there would be men present as well as women. And yet in *v.* 16 St Luke says 'And it came to pass as we were going to *the proseuchē*[1],' i e. the prayer-house, the synagogue.

A convert was won (*v.* 14), a seller of purple-dyed garments from Thyatira in Lydia, her name Lydia having no doubt been given her from her native land. She and her whole household were baptized; and she eagerly persuaded the missionaries to stay at her house (*v.* 15). But, as in Phrygia and Lycaonia, trouble followed immediately. *vv.* 16–18. While walking one Sabbath day to the synagogue, they were met by a slave girl who was in an abnormal condition of excited susceptibility. She was a ventriloquist ('she had a spirit of Pythōn' as St Luke puts it) and a fortune teller, and her owners made considerable profit out of her. The character of St Paul, with its electric energy and intense spiritual fervour[2], at once had a psychological effect upon her, and she shouted out after them on the road for several days words corresponding with the thoughts that must have been uppermost in St Paul's mind—'These men are servants of God the Most High, who proclaim to you the way of salvation.' St Paul, like other people of his time, explained all such abnormal states as due to the presence of a 'demon' who had entered into and gained possession of the victim. When he cured the girl by

[1] DHLP and many minuscules have 'going to prayer,' omitting the article.
[2] St Luke says 'he turned in the spirit [i.e filled with a spiritual fervour or ecstasy], and said, I charge thee etc.'

invoking the name of Jesus Christ (an act of exorcism of which there are many authentic examples in the early Christian centuries), he exercised a power over her weakened will which had a sudden and lasting effect upon her, and St Luke, in the language of his day, says that the demon went out of her. *vv.* 19–24. It cannot have been long before her owners discovered that her power of making money for them had left her. They seized St Paul and Silas and dragged them to the local magistrates to the *agora* The hearing of the case before the magistrates is not described. St Luke's next statement is that they were handed on to the Roman officials, the *stratēgoi*, i.e. the duum viri or praetors, on the charge of having broken the Roman law by introducing, as Jews, into a Roman colony religious teaching which was not compatible with the state religion. At about this time all Jews were expelled from Rome by Claudius, and they no doubt suffered from local hostility in various parts of the Empire, so that it was easy in Philippi to rouse popular feeling against the missionaries, the pagans being unable to distinguish Christianity from Judaism. The praetors yielded to the clamour, stripped St Paul and Silas, and ordered the lictors to beat them. (This is the only recorded instance of the three beatings with rods mentioned in 2 Cor. xi. 25) It was a grievous insult to Roman citizens[1], to which St Paul afterwards referred in 1 Thes. ii. 2, 'having suffered before, and been insulted, as ye know, at Philippi ' They did not protest at the moment; perhaps the rush and clamour gave them

---

1 That Silas was a Roman citizen as well as St Paul is shewn in *v* 37 The Lex Valeria (B C 509) had laid it down that no citizen could be beaten, cf Cic *in Verr* II. v. 170: 'facinus est vincire civem Romanum, scelus verberare.'

no opportunity[1]. They were then confined in an inner dungeon, and their feet were secured in the stocks.

[*vv.* 25–34. They sang hymns at midnight, and a sudden earthquake opened the prison doors and broke the stocks which held all the prisoners; none of them, however, attempted to escape. The gaoler awoke, and being responsible for their safe-guarding was about to commit suicide on seeing the doors standing open; but St Paul reassured him. He then sprang down the steps to the lower dungeon with a torch, crying 'Sirs, what must I do to be saved?' Possibly he meant no more than 'What must I do to escape punishment from the authorities?' But St Paul's answer was on a higher plane—'Believe on the Lord Jesus, and thou shalt be saved, thou and thine house.' He at once brought them out to some place, perhaps the courtyard, where there was water, with which he washed their bleeding stripes, which had been left untended since the terrible beating. And he and all his household were immediately baptized. Then he took them into his house, which no doubt adjoined the prison, and gave them a meal]

vv 35–40. The praetors having for the moment satisfied the popular outcry sent the lictors next morning to tell the troublesome Jews that they could go. But now St Paul stood upon his dignity as a Roman citizen, whose rights had been flagrantly violated. He demanded that the praetors themselves should come and release them with due formality,—which they did[2], in a great

[1] Cf Acts xxii 24 f where St Paul managed to protest only just in time to escape the scourging.

[2] D (and similarly 137 syr[hcl]) has 'And coming with many friends to the prison they besought them to depart saying, We did not know the facts concerning you that ye are righteous men And having brought them out they besought

state of fear at having beaten Roman citizens. St Paul and Silas went to Lydia's house to say farewell, and then departed.

From Phil. i. 7, 28–30 we learn that after St Paul had left them his converts continued to share in his sufferings.

The paragraph above has been placed in brackets because *vv.* 25–34 appear to be derived from a source other than that of the rest of the narrative. (1) The praetors act in the morning with no reference to the earthquake; they simply send the lictors to tell the gaoler to release the two prisoners. This was noticed by the scribe of D, who tried to rectify it by writing, 'The praetors came together into the agora, and remembering the earthquake which had occurred they were afraid, and sent the lictors etc.' (2) The narrative of *vv.* 25–34 itself contains difficulties. An opportune earthquake alone would not be a difficulty. But that the criminals imprisoned with the missionaries were so deeply impressed by hearing them singing hymns that they were ready to forgo all attempt to escape is very surprising. And it is also strange that when the gaoler leapt into the dungeon, and had heard the Christian message, he brought St Paul and Silas out regardless of the rest of the prisoners, all of whom the earthquake had freed from their bonds. The scribe of D again sees the difficulty, and adds 'having secured the rest.' The probability must be recognised that in the growth of the Christian tradition received by St Luke some elements were added which can hardly claim the same historical value as the preceding 'We'-section (see p. ix f.).

them saying, Depart out of this city, lest they again gather together to us crying out against you.'

6. PHILIPPI TO THESSALONICA. xvii. 1–9. From Philippi they travelled S.W. along the Via Egnatia by nearly equal stages of about 30 miles to **Amphipolis** and **Apollonia**, and then about 37 miles W. to **Thessalonica**. Why they did not stop and preach at the first two, especially at so important a town as Amphipolis, we cannot tell[1]. Perhaps, indeed, they did, though St Luke's narrative contains no account of it. They may also have stopped at other places not named, since the three stages were unusually long day's walks for pedestrians. At Thessalonica St Paul, 'as his custom was' (v. 2), preached for three Sabbaths in the synagogue. As in other towns Gentiles who were sympathetic towards the Jewish religion[2] were present at the services, and St Paul converted a large number of them, together with some Jews, and several of the leading women. In 1 Thes. i. 9 f , ii. 1 f. he speaks of his successful work among them. Their Christian devotion became known not only in Macedonia and Achaia, but 'everywhere,' i.e. far and wide. Probably, therefore, after the three Sabbaths he preached for some time elsewhere than in the synagogue. A longer stay than three weeks is rendered almost certain by the fact that while he was in Thessalonica the Philippian Christians sent him supplies at least twice (Phil. iv. 16), and also that he found it worth while to settle down to his hand labour (cf Acts xviii. 3, xx 34),

1 That there was no synagogue in either town, and therefore no opportunity of preaching, can hardly be deduced from the next words, 'Thessalonica where was a synagogue of the Jews.'

2 See p 10 AD 13 *al* vulg memph. read τῶν τε σεβομένων καὶ Ἑλλήνων, i.e. not only Gentiles who were devout, or God-fearing, but others also. Possibly this is the true reading. At any rate the conversion of actual heathen is implied in 1 Thes. i. 9, 'ye turned to God *from idols*.'

in order not to be burdensome to the Thessalonians (1 Thes. ii. 9, 2 Thes. iii. 8). It is possible that the period included missionary work as far as the borders of **Illyricum** (Rom. xv. 19). It is not likely that he travelled so far afield on his next visit to Macedonia, when he was in deep anxiety about the Corinthian Church (p 86), or when he returned from Corinth (p. 87) on his way to Jerusalem with the money for the poor.

His great success at Thessalonica, as at Pisidian Antioch (p. 36) enraged the Jews. They collected the rabble of the town and attacked the house of Jason, where the missionaries apparently lodged, and perhaps held their services. Unable to find them they arrested Jason and some other converts, and took them before the magistrates, who are here called *politarchs*, which inscriptions shew to be their correct title. The complaint against them (different from that at Philippi, where Roman citizens charged them with being Jewish propagandists) was that brought by the Jews against our Lord, i.e. sedition against the emperor, because they spoke of 'another king, Jesus.' As the actual preachers, St Paul and Silas, were not caught, they were no doubt condemned by default, which must have given a handle to the Jews in their further endeavours to make the Greeks persecute the Christians for sedition (1 Thes. ii. 14 f.). Jason and his fellow Christians were bound over by a money payment to ensure that such a disturbance should not occur again. Meanwhile St Paul's converts managed to get him and Silas safely away by night, and they went another 20 miles or more W. to **Beroea**.

7. BEROEA. xvii. 10–15. Events here were very similar. They taught in the synagogue, where, however, the Jews were of a much better type than those in Thessa-

lonica. St Luke says that they listened eagerly, and studied their Bibles during the week to satisfy themselves of the truth of St Paul's teaching. Many were converted, together with Gentiles, both men and the rich Greek ladies. But again the storm broke. The Jews from Thessalonica, hearing of the apostle's successful preaching, came and stirred up the rabble as before. His converts had to get him out of the town as fast as possible, and hurried him S E. some 20 miles to the coast, leaving Silas and Timothy behind. His escort went with him, probably by boat, to **Athens**[1], and then returned to Beroea with his instructions to Silas and Timothy to come to him as soon as they could.

During his stay at Beroea, or perhaps afterwards at Corinth, he seems to have made more than one attempt to return to Thessalonica, but 'Satan hindered' him (1 Thes ii 18), which some explain as meaning that he received news that the feeling there was still too strong for him, and the politarchs would not allow him to return If he had, he would have endangered not only his own life but also that of Jason and the others who had been bound over to keep the peace. Some, however, think that he would not have spoken of the action of Roman authorities as a hindrance of Satan, and explain it as illness (cf 2 Cor xii 7) or the pressure of local circumstances at Corinth. In 1 Thes iii. 1–5 he shews his intense sympathy and anxiety for his converts in the trials that they must be suffering.

8. ATHENS. xvii. 16–34. (*a*) *Preaching and Discussion.* In the beautiful centre of pagan intellectual thought, where St Paul passed an anxious interlude of

---

[1] D adds 'And he passed by Thessaly, for he was forbidden to preach the Word unto them '

waiting, he had practically no success at all. The gods and goddesses of the old religion of Greece were dead, killed by the pitiless questionings of philosophers, though their temples, statues, and altars still decorated the city in profusion. Everyone was ready to listen to the latest philosopher, and to engage in dialectical discussions; but it was for the most part in a purely academic spirit, with little moral earnestness or real desire to reach truth. Waiting at Athens for Silas and Timothy, St Paul with his burning religious enthusiasm was stirred to the depths of his soul as he sadly wandered about looking at the sights. St Luke's account is as follows. He preached, as usual, in the synagogues to Jews and to any Greeks who came there, but he also held discussions in the agora with any chance comers who were willing to hold discussions with him. Among these were some Stoics and Epicureans, representatives of the two chief schools of Greek philosophy at the time. Some condemned him at once with a contemptuous epithet implying that he was merely 'an amateur who had picked up some crumbs of learning[1].' Others were rather more interested. When they heard him preach 'Jesus and the Resurrection' (*Anastasis*), they thought that he was introducing yet another god and goddess to the Athenian pantheon. So they took him to the Areopagus, the 'hill of Ares (Mars),' which stood on the South of the agora, the acropolis being on the West. It was the place where trials in the high Court were held in the open air, the seats being cut in the rock. But the narrative is far from suggesting that St Paul was taken before the Court. They took him by the hand[2] in a friendly manner, and led him to some spot on the hill, in, or more probably

1 σπερμολόγος.   2 ἐπιλαβόμενοι αὐτοῦ.

near, the site of the Court, where they could have a quiet discussion with him.

(b) *St Paul's Speech*. This is the last of the three occasions on which St Luke gives the contents of a missionary address delivered by the apostle. 'All things to all men that I might win some' was his motto in missionary work. And St Luke preserves the thought. To Jews at Pisidian Antioch (xiii. 16–41) he naturally sketched the history of Israel; to ignorant pagans at Lystra (xiv. 15–17) he spoke of Nature and the God of Nature; and to cultured pagans in 'Athens the eye of Greece, mother of arts' he attempts a philosophical strain. His text was an inscription which he had seen on an altar in the city, 'To an Unknown God.' He would tell them about this God, of whom they were ignorant while they gave Him reverence. He does not need temples made with hands (cf. vii. 48), for (as he had said at Lystra, xiv 15) He is the Creator (alluding to Exod. xx. 11), and the Source of all life (perhaps alluding to Is xlii. 5 b), and the Appointer of the boundaries of all nations (cf. Deut xxxii. 8) He wanted men to 'touch Him and find Him,' though He is at the same time an immanent Being (as the Greeks taught), the spiritual Principle 'in Whom we live and move and exist'; or, to quote one of their own poets, 'For we are also His race.' God, then, being spiritual like ourselves, obviously cannot be represented by gold, silver, or stone, graven by art and man's device.—Having so far spoken in a philosophical vein, he suddenly brought before his hearers the Christian truth. This transcendent Creator, Who is also the immanent Principle of life, overlooked pagan ignorance in the past (as St Paul had said at Lystra, xiv 16); but He now calls men to repentance, because a day of judgment is very near when He will judge the world in righteousness in the person of a Man appointed for the purpose; and has assured men of the certainty of this by raising this Man from the dead (cf ii. 24–32).

As before, the mention of *Anastasis* made some of them treat him with ridicule, while others, perhaps with only a thin veil of politeness, said they would like to hear him again another time. A few converts are mentioned, among them a woman named Damaris, and a member of the high Court named Dionysius, both otherwise unknown[1]. The apostle's work at Athens was much less successful than elsewhere; and from what he afterwards wrote to the Corinthians (1 Cor. ii. 1–6) about 'persuasive words of wisdom,' 'the wisdom of men,' 'the wisdom of this world,' he shews that he realised, what is as true to-day as then, that mere academic argument on behalf of Christianity seldom converts anybody.

There can be little doubt that St Luke rightly represents the *tone* of the speech That it is in any sense a verbatim report is, of course, impossible; St Paul under such circumstances would speak at considerable length, while St Luke compresses it into nine verses and a half But it is probable that the shape and outline are St Luke's. Parallels are to be seen in other Greek writings; and there are similarities not only with St Paul's own words at Lystra, but also with the speeches of St Peter and St Stephen. A certain conventionality of form (if it may be so called) has been observed in religious

---

[1] St Luke made use of a tradition which apparently conflicts with St Paul's statement that the household of Stephanas was 'the firstfruits of Achaia' (1 Cor. xvi. 15). If that statement is to be taken literally, no converts were won at Athens.

speeches of ancient times[1], by which St Luke is perhaps to some extent influenced. He has well caught the Stoic tone in some of St Paul's remarks: 'He is not served by human hands as though He needed anything'; the 'feeling' or 'touching' God; 'though He is not far from each one of us'; 'for in Him we live and move and exist'; and the quotation 'for we are also His race' is from a Stoic poet Aratus. It is also interesting to note that in the Dialogue concerning Sacrifices, attributed by Philostratus to Apollonius, the religiousness of Athens is indicated by an altar 'Of unknown Demons'; and Pausanias (I. i. 4) speaks of 'altars of Gods called Unknown.' The singular which St Luke gives affords the opportunity for St Paul's words about the one true God.

(c) *The Movements of Silas and Timothy.* It is not easy at this point to trace their movements clearly. St Paul had sent them a message, by the Beroeans who had brought him to Athens, to rejoin him as soon as possible. According to Acts xviii. 5 Silas and Timothy came to him from Macedonia *after he had gone on to Corinth* from Athens. But in I Thes. iii. 1–6 St Paul says that in his deep affection for the Thessalonians, and his longing to hear that they had remained true to him under trial, he had made up his mind to deny himself Timothy's presence and help: 'we thought it good to be left at Athens alone, and sent Timothy...to establish you....For this cause I also, when I could bear it no longer, sent to know your faith. But when Timothy

[1] This is the principal result reached by Norden, *Agnostos Theos.* He provides much interesting material in a little known field of study, though, like many writers with an original theory, he tends to run it to death, and to prove too much.

came even now unto us from you...we were comforted.' That is to say, *while St Paul was still at Athens* Timothy had joined him, and was sent back to Thessalonica, and then rejoined him at Corinth. The statement, therefore, about Timothy in Acts xviii. 5 omits his first arrival from Thessalonica and his return thither.

With regard to Silas, who came, according to Acts xviii. 5, with Timothy to Corinth (cf. 2 Cor. i. 19, 'the Son of God, Jesus Christ, who was preached among you by us, by me and Silvanus [Silas] and Timothy'), it is uncertain from St Paul's language whether he came with Timothy to Athens or not. The 1st person plural in 1 Thes. ('*we* thought it good to be left at Athens alone') may imply that he did so, and was left with St Paul at Athens when Timothy went back. But (1) it is probable that like other late Greek letter writers St Paul not infrequently wrote in the plural when he meant 'I' only; in *v.* 5 he uses the singular, and in *v.* 6 the plural again. (2) If Silas was left with St Paul at Athens, and if at the same time Acts xviii. 5 is correct, Silas also must have been sent back to Macedonia for some purpose, and then he and Timothy came to Corinth together, whither St Paul had meantime gone alone. But of this sending of Silas nothing whatever is said either in the *Acts* or by St Paul. The difficulties, which are not of serious importance, and of which other possible solutions have been suggested[1], arise from St Luke's characteristic vagueness in matters of chronology. The chief fact which St Paul makes quite clear is that Timothy had been sent back to Thessalonica, and that on his return to St Paul he reported to him the condition of

[1] Lake, *The Earlier Epistles of St Paul*, p. 74 f., gives the above solution and mentions others.

the Christians in that town, and that the report led the apostle to write 1 *Thessalonians* (see p. 123). Trusting in Acts xviii. 5 we can add that he wrote it when he was at Corinth. And the close similarities of style and language make it probable that he wrote 2 *Thessalonians* (see p. 129) almost at the same time.

9. CORINTH. xviii. 1–17. (*a*) *The City.* Corinth had three main attractions for its mixed and shifting population (1) Commerce. It stood on a narrow isthmus[1], 1½ miles from Lechaeon its western port, for Italian trade, and 9 miles from Cenchreae its eastern port, for Asiatic trade. (2) The Isthmian games, which drew crowds of visitors. (3) The worship of Aphrodite, an integral part of which was immorality. Thus there were to be found there hard-headed merchants, fashionable patrons of sport, and decadent devotees of systematized vice. Nationalities were no less mixed. The masses were Greek, but the aristocrats—descendants of the original colonists under Julius Caesar—were Roman, together with government officials and many merchants. And these were interspersed with commercial Jews and a motley of representatives of every nation in the Empire. St Paul seems to have considered earnestly within himself in what form he could best present his message to such a population; and he determined (1 Cor. ii. 1–6) not to follow the academic method that he had adopted at Athens, but to put before them the very heart and kernel of the Gospel—'Jesus Christ, and Him crucified,' and to trust not to argument but to 'the demonstration of Spirit and of power.'

(*b*) *Aquila and Priscilla* Corinth being thus a main artery of cosmopolitan pagan life, St Paul's work there,

[1] Hence Ovid and Horace both speak of it as 'bimaris.'

which lasted 18 months, must have been of great importance for Christianity. But St Luke's account of it is very brief. On his arrival the apostle found living in Corinth a Jew named Aquila and his wife Priscilla[1] (or Prisca, as she is called in the epistles, Rom. xvi. 3, 1 Cor. xvi. 19, 2 Tim. iv. 19). He was from the country of Pontus in the N.E. of Asia Minor. They had lately (see p. xviii) been banished from Rome by the decree of Claudius[2]. St Paul took up his lodging in their house because they were of the same handicraft as himself, 'tent-makers,' the exact meaning of which is uncertain[3]. As at Thessalonica (see p. 62), though engaged the greater part of the day in mission preaching he laboured during the rest of it, and far on into the night, in order to be independent of help from others (cf. Acts xx. 34).

(c) *Separation from the Synagogue.* He began his mission work, as always, in the synagogue, preaching to Jews and Gentiles (v 4). And the arrival of Silas and Timothy from Macedonia (see p. 68), with their report of the faithfulness of the Thessalonians in the face of Jewish persecution, roused his feelings to the highest pitch, so that he felt more than ever 'gripped' by the

[1] Various conjectures have been made with regard to them See Ramsay's art 'Pontus,' and Headlam's 'Prisca' in Hastings' *DB*.

[2] 'Judaeos impulsore Chresto assidue tumultuantes Roma expulit.' Suet. *Claud* 25

[3] Syr[pesh], an Old Latin MS h, and Chrysostom contain a tradition that they were workers in leather Possibly they sewed strips of skin together to form material for tents. The manufacture of felt was a flourishing industry in Cilicia, where St Paul could have learnt it. And in Rome the *tabernacularii* formed themselves into a corporation. The Jews, who mostly provided that their sons should learn a trade, thought of hand labour very differently from the Greeks, to whom it appeared mean and slavish. D omits 'for by their trade they were tent-makers.'

message which he had to deliver[1] (*v.* 5). But the more vehemently he preached the stronger grew the Jewish opposition. At last in a burst of indignation he declared, as at Pisidian Antioch (p. 36), that he would now confine his work to the Gentiles in the city (*v.* 6). From this time he preached[2] in the house of Titius[3] Justus adjoining the synagogue, a Gentile who had already been one who reverenced God (*v.* 7). The close proximity of the house must have made endless opportunities for the Jews to shew their hostility. Crispus the ruler of the synagogue and many others were converted (*v.* 8). St Luke then relates that St Paul had a vision in which the Lord encouraged him to preach boldly, for no one in the city would harm him (*vv.* 9, 10). So he stayed in Corinth for 18 months[4] (*v.* 11).

(*d*) *Gallio.* Some time ('many days,' *v.* 18) before his departure an incident occurred (*vv.* 12–17) which gives St Luke the opportunity, which he never fails to use, of illustrating the favourable attitude of Roman officials towards St Paul. Gallio had just become proconsul of Achaia,—so *v.* 12 seems to imply, though the words

[1] The true reading 'by the Word' is more vivid than 'in the spirit' which is found in HLP, most minuscules, syr[hcl marg] arm.

[2] D* and the minuscule 37 have 'he removed from Aquila,' i.e. he not only preached but henceforth lodged in the house of Titius Justus. Whether the reading is correct or not, it relates what is possibly a fact. It would further emphasize the apostle's renouncement of contact with the Jews. It need not have prevented Aquila and Priscilla from being converted afterwards. There is nothing to shew that they were Christians when St Paul went to lodge with them

[3] Not Titus, as in the English versions, following ℵE, five minuscules, vulg. pesh[MSS]. memph. sah. arm

[4] This seems to mean 18 months after the vision; but St Luke possibly intends to include the whole time of his stay in Corinth till Gallio's arrival.

strictly mean only 'in the proconsulship of Gallio' (see pp. xv–xvii). He was the brother of the philosopher Seneca, who sums up his character in the word *dulcis*, 'gentle.' The Jews apparently thought that the new official would let them have their way. So they brought St Paul before him on the charge of 'persuading men to worship God contrary to the Law' (*v.* 13). This can hardly have been the exact charge that they brought; but St Luke expresses the sort of thing that their complaints actually amounted to, as Gallio discovered in the course of the examination. But when St Paul was about to make his defence, Gallio declared that he was there to judge criminal offences and not religious squabbles of Jews, and he drove them[1], with true Roman scorn, out of the court (*vv.* 14–16). *V.* 17 is difficult: 'And all laid hold on Sosthenes the ruler of the synagogue, and beat him before the judgment seat.' Sosthenes, we may suppose, succeeded Crispus in his office when the latter became a Christian. But it is impossible to suppose that the Jews beat their own synagogue official. 'All' may mean the whole audience of Gentiles who were listening to the trial. (The reading 'all the Greeks' in several authorities is probably a correct gloss, if not the true reading.) But Gallio still treated this as part of the squabble, and refused to take any notice of it. If Sosthenes was the same person that joined with St Paul at a later time in writing 1 *Corinthians* (i. 1), he must have been converted after this incident. But there is no evidence of it; nor that he was already a Christian, nor that the Jews beat him in a rage for having been foiled in their attempt on St Paul.

1 ἀπήλασεν. D* (not d) 133 have the less strong ἀπέλυσεν, 'dismissed.'

10. THE RETURN TO SYRIA. xviii. 18–22. Having founded the Church in Corinth St Paul travelled without delay back to Antioch in Syria. The traditions which reached St Luke contained practically no incidents in connexion with the journey; he therefore gives an extremely rapid sketch, so condensed as to be obscure. And he no longer mentions Silas and Timothy[1].

St Paul 'sailed for Syria,' i.e. started by boat on his journey back to Syria, in company with Aquila and Priscilla. That they had become Christians is shewn by a later incident (v 26), but St Luke nowhere relates the fact of their conversion. They went to the eastern harbour, **Cenchreae**. St Luke's words are 'he sailed thence for Syria, and with him Priscilla and Aquila, having shorn his head in Cenchreae, for he had a vow.' The meaning of this is entirely doubtful. The sentence, thrown in by St Luke in a curiously incidental manner, is usually explained to mean that St Paul cut his hair because he had completed a period of a Nazirite vow (cf. Num. vi. 18). But though, for a special purpose, he afterwards played a part in a similar ceremony with four Jewish Christians in Jerusalem (xxi. 23–26), it is very doubtful if he would have submitted himself voluntarily to a Jewish ordinance at any time, still less in a pagan town after he had publicly renounced the Jews. It is also improbable that he would have allowed his hair to grow long, in view of his words to the Corinthians (1 Cor. xi. 14), 'Doth not even nature itself teach you that if a man have long hair it is a dishonour to him?' Some suggest that

[1] Of the movements of the former nothing more is heard. In 2 Cor i 19 St Paul alludes to his preaching with himself and Timothy at Corinth, but does not mention him again. The next appearance of Timothy is with St Paul at Ephesus (Acts xix. 22).

it was the *beginning* of a vow[1], the hair being closely shaved as an offering. Others think that the words 'having shaved his head etc' are said not of St Paul but of Aquila, as indeed the grammar of the sentence strictly requires. The matter remains at present an unsolved problem.

They sailed straight across the Aegean Sea to **Ephesus** (xviii. 19–21), where the apostle had never yet preached. There he left Aquila and Priscilla, and hurried away, perhaps in the same boat as before, which had given him only a short time on land while it unladed and took in cargo (cf. xxi. 3, 4). In that short time, however, he preached in the synagogue and reasoned with Jews. They wanted him to stay longer, but he said he would come back to them again, God willing In xix. 21 we see St Paul hurrying to Jerusalem for Pentecost, and it is possible that he was now hurrying similarly to be in time for the Passover[2]. The account gives the impression of haste, and is itself slightly obscure, since it relates that St Paul left Aquila and Priscilla *before* he went into the synagogue

Then came the longest part of the voyage—round the S.W. coast of Asia Minor, probably to Patara or Myra (cf. xxi. 1), and then across the open sea to Syria, where he finally landed at **Caesarea** (*v.* 22 a). If St Paul was hurrying to Jerusalem for the Passover, it was in the early spring, when the weather might be very stormy. In any case it is quite possible that in the course of this

[1] Josephus, *Jewish War*, ii. xv 1, speaks of this ceremony at the beginning of a thirty days' vow as usually performed by those in sickness or other distresses

[2] This is actually suggested in DHLP, most minuscules, pesh. aeth, 'I must by all means keep the coming feast at Jerusalem.'

voyage one of St Paul's three shipwrecks (2 Cor. xi. 25) took place. This is his last voyage recorded in the *Acts*—though not the last that he actually made (see p. 140)—before he wrote that passage.

Arrived in Syria 'he went up and saluted the Church.' Apart from the conjecture that he was going for the Passover, this probably means the mother Church in **Jerusalem**. 'Went up' was the usual expression for going to Jerusalem. The corresponding 'went down' in the following clause renders very improbable the explanation that he simply went up from the harbour at Caesarea to visit the Christian community in that town. The slight obscurity is owing to the speed with which St Luke carries the reader over the ground. Finally he relates that the apostle 'went down to **Antioch**[1]' in Syria, merely stating the bare fact with no incidents, though it was a journey of some 350 miles from Jerusalem.

CHAPTER XI

ST PAUL'S THIRD MISSIONARY TOUR

Acts xviii. 23–xxi 16

1. The greater part of this period was spent at the city of **Ephesus**, a place of first-rate importance, the Asiatic counterpart of Corinth. St Paul seems to have worked here on a larger scale than elsewhere, and the city

---

[1] Some early scribes made the curious mistake of confusing this with Pisidian Antioch. Hence the scribe of D, who has the reference to the feast at Jerusalem in *v*. 21, is forced to add a gloss (found also in syr[hcl marg]) in xix. 1: 'And when Paul wished, according to his own plan, to go to Jerusalem, the Spirit told him to turn aside into Asia. And passing through the upper parts he cometh etc.' This confusion of the two Antiochs is made also by Asterius of Amaseia in Pontus, *c*. 360–400, and Euthalius an Egyptian deacon, *c*. 458.

became through his influence the centre of Christian mission work over a wide area (xix. 10), and that in the face of the most violent opposition and danger to himself (1 Cor. xv. 32; see p. 85 f.) and to some of his converts (Rom. xvi 4, Acts xix. 29). But of all this activity St Luke tells us very little. The rapidity of his narrative in the last section continues, and he confines himself to a few striking incidents which tradition preserved for him, until the next 'We'-section begins (xx. 5) when his story at once becomes full of interesting details.

Beside the work at Ephesus, the period of the third tour is one of great interest for the student of St Paul, because in it more than in any other period we gain a picture of him from his own letters, his sufferings for the Cross of Christ, his restless energy, and his alternating extremes of human emotion. He paid a visit to the *Corinthians* which is not recorded in the *Acts*, and wrote no less than four letters to them (see pp. 137 f., 143 ff.); he wrote also to the *Romans* (p 181 f), and perhaps to the *Galatians* (pp. 168–173), and the *Philippians* (pp. 226–232).

2. THE ROUTE TO EPHESUS. xviii. 23. After spending some time at Antioch, St Paul re-traversed the route (here described as the Galatic region and Phrygia[1])

---

[1] Ramsay lays stress on the difference between the expression used here and that in xvi. 6, 'the Phrygian-Galatic region.' There it described the district in which Iconium and Antioch lay, through which St Paul and Silas passed after leaving Derbe and Lystra which lay in the Lycaonian-Galatic region, when they confined their work to the province of Galatia because they were forbidden to preach in that of Asia. But now the apostle being under no such prohibition was able to work not only in Galatia but also in 'Phrygia,' i e. that part of it which lay in Asia. Whether the geographical term was intended to convey precisely this distinction or not, it suggests clearly enough the route that he took.

78 THE LIFE OF ST PAUL [CH.

which he had taken with Silas on the second tour, visiting and strengthening in their Christian life the converts in Derbe, Lystra, Iconium, and Pisidian Antioch. This was his third visit to the Galatian churches. From thence he passed on further westward, into the country where the divine Spirit had prevented him from preaching on the second tour, on the way to Ephesus.

3. APOLLOS. xviii. 24–28. Before stating St Paul's arrival at Ephesus, St Luke relates events which had previously occurred there, and which he seems to view as having a connexion with St Paul's action in xix. 1–7. More important is their connexion with the work and influence of Apollos at Corinth, evidenced in 1 Cor. i.–iv.

Apollos (an abbreviated form of Apollonius), a learned Alexandrian Jew, well versed in the Scriptures, i e. the Greek Old Testament, had come to Ephesus. He had been 'instructed[1] in the way of the Lord, and being fervent in spirit he spake and taught accurately the things concerning Jesus, knowing only the baptism of John.' What this exactly means is not clear. But probably he had learnt the manner of life, the morals and duties of Christians ('the Way,' see p 13, n 1), and also the primary truths of the Death and Resurrection of Jesus, and of His Messiahship and near Advent to inaugurate the divine Kingdom and to judge the world[2]. But he had not learnt that Christian converts were baptized into the name of Jesus, and all that that meant for the corporate life of the Church, having heard only of the baptism of John This important part of 'the Way'

[1] D and an Old Latin MS add 'in his own country.'
[2] Cf. xxviii 31, where 'the things concerning the Lord Jesus Christ' is explained in syr[hcl] by the words 'saying that this is Christ Jesus the Son of God through whom the whole world is about to be judged'; and similarly in two Vulg. MSS.

XI] THE THIRD MISSIONARY TOUR 79

was now taught him by Priscilla and Aquila whom St Paul had left at Ephesus. When Apollos departed to go to Achaia[1], the Ephesian Christians wrote a commendatory letter on his behalf to the Christians at Corinth, and there he preached with convincing eloquence to the Jews.

4. DISCIPLES AT EPHESUS. xix. 1–7. After Apollos had left Ephesus St Paul reached it[2], 'passing through the upper parts,' i e. probably along the high ground nearly due West from Pisidian Antioch[3], instead of along the lower main road, through Apameia, Colossae, and Laodicea.

During his stay in the city, the apostle found certain men, about twelve (v. 7), who were 'disciples,' i.e adherents of Christianity, but in much the same semi-instructed state as Apollos before Priscilla and Aquila taught him. These disciples had not received an outpouring of the Spirit when they 'believed,' i e. became believers in Christ, and knew nothing of the possibility of such an outpouring. They had been baptized with John's baptism. St Paul now taught them a fuller Christianity, they received Christian baptism 'into the

[1] D has 'And certain Corinthians staying in Ephesus, and having heard him, besought him to go with them to their country And when he consented, the Ephesians wrote to the disciples at Corinth that they should receive the man'

[2] D has 'And when Paul wished, according to his own plan, to go to Jerusalem, the Spirit told him to turn aside into Asia. And passing through the upper parts he cometh etc.'

[3] This is the meaning suggested by Ramsay for the vague expression. It might simply mean the higher parts of the province of Asia, i e those remote from the sea. But the expression is unique, and St Luke seems to have intended it to bear a more definite meaning Those who adhere to the North-Galatian theory (see p 51 f.) usually explain it as a route S.W through Lydia

name of the Lord Jesus,' and when the apostle laid his hands on them they received the outpouring of the Spirit, and spake with tongues and prophesied. It is not stated that they had been converted by Apollos. If they were, it is natural that they were not better instructed than he had been. But St Luke seems merely to have placed together two passages in which his traditions spoke of people who had received John's baptism[1].

5. SEPARATION FROM THE SYNAGOGUE. xix. 8–10. Having related this incident, St Luke describes St Paul's work as a whole, during the time that he stayed in the city. He started, as always, in the synagogue, where he taught for three months But, as at Pisidian Antioch and Corinth, the opposition of the Jews forced him to go elsewhere. He held daily discussions[2] in the lecture room of a certain Greek teacher of rhetoric or philosophy named Tyrannus. This continued for two years, and the knowledge of Christianity was spread by his converts far and wide among both Jews and Gentiles in the province of Asia. This is the only hint that St Luke

[1] These were not necessarily 'disciples of John.' There was such a body in our Lord's day (Mk ii 18, vi 29, Lk. vii. 18, xi. 1), but it by no means included all who had been baptized by John, and clear evidence is wanting that as a body it survived so long, or was extended beyond Palestine. The marked emphasis laid in the Fourth Gospel on the subordination of the Baptist to our Lord, particularly in iii. 22–36 where the Baptist's declaration of his inferiority arises out of a dispute on the values of different kinds of baptism, suggests that some persons, at the time when that gospel was written (which a widespread early tradition connected with Ephesus), either called themselves 'disciples of John,' or, more probably, preferred the simple 'baptism of John'— 'a baptism of repentance for the remission of sins'—to Christian baptism in the name of Jesus

[2] D adds 'from the fifth hour [11 a m.] until the tenth [4 p.m.].'

XI] THE THIRD MISSIONARY TOUR 81

gives of what must have been important and carefully organized mission work. It was no doubt by this means that Christian communities were formed in the towns of the Lycus valley, such as Laodicea and Colossae (see p. 203 f.). In xx. 31 St Paul is represented as saying that he taught in Ephesus 'for three years.' That is a round number. As we shall see (p. 140 f.), he did not remain there quite continuously even during the two years and three months mentioned in the present chapter.

6. MIRACLES AND THEIR EFFECTS. XIX. 11–20. St Luke here inserts further illustrations of the success of St Paul's work. The first which he gives is in character not unlike the cure of the woman with the issue of blood who touched the tassel on our Lord's cloak (Mk v. 25–34) The power of a strong spiritual character was, in each case, so great that those who were diseased felt certain that to touch the garments of the wonder-worker would procure healing; and the co-operation of their faith did really gain what they wished. In St Paul's case handkerchiefs and aprons were made to touch him, and on being carried to the sick brought about the cure. Since the diseases were understood to be the result of possession by evil spirits or demons, the cure is described as consisting in their expulsion.

But a similar faith was put, quite as effectively, in 'exorcism,' wrought by invoking over the diseased the name of Jesus. This was of course seriously liable to abuse. Jewish charlatans or quacks used to go about exorcising, often probably for payment. The present instance was one in which seven sons of a certain Sceva, a member of a high-priestly family, tried to exorcise by means of the name of Jesus, and failed disastrously, because the invalid, who was subject to violent fits, was only roused to rage by their attempt, he 'leaped on them, and mastered all[1] of them, and prevailed against them, so that they fled out of that house naked and wounded.' This failure of unauthorised persons only enhanced the prestige of St Paul, and, as St Luke relates, convinced many of the truth of Christianity. Magical arts were so widely practised in Ephesus that writings containing magical formulas and incantations came to be known as 'Ephesian writings.' Many magicians now brought their copies of these writings and burnt them in public. They were so highly valued that their price was reckoned as 50,000 pieces of silver, i.e. denarii, or about £1980.

7. ST PAUL'S PLANS. xix. 21, 22 St Paul intended to pass through Macedonia and Achaia. He would reach the former by sailing up the coast to Troas, and thence, as on the second tour, across to Neapolis. After that, he hoped to go to Jerusalem (for Pentecost, xx. 16), and then to reach the goal of his ambition by visiting Rome. Meantime he sent to Macedonia Timothy and Erastus (see p. 139). The latter can hardly have been the 'treasurer' of the city of Corinth named in Rom. xvi. 23 (cf. 2 Tim. iv. 20). He has not hitherto been mentioned, and was probably a resident in Ephesus, recently converted by St Paul. He seems to have been a young man, since he and Timothy are described as 'two of those who were ministering to him.'

8. THE RIOT. XIX. 23-41. Ephesus was specially devoted to the worship of Artemis, the Latin Diana, as

---

1 The word is ἀμφοτέρων, which in classical Greek means 'both' (so R.V.); hence αὐτῶν ('them') is read in HLP, many minuscules, and syr[pesh]. But papyri shew that in late Greek 'all' was a possible meaning. See Moulton-Milligan, *Vocab. of the Greek Test. s.v.*

THE THIRD MISSIONARY TOUR

Corinth was to that of Aphrodite. The city is described on inscriptions and coins as the '*neōkoros* (temple-keeper or slave) of Artemis[1].' The pride which the citizens felt in the title is shewn in *v.* 35. A guild of silversmiths made large sums by the manufacture of silver models[2], 'small shrines (*naoi*) for votaries to dedicate in the temple, representing the Goddess Artemis sitting in a niche or *naiskos*, with her lions beside her' (Ramsay). One of these silversmiths, Demetrius, called the members of the guild together, and by an inflammatory speech roused them against St Paul, who, he said, was making so many converts that the worship of Artemis, and therefore their trade, was beginning to suffer. They raised a general riot, arrested Gaius and Aristarchus, Macedonians[3] whom St Luke speaks of as 'Paul's fellow travellers[4],' and rushed into the theatre, most of the crowd being quite ignorant of the real cause of the disturbance. St Paul wanted to go into the theatre to address the mob, but was dissuaded by the Christians in the city, and by some of the local officials called 'Asiarchs[5].'

[1] See J T. Wood, *Discoveries at Ephesus*, Append. 6, p. 50.
[2] *ibid*, Append 6, p. 10 f.
[3] Possibly the singular should be read, referring only to Aristarchus (see p 88 n.).
[4] They have not been hitherto mentioned as accompanying St Paul. They may have joined him at some previous stage of his tour, and St Luke in his hasty sketch of the apostle's movements up to this point omitted to mention the fact. But perhaps it means that they accompanied him from this point. They may have been recently converted in Ephesus, and had now arranged to travel with him back to their own country. The mob evidently found them somewhere without St Paul but knew them to be friends of his.
[5] They were religious officials, appointed by Rome to superintend the imperial religion in the province of Asia. They were therefore not in sympathy with the native Artemis worship, and were willing to act favourably towards a Roman citizen.

The Jews in the crowd put up one of their number, named Alexander, to make a speech. The narrative at this point is a little obscure, and St Luke does not seem to have received a precise account of all the details[1]. But Alexander was probably put forward to state that although the Christian missionaries were Jews, the Jewish inhabitants of the city repudiated their teaching. But the Greeks who formed the larger part of the crowd would not distinguish between Jews who were Christians and Jews who were not. For two hours they shouted 'Great is Artemis of the Ephesians[2]!' Then the town clerk, an important native official, who must have been held in high respect, managed to still the shouting, and made a speech which put an end to the trouble In the words which St Luke attributes to him he makes four points. (1) He put them into a good humour by saying that everyone was agreed as to the honourable position of Ephesus as temple-keeper of Artemis, the goddess who fell from Zeus[3]; since this was obvious and undeniable, there was no need for excitement. (2) The prisoners whom they had arrested had committed no crime, either by robbing temples or by speaking evil of Artemis[4].

[1] Alexander is introduced as though he were already known to the reader It is possible that he followed a trade similar to that of Demetrius If, as Ramsay suggests, the silversmiths were only one of the trade guilds concerned, and models of Artemis were made also in other materials than silver, his conjecture that Alexander may have been the worker in bronze (E.V. 'coppersmith'), mentioned in 2 Tim. iv 14 as doing St Paul much harm, is attractive (see p. 259).
[2] The first hand of D has 'Great Artemis of the Eph.,' omitting the predicative article.
[3] Or perhaps 'from the sky.'
[4] The first and the last two points are such as might well have been made in the circumstances, but in the second St Luke rather than the town clerk seems to speak. Demetrius had no doubt been quite correct in saying that the mission-

(3) If a complaint was to be made against anyone, the municipal courts were available, and the Roman officials also could take cognisance of it. Formal legal action and not angry rioting was the right procedure. (4) The Roman officials might very likely hold the city responsible for the riot, and in that case they would find themselves in a serious predicament, because they could offer no good excuse for it.

9. SUFFERINGS IN EPHESUS. With the exception of the riot St Luke says nothing of St Paul's sufferings in Ephesus. But from the epistles to the Corinthians we gather a vivid picture of them. In 1 Cor. xv. 32 the apostle says 'If after the manner of men I fought with beasts at Ephesus etc.' This is perhaps not literal, for a Roman citizen could not be condemned to fight with beasts in the arena. If it is metaphorical, he refers to the wild unreasoning opposition that he encountered[1]. But the words may mean 'If...I *had* fought with beasts at Ephesus, what advantage would it have been to me?' He may actually have been condemned to the arena, but managed to escape by convincing them that he was a Roman citizen. In that case it is very likely that he was for a time in prison (see p. 231) If the words refer to the riot, he suffered from it as well as Gaius and Aristarchus, which St Luke does not relate. But his

aries preached that 'they be no gods which are made with hands' (v. 26). This would be speaking evil of Artemis, and was, in fact, the cause of the riot The town clerk's denial of this 'crime' would only have roused greater fury That Jews were sometimes guilty of robbing temples is shewn in Rom. 11 22.

[1] Ignatius, on his way to Rome to be thrown to the beasts, uses the words 'I fight with wild beasts' metaphorically of the soldiers ('leopards' as he calls them) who guarded him on the journey (*Rom.* 5).

agonies of mind and body were, in fact, incessant during his stay at Ephesus. He calls them (2 Cor. i. 8) 'our affliction which befell us in Asia,' which drove him almost to despair of life. And in 1 Cor. iv. 9–13, 2 Cor. iv. 8–12 he reiterates with anguish all that he had to undergo. See also 2 Cor. vi. 4, 5, xi. 23–27, where he speaks more generally of his sufferings in the course of his missionary work up to this point. If St Luke knew these passages, he omitted all the details because his object was to write, not a biography of the apostle but, a sketch of the expansion of Christianity. But very possibly he did not know them. He sums up the period at Ephesus in the colourless words that St Paul after sending away Timothy and Erastus 'himself stayed in Asia for a while' (Acts xix. 22).

10. MACEDONIA TO GREECE AND BACK. XX. 1–4. In these four verses, before the next 'We'-section begins, St Luke continues his lightning sketch of St Paul's movements. St Paul said farewell to the Christians at Ephesus, and, in accordance with the intention of which St Luke spoke in xix. 21, went to **Macedonia** and **Greece**. The route is not stated; but he no doubt sailed northwards, coasting along the western shore of Asia Minor to Troas (see 2 Cor. ii. 12, and cf. the converse route described in Acts xx. 13-15), and across to Neapolis. Thence he may have followed the route which he took on the second tour, by land *via* Philippi, Apollonia, Thessalonica and Beroea. But possibly, though not probably (see p. 63), he broke away from this route at some point, and journeyed further inland to the borders of the district of **Illyricum**, which he soon afterwards (Rom. xv. 19) names as the limit of his missionary work before the time that he wrote. While passing

through Macedonia he gave 'much exhortation' to his former converts, to whom he was greatly attached. And before he reached Greece he wrote 2 *Corinthians* (see p. 136). St Luke's sketch is so hasty that we are not even told at what town in Greece he arrived, but it was doubtless **Corinth**, where he stayed three months, and wrote perhaps *Galatians* and probably *Romans* (see pp. 172 f. and 181 f.).

At the end of the three months he was preparing to start by sea for Syria, still in accordance with the plan mentioned in xix. 21, when he learnt that Jews in the city were plotting against him. The nature of the plot is not told us, but it made him change his mind, and instead of going by sea, which would perhaps have involved waiting a few days for a ship, he travelled back by the land route through **Macedonia**[1].

He journeyed[2] with seven companions: Sopater a Beroean (who may be the Jew, St Paul's 'kinsman' Sosipater, who sends greeting from Corinth in Rom. xvi. 21); two from Thessalonica, Aristarchus and Secundus (the latter otherwise unknown); two from Galatia, Gaius a Derbaean and Timothy (whose native town Lystra is not named, having been already stated in Acts xvi. 1); and two from the province of Asia, Tychicus and Trophimus. It is natural to suppose that these were representatives of the several churches to carry their contributions for the poor in the Christian community at Jerusalem. St Paul had suggested to the Corinthians that their money should be carried by delegates, and

---

1 D syr[hcl marg] have 'he wanted to sail to Syria, but the Spirit told him to return through Macedonia.'

2 The words 'as far as Asia,' added in R V, must be omitted with אB vulg. memph. sah. Aristarchus at least went further than Asia (xxvii. 2).

that he might perhaps accompany them (1 Cor. xvi. 3, 4). But it is curious that among these seven companions no Corinthians are included[1]; also that Tychicus and Trophimus, if they were the Asiatic delegates, must have sailed across to St Paul at Corinth carrying their money with them, instead of waiting for him at Ephesus or meeting him in Syria, as we should have thought more natural. St Luke makes no reference to the contribution, which was St Paul's principal object in going to Jerusalem (Rom. xv 25–27), except in the words which he attributes to the apostle in his speech before Felix (Acts xxiv 17)

11 PHILIPPI TO TROAS xx. 5–12. At this point begins the second of the 'We'-sections (see p x). Since in the first the events are related as far as Philippi on the second tour, and this one begins at Philippi on the third tour, many have drawn the rather precarious conclusion that St Luke had stayed in that town during the intervening period, or even that he was himself a Philippian

St Paul's seven companions sailed to Troas without him, and there waited for him and St Luke. The apostle probably found it difficult to tear himself away from his favourite converts, and therefore postponed his departure till the end of the days of Unleavened Bread. When he sailed, the wind must have been against him,

[1] One Corinthian would be included if Gaius were the person whom St Paul names as his 'host' in Corinth (Rom. xvi 23), but in that case St Luke is mistaken in calling him a Derbaean, unless the text is corrupt. The Gaius who was one of St Paul's 'fellow travellers' was a Macedonian according to Acts xix. 29 But the plural Μακεδόνας should probably be corrected (as is done in a few minuscules) to the singular Μακεδόνα, referring only to Aristarchus, the σ of the following συνεκδήμους having been accidentally doubled.

XI] THE THIRD MISSIONARY TOUR 89

since the crossing to **Troas** occupied five days, whereas he had, on the first tour, covered the distance in the converse direction apparently in two (xvi. 11).

At Troas (*vv.* 7–12), where they stayed a week, a glimpse is afforded of a Christian assembly. On the Sabbath St Paul may have preached in the synagogue, but on Sunday, the day before his departure, he preached to Christians in a house. They gathered to 'break bread,' i.e. to partake of the Lord's Supper, according to the custom of the Church from the earliest days. It was evening, many lamps were lit, and St Paul discoursed at great length, until a young man named Eutychus, sitting in a window seat (the room was on the third storey), was 'borne down with deep sleep' and fell to the ground. St Luke says he was 'taken up dead.' This may mean that he was actually dead, and that St Paul raised him to life But it may equally mean that when he was lifted up everyone thought he was dead (cf. Mk ix. 26, Acts xiv. 19), but St Paul went down and discovered that he was not So they returned to the room, and St Paul 'broke bread,' after which they all conversed with him till daybreak, when he departed.

The fragmentariness of the record in the *Acts* is illustrated by the fact that St Luke nowhere tells us when and how a Christian community was formed in Troas. It was not on the first tour, when St Paul saw the vision of the man of Macedonia (xvi. 9), for he had been forbidden to preach in the province of Asia (*v.* 6) in which Troas lay. Of the second time that he went there St Luke says nothing (see xx. 1). But St Paul himself relates (2 Cor. ii. 12, 13) that he 'came to Troas for the gospel of Christ,' and that 'a door was opened unto me n the Lord.' He did not stay long because he was overwhelmed with anxiety about the Corinthians (see p. 143), and therefore passed on to Macedonia to find Titus. But even in his short stay he made some converts.

12. TROAS TO MILETUS. xx. 13–16. St Paul now bade his companions, for the second time, to go on ahead. They went by a coasting vessel (cf. xxvii. 2) round the promontory of Lectum to Assos, while he walked across by himself[1], perhaps starting a little later than the boat. He would no doubt enjoy the solitary walk as an opportunity for restful thought and prayer. He joined them at **Assos** (*v.* 13), and they sailed to **Mitylene** (*v.* 14), the chief town in the island of Lesbos, lying on its eastern coast[2]. An early start would be made each morning before sunrise, to get the full benefit of the North wind which in the Aegean Sea generally falls in the afternoon during the summer. On the three following days they reached successively (*v.* 15) a point on the mainland **opposite the island of Chios**, the eastern coast of the island of **Samos**, and the town of **Miletus** on the mainland. Notice that the words are we 'came' opposite Chios, and we 'came' to Miletus, but we 'touched at' Samos, implying that they did not stay the night there. This led to the reading in some manuscripts[3], followed in the A.V., 'and having stayed at **Trogyllium**, on the next day we came to Miletus.' The writer of the words, if they are not original, may have known by experience that it was the usual stopping-place for voyagers down the coast. The promontory of Trogyllium on the mainland projected opposite the eastern promontory of Samos, forming a strait less than a mile in width.

[1] For the suggestion that this was the occasion on which he left his cloak with Carpus (2 Tim iv 13) see p. 259 f.
[2] The whole island is now called Mitylene.
[3] DHLP, most minuscules, syr$^{pesh\ hcl}$ sah

St Luke's remark (*v.* 16) that in order to save time 'Paul had determined to sail past Ephesus' possibly implies that the boat was a hired one, and at his disposal. The Christians at Troas might have chartered it for him, or he and his companions pooled their funds. But it is simpler to suppose that he had purposely chosen a boat which was not due to put in at Ephesus. The channel up the river to the city was at that time becoming narrow and difficult, and boats mostly avoided it (Ramsay). Not only would it occupy time to reach the city, but once there the apostle might find it difficult to hurry away from his numerous friends. That he was afraid of violence or disturbance St Luke in no way suggests, but says that he was hurrying in hopes of reaching Jerusalem for the Feast of Pentecost. The chief reason for this hope probably was that he wished the crowd of Jewish Christians who would come up to the city to realise that he was one who loyally observed the Jewish festival. It is not stated whether he managed to arrive in time, but there are indications that he probably did[1].

[1] The spending of 'several days' at Caesarea (xxi. 10), probably the last stage but one before Jerusalem, may indeed imply either that he had arrived at that town with plenty of time in hand, or that being too late for Pentecost he had no need to hurry. But the former is more probable for three reasons: (1) St James expected that a multitude would assemble (*v.* 22), and they must have been there for the festival. (2) So also were the 'Jews from Asia' (*v* 27) who were in the city after St Paul's arrival. (3) The mention of 'worship' in xxiv. 11 seems to be a reference to Pentecost. St Luke gives the length of most of the stages in the journey from Philippi, but not of the stay at Miletus, the voyage from Patara to Tyre, and the stay at Caesarea. Ramsay, by assuming that St Luke's figures are inclusive, in each case, of the days of departure and of arrival, and giving four days at Miletus and four for the crossing to Tyre, reckons that St Paul reached Caesarea a fortnight before Pentecost.

13. MILETUS. xx. 17–38. At Miletus the boat stayed for a few days, no doubt unloading and taking in cargo. So St Paul had time to send a messenger to Ephesus to summon the presbyters to come to him.

In *vv.* 18–35 St Luke gives a speech addressed to them (see p. x), in which the apostle holds up for their example his own conduct during his stay[1] at Ephesus (*vv.* 18–21). And since he has received divine intimations[2] that he is about to suffer bonds and afflictions in Jerusalem, and is sure that he will not see the Ephesians again[3] (*vv.* 22–25), he protests that he is free from the responsibility of not having done his utmost to save their souls (*vv.* 26, 27), and solemnly charges them in regard to their work as overseers of the Church (*v.* 28), for enemies from outside ('grievous wolves') and also from within the Church itself will try to ruin and pervert their flock (*vv.* 29, 30). They must remember the grief and anxiety with which he admonished them for three years (*v.* 31). He commends them to God (*v.* 32), and reminds them again of his example, in particular of his hand labour for his own living in order not to be a burden upon them, emphasizing it with a saying of our Lord not elsewhere recorded (*vv.* 33–35).

Then they all knelt down and St Paul prayed, and

[1] The words 'from the first day that I set foot in Asia' disregard the fact that St Paul passed through a portion of Asia on his second tour (p 55), long before he visited Ephesus

D here gives the time at Ephesus as 'three years or more' In *v* 31 St Paul speaks of 'three years.' But in xix. 8, 10 it is stated to be two years and three months.

[2] No instances of this are recorded till later, at Tyre (xxi. 4), and Caesarea (xxi. 11).

[3] This does not entirely exclude the possibility that he did after all see them again, but see p 258.

XI] THE THIRD MISSIONARY TOUR 93

after a sorrowful and affectionate farewell they escorted him to the ship (*vv*. 36–38).

14. MILETUS TO TYRE. xxi. 1–6. That day they reached **Cos**, a town on the N.E. shore of the island of Cos, and on the two successive nights they anchored at **Rhodes**, a town at the N.E. corner of the island of Rhodes, and at **Patara** on the Lycian mainland[1]. Their little coasting vessel perhaps turned at this point to retrace its course; at any rate it could not do the long crossing to Phoenicia, so they changed into a larger ship. With the prevailing West wind they were able to take the shortest course, S.W. of Cyprus, instead of sailing under the lee of the island round its eastern shore; and the ship landed at **Tyre** to unload her cargo. Here they stayed a week with the Christians in the town, one of whom, filled with the spirit of ecstasy, advised St Paul not to venture into Jerusalem[2]. On their departure their hosts, with their wives and children, escorted them out of the town to the shore, and as at Miletus knelt for prayer and then bade them farewell.

15. TYRE TO JERUSALEM. xxi. 7–16. They sailed[3] to **Ptolemais**, where they spent the night with the Christians, and thence on the next day to **Caesarea** There they lodged 'several days' (see p. 91 n.) with Philip the evangelist, one of the Seven (cf. vi. 5); he had four un-

---

1 In D sah. the words 'and Myra' (cf. xxvii. 5) are added after Patara. This would be another stage of one day along the Lycian coast

2 R V 'that he should not set foot in Jerusalem,' and A.V. 'that he should not go up to Jerusalem' convey a wrong impression of the meaning

3 Since the Christians at Tyre escorted them to the shore, and, as on the stages along the coast of Asia, they stayed only one night at Ptolemais, it may be concluded that they reached Caesarea by sea, not by land.

married daughters who 'prophesied' in a spirit of ecstasy. They were joined by the 'prophet' Agabus[1] from Jerusalem, who declared that the Jews at the capital would hand St Paul over to the Gentiles, i.e. the Romans, emphasizing his words, like some of the Old Testament prophets, by a symbolic action, binding his own hands and feet with St Paul's girdle. The Christians in the place, and his companions, entreated the apostle not to go, but he replied unshaken that he was ready even to die for the name of the Lord Jesus. So they acquiesced saying 'the will of the Lord be done.'

Accompanied by some of the Christians from Caesarea they now set out for **Jerusalem**, a journey of about 64 miles. They may have ridden on animals, since they can have had very little time at their disposal. Ramsay thinks that the word[2] rendered 'took up our baggage' (R.V.), for which the A.V. has the archaic 'carriages,' means 'equipped, or saddled, animals.' It can mean that, or more generally (as Chrysostom explains it[3]) 'provided ourselves with necessaries,' which might include animals. In v. 16 St Luke says 'Some of the disciples came from Caesarea with us, bringing [us to someone] with whom we might lodge[4], a certain Mnason,

[1] No doubt the same who predicted the famine (xi. 28).
[2] ἐπισκευασάμενοι. R.V. margin 'made ready' follows the Vulgate 'praeparati'; similarly Wiclif and Tyndale.
[3] τὰ πρὸς τὴν ὁδοιπορίαν λαβόντες
[4] This is a legitimate rendering of ἄγοντες παρ' ᾧ ξενισθῶμεν Μνάσωνι κτλ. E. Vv. following the Peshitta have 'bringing [A.V. and brought] *with them* one Mnason etc.' But to bring their intended host with them would be rather a strange proceeding. The rendering adopted above is supported by a gloss added in D syr^{hcl mg} before Mnason's name, παραγενόμενοι εἴς τινα κώμην ἐγενόμεθα παρὰ Μνάσωνι, 'having arrived at a certain village we came to [the house of] Mnason.'

a Cypriot, an original[1] disciple.' Where Mnason lived we have no means of knowing; it may have been anywhere *en route*, so that they broke their journey at his house for the night, or perhaps more probably in or close to Jerusalem, in which case he was to be their host throughout their visit to the capital.

CHAPTER XII

ST PAUL AT JERUSALEM

Acts xxi. 17–xxiii. 30

1. THE PROSPECT OF DANGER. St Paul's fearlessness in appearing openly at Jerusalem at the time of the festival is remarkable. His Gentile converts would not be there to support him, since they did not observe Jewish festivals. The Jewish Christians, present in large numbers, would include the Judaizers who had tried to pervert his converts in Antioch, Galatia, Corinth, and other places; and there was also in the city a multitude of Jews, including those who had tried to kill him at Damascus (ix 23), Jerusalem (ix. 29), Pisidian Antioch (xiii. 50), Iconium (xiv. 5), Lystra (xiv. 19), Thessalonica (xvii. 5), Beroea (xvii. 13), Corinth (xx. 3), and elsewhere (2 Cor. xi. 24). He was fully prepared for trouble (Rom. xv. 31; cf. Acts xx. 23, xxi. 4, 11).

2. RECEPTION BY THE CHURCH. xxi. 17–20 a. On arriving at the city St Paul and his party were gladly received by 'the brethren[2],' which probably means that

---

[1] ἀρχαίῳ μαθητῇ, a Christian since the beginning (ἀρχή) of the Church's history which now seemed so far off.

[2] Whether St Paul's nephew (see xxiii. 16) was of their number we do not know.

some of the resident Christians welcomed them and perhaps gave them hospitality. Next day they were interviewed by St James the Lord's brother, the chief of all Jewish Christians, who had summoned the elders of the Jerusalem Church to meet them. Nothing is said about the handing over of the collection from the Gentile Churches, which St Paul had regarded as a matter of the utmost importance. Those present at the meeting received with gladness his detailed account of what God had done through his ministry among the Gentiles; and the collection which he no doubt presented would serve as an outward sign of it.

3. THE FOUR NAZIRITES. xxi. 20 b–26. But his relations with the 'myriads' of Jewish Christians needed adjustment, as St James pointed out. His opponents had been going about spreading the false report that in his mission work in Gentile countries he had been teaching the Jews of the Dispersion to give up their Judaism. The Jewish Christians in the city would hear that he had arrived, and it would be wise if he could do something to prove to them that he was not so hostile to Judaism as was reported[1]. As suggested on p. 91, that had probably been his purpose in hurrying to the city for Pentecost. But an opportunity offered of giving them a more distinct object lesson[2].

[1] It would hardly prove as much as v. 24 b suggests, and was in fact not enough to allay Jewish hostility

[2] At this point St James is represented as saying, in a curiously parenthetical manner (v 25), that the decrees of the Council (cf xv. 28, 29) had been sent to (or enjoined upon) the Gentile Christians He states it as though St Paul had not known all about it, and himself published the decrees In D an attempt seems to be made to smooth the difficulty by the reading, 'But concerning the Gentiles who have become believers they have nothing to say to thee, for we sent etc.'

AT JERUSALEM

It was no doubt distinct to them, but unfortunately it is somewhat obscure to us. Four Jewish Christians were in the city who were under a vow, which they had probably timed to come to an end before the festival. And St Paul was advised to shew his loyalty to Jewish customs by joining with them in taking upon him for a short period a similar vow, so that he could share in the public ceremony which would form the conclusion of it. 'Be at charges with them (i e. pay money for them) that they may shave their heads' suggests that it was a Nazirite vow, and that he was to pay for the animals etc. for the necessary sacrifices (see Num. vi. 13–20)[1]. What he did is described in $v.$ 26: 'Then Paul having taken the men on the following day having been purified with them went in [the verb is imperfect] to the temple declaring the completion of the days of purification until the offering was offered on behalf of each one of them' The expressions 'having been purified' and 'the days of purification' do not refer to an act of ceremonial cleansing, the former means that St Paul took the vow upon him, the latter means the whole period of their vow. St Luke adopts the language of Num. vi. 2, 5[2]. The imperfect 'went in[3],' and the words 'declaring etc' seem to refer to a custom otherwise unknown; they appear to describe a repeated action, as though the four men completed their vows on different days, all of which fell within St Paul's short Nazirite-

---

[1] In Josephus, *Antiq* XIX vi 1, Agrippa I is said to have done the same for a large number of Nazirites

[2] In v 2 ἀφαγνίσασθαι ἁγνείαν is the equivalent of Hebrew words which mean ' to separate himself as a Nazirite,' and in $v.$ 5 τὰς ἡμέρας τοῦ ἁγνισμοῦ stands for 'the days of the vow of his separation.'

[3] εἰσῄει.

ship, and he entered the temple on those four days, and made a public declaration on behalf of each man that the period of his vow had expired. A further difficulty is caused by the opening words of *v.* 27: 'But when the seven days were about to be accomplished.' St Luke has previously said nothing about seven days, but assumes that his readers will understand the allusion. It perhaps implies that, according to the custom of the time, of which however there is, again, no other evidence, seven days was the shortest time for which the Nazirite vow could be taken.

4. THE RIOT. xxi. 27–40. Among those who had come up for the festival were some Jews 'from Asia,' i e. from Ephesus, as *v.* 29 suggests. They were the same who had tried in the Ephesian riot to put up Alexander to tell the mob that, as Jews, they repudiated all connexion with St Paul (xix. 33). They recognised, or perhaps thought they recognised, Trophimus in his company, whom they had seen with him in Ephesus, and mistakenly imagined, or falsely pretended, that he had taken him into the temple, which would be a defilement to the sacred building, since Trophimus was a Gentile They ought, by Jewish law, to have arrested and killed Trophimus if they had really found him there, but they only made it an opportunity of catching St Paul. They stirred up the mob by saying that he taught everywhere against the chosen people, the Mosaic Law, and the temple (cf vi. 13), and that he had taken Gentiles into the temple. The crowd rushed upon him in the temple, dragged him out, and would have beaten him to death had not the Roman authorities intervened[1].

[1] The events in Jerusalem give St Luke a good opportunity of introducing his favourite theme, that the Romans were

AT JERUSALEM

A cohort under command of a 'chiliarch' or tribune was permanently quartered in the castle of Antonia for the purpose of keeping the turbulent Jews in control. The castle stood at the N.W. corner of the temple court, connected with it at two points by steps. And during the great festivals guards were stationed in the corridors surrounding the temple, ready to act at a moment's notice[1].

When the disturbance, therefore, became known to the chiliarch (who was named Claudius Lysias, xxiii 26), he ran down the steps with some soldiers, and the mob ceased beating St Paul. He ordered him to be chained by the wrists, and asked what he had been doing. Unable to get a coherent answer from the crowd he ordered the soldiers to take the prisoner into the castle A rush was made at him, so that the soldiers had to carry him up the steps to keep him from being lynched. At the door of the castle he surprised the chiliarch by asking him, in Greek, to give him leave to address the mob. The chiliarch supposed that he was a notorious Egyptian rebel, who, as Josephus[2] relates, had recently given himself out as a prophet, and had drawn after him a band of desperate followers whom St Luke describes as *sicarii* or assassins. Many of them had been killed or captured, but the impostor himself had escaped. St Luke gives their number as 4000, Josephus as 30,000. St Paul replied that he was no Egyptian, but 'a Jew, a Tarsian of Cilicia, a citizen of no mean city.' And with the chiliarch's permission he stood on the stairs and

usually favourable to St Paul, and this perhaps accounts for the large space occupied with events connected with Roman authorities (chs. xxi–xxvi)

1 Josephus, *Jewish War*, v. v. 8.
2 *Antiq.* xx. viii. 6, *Jewish War*, ii. xiii. 5.

addressed the crowd, attracting their attention by speaking in 'Hebrew.' i.e. their native Aramaic (xxii. 2).

5. ST PAUL'S SPEECH AND ITS SEQUEL. xxii. 3–29. He told them that he had been a strict Jew, taught by Gamaliel, and that he had persecuted the Christians with the authority of the Sanhedrin, until he was converted by the vision on the way to Damascus. See p. 14 f. He reached the point where God told him to preach to the Gentiles. But at that, the mob interrupted with furious shouts, and the chiliarch ordered him to be taken into the castle, that a confession might be forced from him by the terrible torture of scourging. He was being bound, probably to a pillar[1], when he startled the chiliarch by claiming to be a Roman citizen, and that by birth and not, as the chiliarch had gained the privilege, by a large payment[2]. The scourging, of course, did not take place. Even to have bound him was a punishable offence[3].

6 ST PAUL BEFORE THE SANHEDRIN. xxii. 30–xxiii. 11. Next morning the chiliarch summoned the Sanhedrin, the chief Jewish court of judgment, consisting of the high priests, and some scribes and elders, and St Paul was brought up before them. He had just begun his speech when the high priest Ananias, the president of the court, commanded him to be struck on the mouth. St Paul replied very angrily, but then apologized, saying

[1] $\pi\rho o \acute{\epsilon}\tau\epsilon\iota\nu\alpha\nu$ suggests that his arms were stretched and tied at full length above his head. The victim of the punishment was sometimes suspended with the feet above the ground, cf Terence, *Phorm* I iv. 43.

[2] 'For a great sum I obtained the citizenship' D has 'I know for how great a sum etc' He seems to have thought that St Paul could not possibly have afforded to pay for the privilege, and that he was telling a lie

[3] See p 59 n.

that he did not know it was the high priest¹. He soon
realised that beside the priestly, Sadducean, members
of the court there were also Pharisees present among
the number of the scribes and elders, so he decided on
a tactical move, and cried out that he was a Pharisee,
and that he was being tried 'concerning the hope
and the resurrection of the dead².' This split the court
into two opposing parties, since a resurrection was
one of the subjects on which Pharisees and Sadducees
were in strong disagreement. And St Luke draws the
strange picture of the august Sanhedrin transformed

---

1 The circumstances are not told clearly enough for us to understand how St Paul (even if, as some conjecture, his eyesight was bad) could make this extraordinary mistake. But whatever the circumstances were, his retort is in strong contrast with the patient and dignified silence of our Lord at His trial. St Paul was very human, and highly strung; he had been beaten by the mob on the previous day, and must have been still in pain, and at the gratuitous insult he momentarily lost his self-control

2 'The hope' seems to be a reference to the Messiah (cf. xxvi 6 'the hope of the promise made by God unto our fathers,' xxviii. 20 'the hope of Israel') It is omitted in St Paul's subsequent reference to his speech (xxiv. 21), but an assertion of the resurrection of Jesus formed part of the charge against him as it reached the ears of Festus (xxv. 19). St Paul's statement here is difficult. He was arrested by the Jews not on a charge of believing in a resurrection—which was an accepted doctrine of the Pharisees and most orthodox Jews, as the narrative itself shews—but of teaching things contrary to the Jewish religion, and of defiling the temple. The Sanhedrin could not have been unaware of the causes of his arrest, but the narrative seems to represent St Paul as trying to divert their mind from the real issue by raising a side question Some have thought that St Luke must have compiled his story of the events in Jerusalem from different sources The question of the resurrection probably came up in the course of the enquiry as to St Paul's teaching, and he seized upon it as a way of escape, but St Luke, who was, of course, not present at the trial, received in his traditions confused accounts of what took place.

into a mob which would have torn St Paul in pieces between them if the chiliarch had not rescued him a second time by soldiers who took him back into the castle.

But that night St Paul received the encouragement of a vision, in which the Lord told him that he would witness for Him at Rome as he had at Jerusalem.

CHAPTER XIII

ST PAUL'S IMPRISONMENT AT CAESAREA

Acts xxiii. 12–xxvi. 32

1. ST PAUL SENT TO CAESAREA. xxiii. 12–30. The Jews were furious at being baulked of their prey, and more than forty of them bound themselves by a vow not to eat or drink till they had killed St Paul. But a nephew of his told him of the plot[1], and St Paul contrived, probably by payment, to persuade a soldier to take the young man to the chiliarch. Lysias, hearing his news, ordered a body of soldiers to take him to Caesarea to Felix the procurator, and to start at 9 p.m. in order to travel by night. He sent a letter by them to Felix, stating that he had rescued the prisoner from the violence of the Jews, 'having learned that he was a Roman' (naturally concealing the fact that he had bound and nearly scourged him!); that the Jewish court charged him only with matters concerning their law, which did

---

[1] This need not imply that his nephew was a Christian; he might naturally wish to rescue his uncle It is possible that St Paul's family came to live in Jerusalem while he was learning from Gamaliel, and that his sister was married there

not constitute a crime worthy of death, or even a misdemeanour deserving of imprisonment; but that because they were plotting against him he was now sending him to Felix, and had ordered the Jews to state their accusations in his court

The cavalcade travelled all night to **Antipatris**, which lay about 40 miles from Jerusalem between Lydda and Caesarea, and the horsemen took the prisoner on, while the rest returned to Jerusalem. He was handed over to the procurator, who asked to what province he belonged[1]; and then, until the arrival of his accusers, confined him in Herod's palace which he used as his own 'praetorium' or official residence.

2. FELIX. xxiv. The Jews were not long in discovering that the prisoner had again escaped their clutches. In five days the high priest and certain elders arrived at Caesarea, bringing with them a professional counsel for the prosecution, a Roman *causidicus* named Tertullus. He made a speech (*vv.* 2-8) in which, after a formal compliment to the procurator, he charged St Paul for the first time with a really indictable offence, that of being the ringleader of an insurrectionary sect named Nazarenes, one who had caused disturbances in all parts of the Empire[2], his latest exploit being the profanation of the temple,—which Tertullus treated as only another instance of deliberate creation of disturbance. And the Jews, of course, agreed with what he said

St Paul's reply falls into two parts (*vv.* 10–16 and 17–21) which cover almost entirely the same ground,

---

1 Roman law allowed the trial to take place either in the native country of the accused, or in that in which the alleged crime was committed.
2 τὴν οἰκουμένην, the civilized world.

and are possibly different versions of the same speech. Four chief points appear in both: (a) St Paul's reason for going to Jerusalem was a religious one, in harmony with, and not opposed to, the Jewish religion. (b) Denial of making a disturbance. (c) Challenge to the prosecutors. (d) Admission regarding a resurrection.

(1) *vv.* 10–16. St Paul began, like Tertullus, with a compliment to Felix. He was happy to make his defence before him because, having governed Jews for so long, the procurator would understand that it was only twelve days since he (a) went to Jerusalem for worship, i.e. to attend the festival of Pentecost. (b) He denied having made any disturbance in the temple, the synagogues, or in any part of the city; and (c) challenged the prosecutors to prove their accusations. He admitted being a member of a body of people who followed a certain 'Way' of living and teaching, and were called by their opponents a 'sect,' but he believed in the Scriptures, and (d) hoped, as did his accusers, for a resurrection of righteous and unrighteous.

(2) *vv.* 17–21. After many years, i.e. after a long absence from Jerusalem, he came (a) to do the Jews a kindness by bringing them alms, and also to make offerings in the temple[1]. (b) He was in the temple with no desire to make a disturbance, but 'purified' and stirring up no crowd or tumult. 'But certain Jews from Asia[2]

[1] The alms were the contribution from the churches, to which this is St Luke's sole reference in the *Acts*. The offerings were probably the sacrifices for himself and the four Nazirites; but the verse is so condensed that it makes it appear as though these offerings, as well as the alms, were part of the apostle's previous intention in coming to Jerusalem.

[2] St Paul probably related their violent and unwarranted act in arresting him. Their absence from the court now made conviction impossible.

[the sentence is here broken, and something has probably been lost]—who ought to have been here before thee, and to make accusation if they had aught against me' (c) But he challenged Ananias and the elders to declare any wrong-doing of which the Sanhedrin had convicted him, unless (d) it were his plea that he believed in a resurrection.

Felix, who knew enough about the 'Way'—the Christian manner of life—to understand that it was not the prisoner's Christianity which could make him a criminal, adjourned the trial till Claudius Lysias the chiliarch should come from Jerusalem, and ordered that St Paul, as a Roman citizen, should receive favourable treatment[1] while in custody, and be allowed to receive visits from his friends (vv 22, 23). So far as we are told, the chiliarch never appeared, and no further trial under Felix took place But one other incident is related.

Some time afterwards Felix, who had left Caesarea, came back with his wife Drusilla, a beautiful young Jewish girl, daughter of Agrippa I, whom he had, with the help of a magician, enticed to marry him, deserting her husband Azizus, king of Emesa[2]. He made St Paul talk to him about Christianity. To a man of his infamous character[3], 'righteousness and self-control' were abhor-

[1] As said above, this attitude of Roman officials towards St Paul is a favourite theme of St Luke.
[2] Josephus, *Antiq.* xx. vii 2.
[3] He was a freed slave of Claudius, over whom he had gained such an influence that he was actually given a procuratorship, to the disgust of properly minded people Two sentences of Tacitus illustrate what was thought of him: *Hist* v. 9, 'With all manner of cruelty and lust he exercised royal functions in the spirit of a slave' *Annals*, xii. 54, 'Backed by such influence [that of his powerful brother Pallas], he thought he could commit all kinds of enormities with impunity.'

rent, and St Paul's warning of the near approach of the divine Judgment was frightening. But cupidity being stronger than conscience, he did not release the prisoner during his remaining two years of office, but talked with him frequently, hoping he would bribe him. Failing in this, he tried to curry favour with the Jews by leaving him imprisoned when Nero recalled him and Festus succeeded to the procuratorship (*vv.* 24–27).

3. FESTUS AND AGRIPPA. xxv., xxvi. Porcius Festus was a man of a much better type. He went to Jerusalem, where the Jews at once brought charges against St Paul, and asked him to bring him to Jerusalem, hoping to waylay and assassinate him. But Festus said they must come to Caesarea, and he would put him on his trial (xxv. 1–5). Eight or ten days later, therefore, the trial was held. The old charges were brought up again—offences against the Mosaic Law and the temple, and sedition against the Emperor. But no proof of these things could be brought. Festus who, like all Roman governors of Judaea, was anxious to gain the goodwill of the difficult nation, asked St Paul if he would go and be tried before him at Jerusalem. But St Paul, who had been virtually acquitted at one trial after another, now saw that his only chance was to get away from Palestine; so he boldly appealed to the Emperor, as every Roman citizen had a right to do. Festus consulted with his assessors in the court[1], and decided to allow the appeal (*vv.* 6–12).

Some days afterwards Agrippa II arrived at Caesarea with his sister Bernice (or Berenice)[2], probably to pay

[1] Sueton *Tiber* 33. See Schurer, *Hist. of the Jewish People*, I. ii. 60.

[2] Agrippa II was the son of Agrippa I, and brother of Drusilla; he held the tetrarchy of Trachonitis, Gaulonitis,

XIII]   IMPRISONMENT AT CAESAREA   107

their respects to Festus on his succeeding to the procuratorship. The latter told them about the prisoner whom Felix had left in his charge, stating that the complaint against him was concerned with questions of the Jewish religion, in particular with the resurrection from the dead of a certain Jesus[1]. Not knowing how to deal with such a matter, he had asked the prisoner if he would go to Jerusalem for trial[2]; but he had appealed to the Emperor, so he was keeping him till he could send him to Rome (*vv.* 13–21). On Agrippa expressing a wish to hear him himself, St Paul was brought before the two rulers on the next day, when Festus formally repeated the facts, and asked Agrippa to examine him, so that he might have something definite to report to the Emperor (*vv.* 22–27).

Receiving permission to speak, St Paul stated, as he did to the mob at Jerusalem, that he had been a strict Pharisee, adding that he was now on trial for adhering to the universal Jewish hope of the Messianic kingdom and the resurrection. In support of the latter he related his vision of the risen Christ on the road to Damascus (see p 14 f.), and his subsequent preaching in Damascus, Jerusalem, Judaea, and then to the Gentiles, of the great facts which formed the basis of Christianity, and which had been foretold throughout the whole of the Old Testament (xxvi. 1–23).

It had become more of a sermon than a speech in self-

---

and other districts. Bernice was the widow of her uncle Herod of Chalcis, and a woman of infamous reputation.

1 This is not the charge to which St Paul replies in *v.* 8, but is analogous to that which he states to the Sanhedrin before Claudius Lysias (xxiii. 6) and to Felix (xxiv 15).

2 The reason which St Luke gives (*v.* 9) for his asking this question is very different.

defence. As one inspired, St Paul seems to have raised his voice higher and higher as he tried with all his fervid spiritual energy, pent up during two years' imprisonment, to persuade these two rulers, the Gentile procurator and the Jewish king, to accept the truth which filled his own soul. To Festus this seemed only the raving of one whose brain was turned by excessive study, and he harshly broke in by saying so in a loud voice. St Paul dropped from the high plane of his speech, and shewed that he was not mad by the quiet dignity of his reply, adding that Agrippa would bear him out as regards the facts that he had stated, since they were 'not done in a corner,' but were widely known. And he then appealed to Agrippa's Jewish knowledge of, and belief in, the prophets who had foretold these things. The exact force of Agrippa's reply is uncertain, but the general meaning is probably represented better by the R.V. than the A V.[1] St Paul's earnest and pathetic rejoinder closed the conversation (vv. 24-29).

After consulting with Festus in private, Agrippa declared that the prisoner could have been set at liberty if he had not appealed to the Emperor (vv. 30-32).

[1] R.V 'With but little persuasion thou wouldest fain make me a Christian.' A V 'Almost thou persuadest me to be a Christian' The best reading (followed by the R.V.) is ἐν ὀλίγῳ με πείθεις Χριστιανὸν ποιῆσαι. Apart from the first two words, which can mean 'in a short time,' the only grammatical rendering is 'Thou persuadest me to make a Christian,' i.e. either 'to make a Christian of myself' or 'in order to make a Christian of me.' A reads πείθῃ 'Thou art persuaded, or confident,' EHLP read γενέσθαι (taken from the following verse) for ποιῆσαι Both are corrections to smooth the difficulty For an ingenious suggestion see *J. Th. S.* Oct. 1913. Notice that Agrippa does not use the term 'Nazarene' which Jews usually applied to the 'sect,' but the contemptuous nickname which had come into use in early days at Antioch.

CHAPTER XIV

ST PAUL'S JOURNEY TO ROME AND HIS WORK THERE

Acts xxvii, xxviii.

1. CAESAREA TO MYRA. xxvii. 1–5. St Paul and some other prisoners who were to be sent to Rome—some of them perhaps criminals to be exposed to wild beasts in the arena—were placed in charge of a centurion named Julius of the 'Augustan cohort[1].' He put them on board a vessel which had come round the shore of Asia Minor from Adramyttium, and was about to make the return voyage. Aristarchus from Thessalonica and St Luke accompanied the apostle,—according to Ramsay as his slaves, since they would not be allowed to travel with a prisoner in any other capacity. They sailed up the coast to **Sidon**, where St Paul, no doubt in charge of a soldier, was allowed to visit his friends till the ship was ready to proceed. The prevailing westerly wind forced them, as was often the case, to go to the East of Cyprus[2], and they reached **Myra** on the Lycian coast.

2. MYRA TO FAIR HAVENS *vv* 6–8. There they found a larger vessel, hailing from Alexandria, perhaps carry-

---

[1] Authorities are divided as to whether this was one of the legionary or the auxiliary cohorts. The latter bore names (cf. x. 1), and consisted of Romans living in the provinces. Ramsay (*St Paul the Traveller*, p 315) contends that an auxiliary centurion would not conduct prisoners, and thinks, following Mommsen, that St Luke inaccurately describes a *frumentarius*, 'a legionary centurion on detached service for communication between the Emperor and his armies in the provinces'

[2] Not to the West of that island, as St Paul had previously sailed, with the same wind, from Lycia to Syria (see p. 93).

ing corn, on her way to Italy. At first they coasted along very slowly westward in the teeth of the wind, till they reached the outermost point of a long narrow peninsula where the town of **Cnidus** stood. When there was no longer any shelter from the land they could not keep a straight course further westward, but were obliged to run nearly South to get under the lee of **Crete**, the first point which afforded them shelter being Cape Salmone. To coast along the southern shore of the island was an operation as difficult as to coast from Myra to Cnidus, but they managed to reach a harbour named **Fair Havens** near the town of Lasea.

3. CAUDA AND THE OPEN SEA. *vv.* 9–26. The Fast, i.e. the Day of Atonement, was already past; it was therefore well into October, and sailing was becoming daily more dangerous. St Paul, though not a sailor, was at any rate an experienced traveller; and he advised them to lay up the ship there for the winter. But since the harbour was inconvenient—it afforded little protection from winter storms—the ship's pilot and commander[1] disagreed with him, and the centurion naturally accepted their expert opinion. A discussion was held, and the majority of those who took part in it were in favour of moving to the harbour of Phoenix[2], a few

[1] The 'owner of the ship' (E V.) correctly represents the word ναύκληρος, but he commonly acted as his own commander or skipper.

[2] The harbour is described by St Luke as 'facing down the S.W. and down the N.W. wind' (see R V. margin). But if it is rightly identified with the modern Lutro, which is said to be the only harbour in the neighbourhood capable of sheltering a large ship for the winter, it faces East. It is sometimes explained as facing down the direction in which the two winds blow, i.e. N.E. and S.E ; but that is against the ordinary usage of the Greek preposition κατά. If St Luke has not made a mistake, he may be referring to a smaller

miles further up the coast, and to winter there. When a gentle South wind sprang up they seized their chance, and edged close along the shore. But they had not gone far, probably just beyond Cape Matala into the Gulf of Messara, when 'a typhonic wind called Euraquilo¹' (i e. a N.E. wind) suddenly burst upon them. They could do nothing but run before it, being thus driven S.W. to the little island of **Cauda** (or Clauda), under the lee of which they managed to haul in the small boat which had been towing behind when the squall struck them, and also 'used helps, undergirding the ship,' which is explained to mean that they placed girders round her from stem to stern to strengthen the timbers. The 'helps' may have been some mechanical contrivance for manipulating the ropes, or a term used for the ropes themselves. The next expression is also obscure. 'They lowered the gear²' (R.V), 'strake sail' (A.V) is explained by Jas Smith (*The Voyage and Shipwreck of St Paul*, p. 112) to mean that they lowered the yard with the sail attached to it; nothing but a minimum of storm sail was set. Others think it means the letting down from the stern into the sea (and dragging along the bottom) of some heavy weight, to retard the pace³. Whichever it was, St Luke gives it as a method of avoiding what was their chief fear, the certain destruction which they would meet if they were driven upon the

harbour which lies, facing West, on the other side of the narrow Lutro isthmus. In that case it must have been a larger and better harbour than it is now.

1 'Euroclydon' (A V) is a mere corruption in some late MSS.

2 χαλάσαντες τὸ σκεῦος. Cf. the use of σκεῦος, a 'sheet' or 'sail' (R.V. 'vessel') in x 11, 16.

3 Plutarch, *Moral. de Garrulitate*, x., speaks of the use of ropes and anchors for this purpose.

Syrtes, the quicksands on the coast of Africa. But neither operation in itself, necessary as it might be in any storm, would avoid this. St Luke as a landsman describes what struck his eye, but he does not mention the all-important steering. With a N.E. wind the only thing that would prevent the ship from being driven straight across to the African coast was to keep her head as close to the wind as safety would allow, so that she would drift to port, as much North of West as possible. On the next day they lightened the ship by heaving the cargo overboard; and on the following day all the ship's fittings. Sun and stars were blotted out for days, and the gale blew as hard as ever. None on board could bring himself even to take food. But St Paul told them that in a vision that night God had assured him that no lives would be lost, but only the ship; and he predicted that they would be cast upon an island.

4. THE SHIPWRECK. *vv.* 27–44. For a whole fortnight they had been storm-tossed[1] in Adria[2], i e the sea between Crete and Sicily, when the sailors began to perceive at midnight that land was near[3] On sounding they found that they were in 20 fathoms, and soon afterwards in 15; and in fear of dashing upon rocks they anchored with four anchors at the stern, so that the ship could

[1] R.V. 'as we were driven to and fro' gives a wrong impression If the suggestion made above is correct, that the ship was kept *drifting* to port, it would move in a uniform direction, though tossed about.

[2] The name was extended from the northern portion of the Adriatic so as to include first the Ionian Sea and then also the Sicilian or Ausonian Sea. Using the name in its early narrow meaning, some have held very improbably that an island called Melita (now Meleda) off the Illyrian coast was the scene of the shipwreck.

[3] Lit. 'was approaching them,' a picturesque expression which led to alterations in some MSS.

XIV] THE JOURNEY TO ROME 113

not turn towards the wind, and when the longed-for daylight arrived she could at once run straight ahead. Having done this, the sailors lowered the ship's boat, pretending that they were going to pull out the bow anchors as far from the ship as they could before dropping them, but in reality to escape. St Paul discovered their real object, and pointed out to the centurion and the soldiers that with only landsmen left to manage the ship destruction was certain. They therefore cut the boat adrift before the sailors entered it.

When dawn was approaching, St Paul encouraged them all to eat some food. And everyone[1] on board was strengthened for the coming peril by joining in the meal[2]. Then they threw overboard the last thing that could be sacrificed, the wheat. Day dawned, but the land which appeared was unknown to any of the sailors. Perhaps if they had visited the island before, which was probably the case, they had never approached it from this point. But daylight revealed a bay[3]—still called St Paul's Bay —with a beach, and the question was whether they could control the ship enough to steer it to this beach, instead of being driven straight across the mouth of the bay. The conditions make it clear that the point aimed at must have been on the western side of the bay, not, as some early interpreters supposed, on the eastern

1 B sah. have 'about seventy-six' from some earlier MS in which it was written numerically as $\overline{\Omega C O s}$; others have 'two hundred and seventy-six,' i.e $\overline{C O s}$.
2 St Luke's language suggests that in those moments of terrible danger it seemed to him like a sacred act, as though St Paul were celebrating the Lord's Supper, although he and his two companions, Luke and Aristarchus, were perhaps the only Christians on board (see, however, p. 260, n. 3). This led to the addition in 137, syr^{hcl}, sah. 'giving also to us.'
3 On the northern coast of the island.

side. They decided to make the attempt. They cast off the four stern anchors and let them drop. The two paddles which served as rudders had been lifted out of the water while the ship was at anchor, and lashed by bands; these bands were now unfastened, so that the rudders could be used Then they hoisted the small foresail (not 'mainsail' A.V.), and steered as best they could for the beach. But they could not see a ridge or bank of mud covered by shallow water, or perhaps usually visible but now concealed by the driving storm. Deep water raged on each side of it[1], so that when, in steering for the beach, they accidentally ran the ship aground at the outermost end of this ridge, and the bow stuck fast in the mud, the stern was soon broken in pieces. The soldiers wanted to kill the prisoners to prevent them from escaping; but Julius the centurion, wishing to save St Paul, refused, and ordered everyone to save himself as best he could. By swimming, or with the help of pieces of wood from the wreck, all managed to reach land in safety.

5. MELITA. xxviii. 1–10. They soon learnt that they were on the island of **Melita**, the modern Malta. The inhabitants, who were mostly of Punic origin, and therefore spoken of by St Luke as 'barbarians,' hospitably made a large fire to warm the perishing company, drenched with sea water, in the cold of mid November, and in pouring rain. All helped to gather wood, including St Paul. But as he was arranging on the fire an

[1] Other less simple explanations have been suggested of the 'place where two seas met' ($\tau \acute{o} \pi o s \ \delta \iota \theta \acute{a} \lambda a \sigma \sigma o s$) That such a ridge does not now run out from the western side of St Paul's Bay matters nothing, it would be subject to constant change from the action of wave and tide, and may long have disappeared.

armful that he had collected, a deadly viper feeling the heat slipped out and curled round his arm; but he shook it off into the fire before it stung him. The simple inhabitants thought he must be a murderer[1], whom the goddess *Dikē*, 'Justice,' having failed to kill by shipwreck was now about to kill by other means. But when they saw that no harm followed, they thought he had worked a miracle, and said that he was a god.

The governor of the island, named Publius, whose title was 'the *Primus*[2]' (R.V. 'the chief man'), gave them hospitality for three days. St Paul cured his father of dysentery, and then all who were ill in various parts of the island were brought to him, and he healed them. The inhabitants in return could not do enough to shew their gratitude[3], and provided their visitors with supplies when the time came to depart.

6. MELITA TO ROME. *vv.* 11–16. They remained on the island for three months, from the middle of November till the middle of February. Ships usually did not sail between November 11 and March 5, but the wind being favourable they started rather earlier. They embarked in an Alexandrian ship, named *Dioscuri*[4], probably a large corn ship, which had been laid up for the winter in the principal harbour of the island, not far from St Paul's Bay. They sailed, no doubt with a South

1 They may have seen that he was under guard as a prisoner.
2 In an inscription a certain Prudens is given the title πρῶτος Μελιταίων
3 'They honoured us with many honours' St Luke does not explain to whom the pronoun refers, nor the nature of the honours, but St Paul, as the public benefactor, must have been the chief recipient
4 In Latin *Gemini*, 'the Twins,' i e. Castor and Pollux (A.V.), two stars which served as a guide to mariners, and were reverenced as deities.

wind, to **Syracuse** on the East coast of Sicily. After three days there, they proceeded[1] to **Rhegium** on the mainland of Italy, near the narrowest point of the Straits of Messina; and within two days after that, again with a South wind, they crossed to **Puteoli** (the modern Pozzuoli, in the Bay of Naples) where they landed. There they found some Christians, by whom they were invited to stay with them for a week[2]. 'And so we came to Rome'—'the Rome,' the object of the arduous journey, and the great goal of all St Paul's longings and labours[3]. During his stay at Puteoli, the Christians had probably sent to the city announcing the day on which the apostle was to arrive, so that Christians from Rome met him

1 R.V. 'made a circuit,' A V 'fetched a compass' represent περιελθόντες, which is very possibly the true reading. Instead of coasting along the Sicilian shore, they stood out to sea and tacked, because the wind had shifted. ℵ*B read περιελόντες, the word rendered 'casting off' in xxvii. 40; some therefore understand it to mean 'weighing anchor.' But this is a superfluous remark which St Luke nowhere else makes in his descriptions of St Paul's voyages; and it is doubtful if the word can have this meaning with the word 'anchor' omitted

2 παρεκλήθημεν παρ' αὐτοῖς ἐπιμεῖναι. This is strange, since St Paul was a prisoner. But if Julius could allow him to visit friends for a night in Sidon (xxvii. 3), he might do so again here; he could be left under guard of a soldier or two, who would bring him to Rome, the centurion having gone straight on with the other prisoners. In H and a few minuscules an attempt is made to lessen the difficulty by reading παρεκλήθημεν ἐπ' (or παρ') αὐτοῖς ἐπιμείναντες, 'we were comforted, staying with them etc.,' which might be supposed to mean that the whole company of prisoners with Julius and the soldiers stayed for a week (which is extremely improbable), and St Paul was allowed to lodge with his friends.

3 This anticipates the actual entrance into the city in v 16, where Rome is without the article. Ramsay improbably suggests that 'the Rome' means the whole Roman district, the *ager Romanus*, while 'Rome' means the city itself.

at the **Forum of Appius**[1], 43 miles from Rome on the Via Appia, and the **Three Taverns**[2], 10 miles nearer the city.

It was a moment of crisis for the apostle which he must have felt acutely, and perhaps with some despondency and depression, when he contrasted his condition as a prisoner with the missionary activity in Rome to which he had so often looked forward. But the welcome which he received at these successive points on the road put new courage into him, and he entered the city with thanksgiving to God in his heart. He was allowed, no doubt owing to the report sent by Festus, to lodge by himself, except that he was always guarded by a soldier, to whom he was chained by the wrist (see *v.* 20). In *v.* 16 after the clause 'And when we entered into Rome' some late MSS[3] insert the words 'the centurion delivered the prisoners to the *stratopedarch.*' St Luke's thoughts were centred on the apostle, and he did not trouble to speak of the other prisoners. If he arrived with St Paul a week later than they, he might not even know what had been done with them. But a scribe, acquainted with the military arrangements in Rome, added what is very probably an accurate statement[4].

[1] It was a place where horses were changed, see the description in Horace, *Sat* 1 v. Since Puteoli is nearly 100 miles from Rome, St Luke evidently does not name all the stopping-places.
[2] Mentioned by Cicero, *Ep.* 11. 10, 12, 13
[3] HLP, most minuscules, syr^{hcl}.
[4] If Julius was a centurion of the *frumentarii* (see p 109), and he handed over the prisoners to his superior officer, the latter was not the prefect of the praetorian guard (see R V. margin), Afranius Burrus, but the chief commander of the detached legions, who, when in Rome waiting to be sent abroad on duty, were quartered in the *castra peregrinorum.* In this case 'the stratopedarch' was the 'princeps castrorum peregrinorum' or 'princeps peregrinorum,' both of which occur in inscriptions, and the latter in g (Gigas), an Old Latin MS of the *Acts*. But this means only that the cen-

7. IMPRISONMENT AT ROME. *vv.* 17–31. St Paul could have no idea how soon his trial might come on. But he was not one to waste time. He had not been in Rome more than three days when he began his missionary work. Following his invariable custom he gave the Jews the first opportunity; and since he could not go to their synagogue, he invited their principal representatives to his lodging or inn[1].

Before he could preach Christianity to them, it was necessary to explain why he was a prisoner. He told them that he had committed no offence against the Jewish nation or their religious practices, and the Roman officials had declared him innocent; but that Jewish opposition compelled him to appeal to the Emperor,— not in order to complain against the Jews, but simply to save his life[2]. He was a prisoner really because he was a Christian, believing that Jesus was the Messiah, 'the hope of Israel' (see p. 101). The Jews replied that they had received no report against him[3], and would like to hear what he had to say about Christianity, i.e. the views of the growing Jewish sect, because they knew that Jews were everywhere opposed to it.

This was hopeful so far as it went; and they arranged to come back on a given date. A large number came, and he spent the day proving to them—as he had tried to prove

turion reported himself, with his prisoners The 'princeps' no doubt handed them over to the praetorian guard, whose duty it was to keep them in custody in the praetorian camp; and St Paul would be guarded in his lodgings by a succession of praetorian soldiers

1 ξενία, v. 23, cf Philem 22.
2 Two minuscules and syr[hcl] make this clearer by adding 'but in order that I might save (lit redeem) my life from death.'
3 This shewed clearly enough that the Sanhedrin at Jerusalem could not even concoct a plausible case against him.

XIV] HIS WORK AT ROME 119

to Agrippa—that the whole of the Old Testament, the Jewish Scriptures, pointed forward to Jesus. As his discourse went on, some of them were gradually convinced, but some continued to disbelieve; and they left him disputing with one another. St Luke relates that he delivered a parting shot by quoting Is. vi. 9, 10, which describes the obtuseness of those to whom the prophet was commissioned to preach, and added that 'to the Gentiles has been sent this salvation of God, and they will listen[1].'

St Paul hired, no doubt as soon as he could, a house of his own, where he conversed with all who were willing to visit him, teaching them about the coming Kingdom of God, and about the Lord Jesus Christ[2], 'openly[3] without hindrance.'

Thus St Luke reached the end of his task. He had shewn how Christianity, starting among Jews in Jerusalem with the Resurrection of Jesus Christ and the outpouring of the Spirit, and proclaimed in other parts of Palestine by the first Jewish Christians, had then—helped rather than hindered by the Roman authorities in various parts of the Empire[4]—spread among Gentiles, chiefly through the labours of his hero St Paul, in Damascus, Antioch, Asia Minor, Macedonia, Greece, and now at last in great Rome itself. The triumphant ring in his closing words 'openly without hindrance' shews the line of thought along which he had planned his writing. The addition of anything further about the

[1] The best MSS omit *v.* 29, added in A V., see R.V margin. It repeats the substance of *v* 25 a.
[2] See p. 78, n 2.
[3] μετὰ πάσης παρρησίας, i e. with all the boldness due to unfettered freedom of speech.
[4] No doubt St Luke, for apologetic purposes, recorded as many instances of this as he could; but it is too much to say, as some writers have said, that it was his main purpose in writing.

apostle of a personal kind, however interesting or important, would have been a literary blemish such as St Luke was too good an artist to commit; having planned a sketch of the expansion of Christianity (cf. Acts i. 8), he would not allow it to become a biography, even of St Paul himself. No other explanation is needed of the fact that the book ends where it does. The explanation that St Luke laid down his pen because he had carried his narrative up to the time of writing is impossible. The *Acts*, according to its opening words, was written later than the Third Gospel, and it is doubtful if the latter can be dated earlier than 80 A.D. Other guesses have been made, as for example that St Luke intended to add more to the *Acts*, or that he intended to write a third volume after the Gospel and the *Acts*, but was prevented by death, perhaps martyrdom[1]; or that the true ending of the *Acts* has been lost by the mutilation of a manuscript. These unnecessary conjectures can be allowed no weight in deciding the problem of the closing events of St Paul's life. It has been held by many writers, patristic and modern, that there are indications which point to the fact that he was released from imprisonment, and after a period of missionary activity was again imprisoned, condemned and executed. This is discussed on pp. 253–261, where the conclusion is reached that the imprisonment recorded in Acts xxviii. ended with his death. After a formal trial, probably on the charge of creating disturbances, he was beheaded in the reign of Nero, before the persecution of Christians in 64 A D. began to rage.

[1] A tradition as to his martyrdom, given by Gregory of Nazianzus (Migne, *Patr Graec*. xxxv 589), dates it in the reign of Domitian, i e some 30 years after the events with which the *Acts* closes.

PART II
THE EPISTLES OF ST PAUL

INTRODUCTION

1. THEIR CHARACTER. To understand St Paul's epistles rightly it is important to realise that they are not treatises, or essays, or sermons, but *letters*. He had no idea that he was writing instruction for future ages. If he had, it is probable that the man himself would not have been so clearly revealed. On the other hand, though letters, arising out of the real circumstances of the moment, they were not, with the single exception of the letter to Philemon, written to individuals[1]. If they had been, much of incalculable value to us must have been absent. They were *spiritual letters*, written by a pastor to his flock, and falling, as all of them do, within the last quarter of his life, they represent his ripe experience. They were designed for public reading (cf. 1 Thes. v. 27, Col. iv. 16), and were intended to apply to each community as a whole. Many of the rebukes and warnings which he offers would not apply to every individual who heard them; and conversely when he writes with joyful acknowledgement of virtues and graces in his flock, there must have been some individuals who were far less worthy of his approbation than others. The wide

---

1 To this exception must probably be added the fragments of personal communications embodied in the Pastoral Epistles, though it is doubtful if those epistles, in their present form, were from his pen.

variety among them often helps to explain the sensitive alternations of his tone and feeling.

St Paul made a practice of writing by an amanuensis[1], and of adding a few words in his own handwriting at the end of the letter as an assurance of its genuineness (2 Thes. iii. 17; cf. Gal. vi. 11, 1 Cor. xvi. 21, Col. iv. 18). Shorthand was a not infrequent accomplishment in those days, and the apostle must sometimes have poured out his thoughts with rapid vehemence,—so rapid that he was sometimes grammatically incoherent; but the incoherence was faithfully reproduced by the amanuensis, and not always corrected by the apostle.

2. THEIR PRESERVATION. There can be no doubt that as a great spiritual leader, with 'the care of all the churches' resting on him, St Paul must have written many more letters than we possess. In 2 Thes. iii. 17 he can write 'which is the token in *every* epistle,' although that is only the second, or possibly the third, of those which have come down to us At the same time we must not exaggerate their probable number. There was no cheap postage; letters could be sent only by hand, so that he would often be obliged to wait till a Christian messenger could be found who was travelling in the desired direction. Still there are clear indications that some of his letters have been wholly or partially lost. Those which we possess owe their preservation to the love and reverence felt for the apostle by his converts, though his letters when first received were not, of course, regarded as sacred scripture, and were therefore not all kept with equal care; of some, only mutilated fragments

---

[1] On this and other points connected with ancient letter writing see Milligan's interesting note on 'St Paul as a Letter-Writer' (*Thessal* pp. 121–130).

survived. But soon after his death a desire was felt to collect every available letter or fragment which had come from his pen[1]. And some of these fragments have reached us attached to, or embedded in, some of his other epistles (see pp. 137, 138, 144–9, 182–4, 234–6).

CHAPTER I

I THESSALONIANS

1. CIRCUMSTANCES AND PLACE. St Paul's doings at Thessalonica and his subsequent movements as far as Corinth on his second missionary tour are related in Acts xvii.–xviii. 1 (see pp. 62–70). Of all his converts those that remained nearest to his heart were the simple and devoted Christians of Macedonia. When he was banished from Thessalonica it was a bereavement (1 Thes. ii. 17) which he felt as an acute sorrow. And when Timothy and Silas (Silvanus) rejoined him at Corinth (Acts xviii. 5; see pp 68–70), he wrote, adding their names with his in the opening salutation (1 1), a letter to the Thessalonians which is the earliest, or perhaps the earliest but one (see pp. 168–173), of those which we possess. The letter was the result of the report, and possibly a letter from them, brought to him by Timothy, relating their spiritual and temporal condition.

[1] Compare the request made by the Philippians to Polycarp regarding the letters of Ignatius immediately after his martyrdom Polycarp replies to them, 'The letters of Ignatius which were sent to us by him, and others as many as we had by us, we send unto you according as ye enjoined' (*ad Phil.* 13) He would, of course, send copies, not the originals, and the same thing would be done by the churches that circulated St Paul's letters.

2. ANALYSIS.
          i. 1. Salutation[1].

A. i. 2–iii. 13. Personal matters.
- i. 2–10. Thanksgiving for the zeal and endurance of the readers.
- ii. 1–12. An *apologia* for his teaching and for his manner of life among them.
- ii. 13–16. Renewed thanksgiving.
- ii 17–iii 10. His relations with them since his banishment. The mission of Timothy and his joyful report.

          iii. 11–13. A Prayer.

B iv. 1–v. 22. Exhortations.
- iv. 1–8. Warning against immorality.
- iv. 9–12. Advice·
  - (a) to increase in mutual love,
  - (b) to keep quietly to themselves,
  - (c) to labour with their hands.
- iv. 13–v. 11. Instructions on Christ's Advent:
  - (a) iv. 13–18. The dead in Christ, no less than the living, shall share in it,
  - (b) v. 1–11. It will be sudden, and therefore demands sober watchfulness.

v. 12–22. Miscellaneous Injunctions.

          v. 23–28. Conclusion.

---

[1] Milligan (*op cit* p. 127) shews by examples from papyri that the general form of the Pauline letters, which 'consists as a rule of an Address or Greeting, a Thanksgiving, Special Contents, Personal Salutations, and an Autographic Conclusion,' closely resembles the structure of an ordinary Greek letter.

3. CONTENTS. A. After the salutation (i 1) the apostle thanks God for their Christian devotion (*vv.* 2, 3), and for the zeal with which they had responded to his teaching, and had made themselves an example to other Christian communities (*vv.* 4–10). This in itself was enough to disprove false charges which had been laid against his preaching. He offers an *apologia* (ii. 1–12): his teaching had been free from error, uncleanness, and guile (*v.* 3), from all wish to be pleasing to men rather than to God (*v.* 4), from flattery, under which covetousness might be concealed (*v.* 5), from a desire for praise, and finally from the domineering spirit which might have insisted on their providing for his maintenance and giving him honour as to an apostle (*vv.* 6, 7 a)[1]. On the contrary, he had been like a nurse treating children with tender sympathy (*vv.* 7 b, 8); he had laboured with his hands that he might not burden them with his maintenance (*v.* 9); and he had exhorted them as a father does his children (*vv.* 10–12).

Having done so much for them, he is the more thankful for the readiness with which they received his teaching (*v.* 13), and for their patience under persecution from their fellow Greeks, stirred up by the Jews who had similarly persecuted the Judaean Christians, had killed the Lord Jesus and the prophets, and had caused his own banishment from Thessalonica (*vv.* 14, 15), whose wicked opposition will very soon receive divine punishment (*v.* 16)[2].

---

1 His self-defence in *vv* 1–7 a perhaps had the further purpose of contrasting his own behaviour with that of other teachers who, as he may have learnt from Timothy, had foisted themselves upon the Thessalonians

2 Some have thought that the last clause is a later addition, written after the fall of Jerusalem But the aorist ἔφθασεν can be prophetic or proleptic as in Mat. xii. 28.

He speaks of his thought for the Thessalonians since his banishment. He had longed to return, but was prevented (*vv*. 17–20); so he had sent Timothy to establish and comfort them, and was overjoyed at the report which he had brought back (iii. 1–10).

This part of the letter ends with a prayer that he may some day see them again (*v*. 11), and that they may advance in Christian love, in readiness for the near 'Advent of our Lord Jesus Christ with all His holy ones[1]' (*vv*. 12, 13).

B. In the second portion of the letter he turns his attention to certain shortcomings which needed correction and advice.

[It must be remembered that his readers were for the most part converts from heathenism, and a few weeks were not enough to lead them to Christian maturity. They were among the best examples of the early Christians—fresh, open-minded, full of spiritual zeal, and personal devotion to their father in God. But they were by no means all on the same level of intellectual or spiritual progress. Some definite instruction, therefore, on particular points was needed.]

The apostle deals with the temptation to immorality with which Christians, living in the midst of pagans, were constantly assailed, especially when they had learned something of the meaning of Christian 'liberty,' but not enough to understand it rightly. He holds up a high ideal of marriage. A man ought to marry a wife ('obtain his vessel') not for the purpose of gratifying his physical lust, but in a state of Christian sanctification, ready to

---

[1] I.e. the angels, cf. Zech. xiv. 5 to which St Paul here alludes. Some think that holy men who have died are also to be included in the term.

treat her honourably (iv. 1–5). And he must not wrong a fellow Christian by his action (v. 6 a). He gives as a reason for this that God will punish (v. 6 b), but then lifts the subject on to the highest plane. The divine purpose in their life, God's 'call,' is sanctification not uncleanness (v. 7); to thwart that purpose is to despise God, whose Holy Spirit has been poured upon them for the purpose of enabling them to be true to their calling (v. 8).

Then follows advice of a different kind. St Paul says he has no need to exhort them to love their fellow Christians; they do that conspicuously already; but still he asks them to abound in it increasingly (vv. 9, 10). But a warning which they really did need was to 'be quiet,' i.e. not to mix themselves up with public pagan life, and to 'do their own business,' i.e. to keep themselves to themselves; also to work with their hands, a duty from which pagans shrank as mean and slavish (v. 11). The objects of both pieces of advice are that as Christians they may create a good impression among non-Christians, and that they may be independent of charity (v. 12).

[This injunction to be independent may be intended as a further warning against those teachers who tried to live at the expense of the community (see note above on ii. 1–7 a). But it seems also to be connected with the following section. St Paul had taught them that the Advent of Jesus the Messiah would occur in the near future. Why then, they may have asked themselves, should they trouble to go on with their work if there was no need to lay by for the future?[1]]

[1] Cf. v 14, where after his teaching on the Advent St Paul returns to the subject of the 'disorderly.'

The next two sections deal with Christ's Advent. A difficulty had arisen, as Timothy had no doubt reported, in the minds of some of them. Certain members of the Thessalonian Church had died, probably since the apostle's banishment, and perhaps as victims of the persecution from which they suffered. If the Messiah was destined to descend from heaven, as some of the Jewish apocalypses had taught, and St Paul also in his preaching at Thessalonica (cf. i. 10, 'to await His Son from heaven'), He would descend upon this earth and its living inhabitants. What, then, was to be the fate of those who had died? St Paul heard that they were seriously troubled about this, thinking that their departed brethren would have no share in the glories of the Advent; they were sorrowing as hopelessly as 'the rest,' i.e. the pagans. St Paul meets this by declaring that Christ's Resurrection is a pledge of the resurrection of Christians, and therefore of their advent with God (v. 14). They will have the first share in the glories of the Advent, and then we that are still alive shall be caught up to meet the descending Lord in the air. So shall we ever be with the Lord (iv. 13–18).

The teaching on the Advent is continued. That it would be as sudden as a thief in the night, or the pangs of childbirth, the apostle had already taught his readers when he was with them. But some of them needed the exhortation to live in accordance with their belief. The allurements of pagan life were making them unready for the great moment as though they belonged to the night darkness instead of being sons of the light of day. And he rouses them with the warning that they were in danger of forfeiting their Christian privilege, i.e their divine appointment—not to 'wrath,' the punishment of sinners at the Last Day, but—to the obtaining of salvation through our Lord Jesus Christ (v. 1–11).

Some miscellaneous injunctions on Christian life and behaviour are added, instances of the ways in which they could 'build each other up' (v. 11) in view of the nearness of the Advent. Obey and honour your Church rulers (vv. 12, 13 a). Do not quarrel (v. 13 b). Help one another in the Christian life, according to the needs of each (v. 14). Do not retaliate when another does you harm, but do your utmost to do good to him and to everyone (v. 15). Rejoice, pray, give thanks (vv 16–18). If you see in any Christian the rush of enthusiasm caused by the outpouring of the Spirit, do not quench it (v. 19). If it takes the form of ecstatic 'prophesying' do not despise it (v. 20). At the same time test these outbursts, for some may not be genuine (v. 21); and avoid every sort that is not (v. 22).

The epistle then ends with a solemn commendatory prayer (vv. 23, 24); a request for their prayers (v. 25); a salutation (v. 26); an injunction to read the letter publicly (v. 27), the Grace (v. 28).

CHAPTER II

II THESSALONIANS

1. CIRCUMSTANCES AND PLACE. The close similarity between parts of this epistle and parts of 1 *Thessalonians* makes it practically certain that if it was written by St Paul it was at the same time and place as the First epistle, i.e. at Corinth in the second missionary tour, when Timothy had reached him bringing his report, and when Timothy and Silas (Silvanus) were both with him (see i. 1).

2. ANALYSIS.

     i. 1, 2 Salutation.
A. i. 3–5. Thanksgiving for the zeal and endurance of the readers. This leads to
 i. 6–10. Instruction on Christ's Advent. They will receive their reward at the Advent of the Lord Jesus with His angels, when sinners shall be destroyed.

     i. 11, 12. A Prayer.
B. ii. 1–12. Instruction on Christ's Advent. The Advent must be preceded by the Lawless One, who is at present checked by a hindering power, but whom Jesus will destroy when He comes. This leads to
 ii. 13–15. Thanksgiving for the spiritual privileges of the readers, and an exhortation to hold fast the Christian tradition.

     ii. 16, 17. A Prayer.
C. iii. 1–5. A request for their prayers, and expressions of confidence.
 iii. 6–15. Injunctions to work quietly for their own living, and to avoid and admonish those Christians who do not.

     iii. 16. A Prayer.
 iii. 17, 18. Autographic conclusion.

The two passages on Christ's Advent are discussed in the following section; but the remainder of the epistle bears in general so close a similarity to passages in the First epistle that further detailed exposition here is hardly necessary.

3 GENUINENESS. Some writers have denied that this is a genuine letter written by St Paul, for two main reasons: (1) The *dissimilarity* of its teaching on Christ's Advent to that of the First epistle; (2) the *similarity* of its remaining portions to portions of the First epistle.

(1) In the First epistle the teaching on the Advent, as we have seen, is one of encouragement regarding Christians who have died and of warning to be in readiness for the great event. Of the dead and of the living alike the future bliss is to be 'ever with the Lord.' In 2 Thes. i. 6–10 much is added to this. The future state of things is described as 'the kingdom of God,' and the bliss spoken of is in particular that of the persecuted Thessalonian Christians, to whom God will recompense 'rest with us,' the writer looking forward joyfully to the future unity with his converts which is at present denied him. The explanation of Schmiedel that the words are due to a later writer who places St Paul on a loftier plane than other Christians is improbable and entirely unnecessary. With regard to the fate of the wicked, the First epistle only hints in the words 'the wrath to come' (i. 10) and 'wrath' (v. 9). But in the Second it is described as 'punishment, eternal destruction from the presence[1] of the Lord, and from the glory of His might ...in that day.' The other passage, ii. 1–12, is thought to contain even clearer marks of spuriousness. It is said to contain teaching (*a*) implying a date later than St Paul, (*b*) not only supplementary but contradictory to that in the First epistle.

(*a*) This passage speaks of 'the Man of sin,' 'the Son of perdition,' 'the Lawless One,' a being who sets himself in the place of God, and imitates Him in his advent,

[1] Lit. 'face,' a Hebraic expression

and self-exaltation, and by false miracles, so that he seduces many to worship him. It is maintained that this is a reference to the belief, current after Nero's death, that he would come to life again and return. If that were the true explanation, its Pauline authorship would be impossible. But it is now generally admitted that the reference is to 'Antichrist' (though St Paul does not use the term), the mysterious Figure which the Jews had long thought of as about to come in order to resist God, as the dragon in the ancient Babylonian legend had resisted the Creator at the beginning of the world[1]. The hindering power, which is spoken of both as neuter, 'that which hindereth,' and masculine, 'he who hindereth,' is probably the Roman power which diffused law and order throughout the civilized world, and which could be thought of also as personified in the Emperor.

(*b*) The contradiction to the teaching in the First epistle is thought to be as follows. In 1 *Thessalonians* St Paul shews that he and his readers expected that the Advent would take place very soon indeed; but here he says that it must be preceded by the general falling away from God[2], and by the coming of the Lawless One, both of which had long been Jewish expectations. And the supposed contradiction is further emphasized in ii. 2 if it is translated 'to the end that ye be not quickly shaken from your mind, nor yet be troubled... as that the day of the Lord is *near*.' The words in this form deny that the day of the Lord is near, whereas in

---

1 See Bousset, *The Antichrist Legend*.
2 This is probably the best explanation of ἡ ἀποστασία. It is not specifically a Jewish apostasy from the Mosaic Law, nor, as some early fathers explained it, a rebellion against Rome. The article '*the* apostasy' implies that it was a well-known expectation.

the First epistle St Paul said that it was. The last word[1], however, means rather 'is *present.*' Some persons had tried to persuade the Thessalonians that the 'day of the Lord,' i.e. the final series of events and catastrophes culminating in the Advent, had actually begun to arrive. This the apostle denies. But he does not thereby contradict what he said in 1 *Thessalonians*. There he wrote as though the End would be soon; here he writes that, though near, it is still strictly in the future, and that certain events must precede it. It is now largely recognised that though the teaching in the two epistles is of a different character, it presents no contradiction.

(2) The other argument against the genuineness of the Second epistle, i.e. its similarity to the First, sounds paradoxical. It has been truly said that if the First epistle had been lost we should have no reason to doubt the genuineness of the Second, it is in every way so thoroughly and unmistakeably Pauline But it is, in fact, difficult, at first sight, to understand why St Paul should have written two letters at the same time to the same church, containing portions so closely similar in language, and yet why he should have left pieces of teaching about the Advent so striking and important as those in 2 Thes. i. 6–10 and ii. 1–12 to be given in a second letter.

Those who deny the genuineness of the Second epistle suppose that a later writer composed these verses and put them into an epistolary framework made up of passages imitated from the First epistle.

But there are features which make the theory of an imitator improbable. His imitation is not really as close as we should expect. For example he makes no refer-

---

1 ἐνέστηκεν.

ence to Christ's death and resurrection (contrast 1 Thes. i. 10, ii. 15, iv. 14, v. 10). Instead of repeating the injunction in 1 Thes. iv. 11, 12 about working quietly with the hands, he adds warnings against those who do not. Apart from this he gives no exhortations as to morals and conduct such as those in 1 Thes. iv. 1-10, v. 12-22. In iii. 17, in which, according to this theory, he impersonates St Paul, he ventures to add 'which is the token in every epistle, so I write'—words which find no parallel elsewhere. He says not a word about his past relations with his readers; and, more generally, he has, on the theory of imitation, failed to reproduce the warmth of friendliness and joy which mark the First epistle.

If, then, St Paul is the author, the question still remains to be answered how it was that he wrote to the same church, at the same time, two letters so similar in language, both treating of the Advent, but treating it differently, and with a somewhat cooler and more official tone in the Second than in the First.

Harnack's explanation is attractive, that while the First epistle was written, as we have seen, to converts from paganism, the Second was written not to the Greek but to the *Jewish* Christians in Thessalonica. They would understand much more readily than Greeks the allusions to Antichrist, which was a Jewish expectation; and the passage, ii. 1-12, which treats of it contains several echoes of Old Testament language. The word 'traditions' (2 Thes ii. 15, iii. 6), which does not occur in the First epistle, is one to which Jews were well accustomed. And perhaps the emphasis on 'all' in iii. 16, 18, 1 Thes v. 26, 27 reveals the fact that the Jewish and Gentile Christians were not on very friendly terms. In 2 Thes. ii. 13 there may be a further support for the theory If the reading given in R.V. margin is right, 'God chose you *as firstfruits* unto salvation,' it could be explained by the fact that Jews in Thessalonica were converted to Christianity before Gentiles. Without this explanation the reading is difficult, since the Thessalonians as a whole were not the first converts even in Macedonia, and scribes easily altered it to the reading adopted in R.V. text 'from the beginning,'[1] i.e. in His divine purpose from the beginning of the world.

If Harnack's suggestion is not right, we are forced to adopt either the view that the Second epistle is not by St Paul, or the difficult alternative that St Paul learnt from some source that the Thessalonians needed the additional teaching about the Advent, and that he wrote off at once, framing the teaching in several remarks similar to those which he had written in the First letter[2].

CHAPTER III

INTRODUCTION TO I AND II CORINTHIANS

1. PLACE. I *Corinthians* was written, during the third missionary tour, at Ephesus or in the immediate neighbourhood. This is indicated by xvi. 8, 9, 'I will tarry at Ephesus until Pentecost, for a great door and effectual is opened unto me, and there are many adversaries', also by the salutations in xvi 19 from the churches of Asia, and from Aquila and Prisca[3] who had travelled

---

[1] The two readings are ἀπαρχήν BFGP, a few minuscules, f. vulg. syr^hcl, and ἀπ' ἀρχῆς ℵDEKL, most minuscules, d e g syr^pesh memph. arm. aeth.

[2] For another suggestion see *Journal of Theol. Studies*, Oct. 1913.

[3] At the end of the verse DEFG add παρ' οἷς καὶ ξενίζομαι 'with whom also I lodge.'

with St Paul to Ephesus and had stayed on there (Acts xviii. 18, 19, 26). It is improbable, therefore, apart from other considerations, that the epistle was written, as some have thought, from Macedonia after he had left Ephesus.

2 *Corinthians* was written from Macedonia after he had left Ephesus. He traces his movements· i. 8, Asia; ii 12, Troas; *v.* 13, Macedonia; and then relates the arrival of Titus in Macedonia (vii 5, 6), speaks of his own boasting 'to them of Macedonia' (ix. 2), and says that he is now sending Titus back to Corinth to arrange for the collection, together with two other brethren (ch. viii)

2. TIME. How long St Paul had been at Ephesus before he wrote 1 *Corinthians* is uncertain. In calculating it we must travel back from a fixed date He left Philippi on his final journey towards Jerusalem 'after the days of Unleavened Bread' (Acts xx 6), i e. about the end of March. Previously to that, he had been for three months in Greece (xx. 3), i.e. Corinth, to which, therefore, he had gone early in January or late in December. Before reaching Corinth, as he passed through Macedonia, he had 'given much exhortation' (xx. 2); he cannot, therefore, have arrived in Macedonia from Ephesus later than perhaps the beginning of November; and it may have been earlier. 2 *Corinthians*, then, was written during November or perhaps earlier. So far, all is fairly clear.

Now, in 2 Cor. viii. 10, ix. 2 he speaks of the collection for the poor of Jerusalem which the Corinthians, as he boasts, had begun 'last year[1]' (not as R.V. 'a year ago,' and 'for a year past'). Did he think of the year as be-

---

1 ἀπὸ πέρυσι.

ginning according to our (Roman) reckoning in January, or did he as a Jew think of it as beginning in the autumn? If the former, he boasts that the Corinthians had begun at least by the December before he left Ephesus for Macedonia. If the latter, there are two possibilities: (*a*) If he reached Macedonia and wrote 2 *Corinthians* before the autumn New Year began, his boast meant, as in the last case, that they had begun by the previous December; (*b*) if after the autumn New Year, he may have thought of any time up to September, just over a month before he wrote.

Lastly, still moving backwards, he clearly implies in 1 Cor. xvi. 1, 2 that when he wrote that epistle the Corinthian collection had not yet been begun. This was written in the spring shortly before Pentecost (*v*. 8), i.e. probably early in May. Thus the two alternatives are that 1 *Corinthians* was written 5 or 6 months before 2 *Corinthians* in the spring of the same Roman year, or 17 or 18 months before it in the spring of the preceding Roman year.

3. THE PREVIOUS LETTER. The letter that we call 1 *Corinthians* was not the first that St Paul wrote to them. In v. 9 he says 'I wrote to you in my letter to have no company with fornicators.' Such advice does not occur in 1 *Corinthians* before this point. He is clearly referring to a previous letter[1], written probably because the news had reached him that his converts were treat-

---

[1] This letter was not known widely enough to have come to the notice of Clement of Rome (96 A D) In *Cor*. xlvii. he writes 'Take up the epistle of the blessed Paul the Apostle. What wrote he first unto you in the beginning of the Gospel? Of a truth he charged you in the Spirit concerning himself and Kephas and Apollos, because that even then ye had made parties.'

ing the sin of immorality, with which Corinth was permeated (see p. 70), in a manner unfitting for Christians. Having received his advice on the subject, some of them misunderstood it, and needed the explanation which he gives in v. 10–13, viz. that he did not mean that they were to separate themselves entirely from all fornicators: to do that, they would have to leave the world altogether; he meant that they must keep clear of any *brother*, i.e. any Christian, who was guilty of the sin. It is far from improbable that though this previous letter as a whole has been lost, yet a fragment of it is to be found in 2 Cor. vi. 14–vii. 1. A brief study of that passage will shew that it might have been misunderstood in the way indicated. Moreover it breaks the close connexion of thought between vi. 11–13 and vii. 2–4, both of which are parts of the apostle's appeal to the readers to open their hearts to him more widely in affection.

4. TIMOTHY SENT TO CORINTH. St Paul heard from 'them of Chloe[1],' i e. probably some of her servants, that the Corinthian Church was split by party factions (1 Cor. i.–iv.) He heard also, perhaps from the same source, that a Christian in Corinth had committed a gross act of immorality (ch. v), that Christians were bringing lawsuits against Christians before heathen, i.e. Roman, courts (vi. 1–11), and, generally, that immorality was to be found among them (vi. 12–20). These were very serious matters; and with regard to the first, at least, he made up his mind, if it could not be set right by other means, to go himself to deal with it sternly (iv. 18–21). But before doing so, he sent Timothy to

---

[1] We may suppose that she was a wealthy Greek lady, living either in Corinth or Ephesus, and sending slaves to one or the other city for commercial or other purposes.

try to put an end to the evil (iv. 17). In xvi. 10, 11 he asks them not to despise Timothy, probably on account of his youth, or youthful appearance, 'but set him forward on his journey in peace, that he may come unto me; for I expect him with the brethren.' These brethren were probably the intended bearers of the letter (1 *Corinthians*) which he was then writing. The wording seems to imply that the bearers would reach Corinth before Timothy, which they could do if they went straight across from Ephesus by sea while Timothy took the longer route round by Macedonia. St Luke perhaps refers to this mission of Timothy in Acts xix. 22, where he relates that St Paul sent Timothy and Erastus to Macedonia, though, if so, it is curious that he says nothing about Corinth, which was Timothy's real destination (see below). And St Paul says nothing about sending Erastus.

5. THE RETURN OF TIMOTHY. It is nowhere stated that Timothy returned to Ephesus We know only that when St Paul wrote 2 *Corinthians* in Macedonia, Timothy joined with him in his salutation (i. 1). There are two divergent views about it, dependent partly on the meaning given to 1 Cor. xvi. 10: '*If* Timothy come' does not necessarily express a doubt as to whether he would reach Corinth; 'if' can mean 'when,' as e.g. in 2 Cor. xiii. 2, 'if I come again I will not spare.' But if it expresses a doubt, Timothy may not have reached Corinth, which would be in accordance with Acts xix. 22 where, as said above, Timothy and Erastus were sent to Macedonia, nothing being said about the continuance of their journey to Corinth. In the former case, Timothy may have returned to Ephesus, bringing a report that the party factions and other abuses at Corinth were very bad; he

had been unable to improve matters, and had perhaps made them worse. In consequence of his report, St Paul paid the visit to Corinth discussed in the next section. In the latter case, Timothy did not return to Ephesus, and brought no report, and St Paul's visit must have been due to a disquieting report which reached him from some other source.

6. ST PAUL'S VISIT TO CORINTH. (The painful visit.) His long absence, or some other cause, had made some of the troublesome Corinthians to be 'puffed up,' and to think that he would not visit them. 'But I will come to you shortly if the Lord will' (1 Cor. iv. 18). 'Shall I come to you with a rod, or in love, and a spirit of meekness?' (iv. 21) 'The rest will I set in order when I come' (xi. 34). And when he came, he would arrange for the transport to Jerusalem of the collection for the poor Christians which he asked them to begin to make; and he would come *via* Macedonia, and perhaps stay the winter at Corinth, but he wanted to stay at Ephesus till Pentecost (xvi. 1–9). But the report which he received about them, either from Timothy or some other source, made him change his plan, and determine to come to them not in the first instance *via* Macedonia, but to *visit them twice*, first from Ephesus straight across the sea, and then, after moving on from them into Macedonia to return to them from thence (2 Cor i 15, 16). The former of these two visits to Corinth was paid, but circumstances postponed the latter. For this postponement, which was his second change of plan, some of the Corinthians accused him of fickleness, against which he defends himself in 2 Cor. 1. 17–ii. 1. The reason was that the former visit was so painful that he could not bring himself to return to them until their relations with him

INTRODUCTION TO I AND II CORINTHIANS

were improved: 'to spare you I came no more[1] to Corinth' (i. 23); 'for I determined this for myself that I would not come again to you in sorrow' (ii. 1), i.e. he would not risk another visit as painful as that which he had just paid. This painful visit (which is not mentioned by St Luke in his brief sketch of the apostle's activities at Ephesus, Acts xix.) is indicated also by St Paul's words 'This is the third time[2] I am ready to come to you' (2 Cor. xii. 14); 'This is the third time I am coming to you...I say beforehand, as [I said] when I was present the second time' (xiii 1, 2)[3].

The painful visit was a sad failure St Paul for some reason was unable to act forcibly. The opposition against him was so strong that authoritative action was, for the moment, rendered impossible. He returned to Ephesus burdened with the miserable sense of failure, and wrote a letter to Corinth expressing his feelings (see section 8).

[1] Not 'I forbare to come' (R.V), or 'I came not as yet' (A V). The former is an incorrect paraphrase, the latter an incorrect rendering, of οὐκέτι ἦλθον,—both due to the wish to avoid the conclusion that St Paul paid a visit which is not recorded in the *Acts*.

[2] The first visit, of course, had been that in the second missionary tour when he had first evangelized Corinth (Acts xviii 1–17).

[3] The latter passage shews that the former cannot mean that he had previously been *twice ready* to come, and had been twice prevented. Those who so explain it are forced to the very unnatural explanation of the latter passage that 'the third time I am coming to you' means 'the third time I am *planning* to come to you,' which ignores the words 'when I was present the second time.'

No objection can be raised against a visit between 1 and 2 *Corinthians* on the ground that there was no time for it. Not less than five or six months intervened between the two epistles (see above), which gives plenty of time. So painful a visit cannot have lasted long, and the voyage from Ephesus would not occupy much more than a week; three weeks, at any rate, would be ample for the voyage to Corinth and back.

7. THE REASON FOR THE VISIT. What the abuse was which St Paul tried to rectify cannot be determined with certainty. It was apparently a wrong-doing by an individual towards another individual (2 Cor. vii. 12: 'he that did the wrong,' and 'he that suffered the wrong'). The apostle's subsequent letter, and the personal efforts of Titus who carried it, finally persuaded the Corinthians, or rather a majority of them, to punish the offender severely (2 Cor. ii. 6). There are three possibilities as to the nature of his offence. (1) It was the crime mentioned in 1 Cor. v. 1, 2: a Christian had committed fornication with his father's wife, and the Corinthians were, at first, puffed up, and shewed no regret in the matter. 'He that suffered the wrong' was in this case the man's father. St Paul said that they ought, publicly and officially, 'to deliver such a one unto Satan for the destruction of the flesh, that the spirit may be saved in the day of the Lord Jesus' (vv. 3–5). If, after writing thus, the apostle on his visit tried to insist on this same punishment of extreme public excommunication, and they refused, it would explain the complete failure of the visit. (2) It was connected with the party factions rebuked in 1 Cor. i.–iv. But though the division of the Corinthian Church into parties might explain the fact that the offender was punished by a majority and not by the whole Church, it does not easily explain his offence, unless, indeed, 'he that suffered the wrong' (2 Cor. vii. 12) was St Paul himself. In this case the heat of party spirit had led one of his opponents, i.e. one of those who refused to say 'I am of Paul' (1 Cor. i. 12), to make a violent, possibly an insulting, attack upon his teaching or reputation (3) It was connected with litigation in heathen courts, which he rebukes in 1 Cor. vi.

The first of these is perhaps the most probable; but it may be that the true explanation is entirely lost to us.

8. ST PAUL'S SORROWFUL LETTER TO CORINTH. After his brief unsuccessful visit the apostle (as said above) did not, as he had intended, go to Macedonia from Corinth and back again (2 Cor. i. 16), but returned straight to Ephesus There he poured out his heart in a letter of sorrowful remonstrance, 'out of much affliction and anguish of spirit, with many tears' (2 Cor. ii. 4). This sad letter was carried by Titus. St Paul was in an agony of mind as to how it would be received; he even had qualms that it had been too stern (vii. 8). He felt so restless and upset that he could not stay at Ephesus surrounded by enemies and perils; so he went to Troas. But Titus had not arrived, and though opportunities for missionary work offered themselves there, he could not stay still, but went on into Macedonia (ii. 12, 13). Even there 'our flesh had no relief, but we were afflicted on every side; without were fightings, within were fears' (vii. 5). But at last Titus met him, and brought him the comforting news that the Corinthians had submitted[1], and had punished the offender The sorrowful letter had done its work; it had made them sorry, but it was the sorrow of repentance issuing in zeal, which caused the apostle a deep feeling of relief and joy, in which Titus shared (vii. 6–16).

It is difficult, however, to determine exactly what had occurred. A majority had inflicted a punishment which St Paul declares 'adequate,' 'so that on the contrary ye should rather forgive him and comfort him,

[1] In vii. 15 he speaks of 'the obedience of you all.' His thankful joy makes him for the moment disregard the minority who were still opposed to him (see next section).

lest by any means such a one should be swallowed up with his excessive sorrow' (ii. 6, 7). The infliction of the punishment by a majority might imply that the minority wanted to inflict either a lesser punishment—perhaps none at all—or one still more severe. In the latter case '*ye* should rather forgive' is addressed to the minority, which is awkward; in the former, more simply, it is addressed to the Corinthian Church as a whole, to whom the letter is written. Those who explain 'ye' as the minority who wanted severer measures, think that they may have been the Paul-party (1 Cor. i 12) who wished jealously to uphold the apostle's authority to the uttermost. But if the minority, as is more probable, still adhered to the attitude rebuked in 1 Cor. v. 2, and refused to acquiesce in St Paul's authority, it is easier to understand the sternness displayed in 2 *Corinthians*, especially in chs. x.–xiii. (see section 9), in spite of the relief and joy which the report of Titus had caused him.

9. Is the Sorrowful Letter lost? Again there are divergent views.

(1) The sorrowful letter is thought to be partly preserved in 2 Cor. x.–xiii. 10.

(*a*) It is pointed out that in chs. 1–ix. St Paul writes in a friendly tone, as though the trouble were all over, and he were quite satisfied with the Corinthians: 'I rejoice that in everything I am of good courage concerning you' (vii. 16); but in chs. x.–xiii he writes in a tone of indignant remonstrance, anger, satire, and self-defence.

(*b*) According to this view he speaks in xii. 20–xiii. 2 of a severe visit that he was shrinking from the necessity of paying, because the former visit had been so painful, and he was relieved from it by the report that Titus brought of the effect of his sorrowful letter.

INTRODUCTION TO I AND II CORINTHIANS

(c) Three passages in chs. x.–xiii. are thought to point *forward* to the possibility of this visit, while three passages written later in chs. i.–ix. point *backward* to the fact that he had not been obliged to pay it.

'Being in readiness to avenge all disobedience when your obedience shall be fulfilled.'—2 Cor. x. 6.	'For to this end also did I write that I might know the proof of you, whether ye are obedient in all things.'—2 Cor. ii. 9.
'If I come again I will not spare'—2 Cor. xiii. 2.	'To spare you I came not to Corinth.'—2 Cor. i 23.
'For this cause I write these things from a distance, that I may not when I come deal sharply.'—2 Cor. xiii. 10.	'And I wrote this same thing that when I come I might not have sorrow.'—2 Cor. ii. 3.

(d) 'Did I take advantage of you by any one of them whom I have sent unto you? I asked Titus to go, and I sent the brother with him Did Titus take any advantage of you? Walked we not by the same spirit, in the same steps?' (2 Cor. xii. 17, 18). According to this view these words occur in the sorrowful letter which Titus himself was taking, and therefore cannot refer to the conduct of Titus in Corinth on the occasion when he took it. Lake paraphrases it thus: 'You know that from the beginning of my intercourse with the Corinthians I have never had a penny of profit from them, and the same is true of my representatives. Titus, who is now coming to you, has never made any profit. Can you deny that he always behaved in this respect in exactly the same way as I did myself?'

(e) 'Are we beginning again to commend ourselves?' (iii. 1). 'We do not again commend ourselves to you' (v. 12). In chs. x.–xiii. St Paul commends himself with the utmost energy. These two passages therefore, according to this view, refer to the sorrowful letter of which chs. x.–xiii. form a part.

(2) The other view, which seems to the present writer on the whole the more probable, is that the sorrowful letter is entirely lost to us, and that 2 *Corinthians* was a complete letter as it stands[1]. The five points noted above can all be explained as easily on this view as on the other.

(*a*) Though the tone of chs. i.–ix. is happier than that of chs. x.–xiii., the former chapters are by no means without indications that all was not yet right at Corinth. St Paul has to defend himself against opponents who brought against him the charge of fickleness (i. 17–22). Some, 'the many,' were still insincerely making profit out of the word of God (ii. 17). Some of his opponents are sharply satirized for needing, and bringing, commendatory letters with them to Corinth (iii. 1). Some still handled the word of God deceitfully (iv. 2), and in complaining that St Paul's preaching was obscure only shewed that their own hearts were still in obscurity (*vv.* 3, 4); and they 'preached themselves, not Christ Jesus as Lord' (*v.* 5). The Corinthians needed an answer 'to them that glory in appearance and not in heart' (v. 12), and scoffed at St Paul as being 'beside himself' (*v.* 13). He still felt that he must as Christ's ambassador intreat them to be reconciled to God (*v.* 20), and not to receive His grace in vain (vi. 1). The hearts of some of them were not opened wide towards him in love (vi. 12, 13, vii. 2). And lastly he was afraid that the collection for the poor of Jerusalem which they had begun, and of which he boasted to the Macedonians, had not really advanced (ix. 6, 10, 11).

[1] With the probable exception (see section 3) of vi. 14–vii. 1.

III] INTRODUCTION TO I AND II CORINTHIANS

While the submission of the Corinthians caused St Paul profound relief, and he spent much of the first nine chapters in expressing it in a tactful and friendly way, yet he was compelled, even in these chapters, to rebuke the serious opposition to his authority and teaching which still remained in a minority of them; and in chs. x.–xiii. he directs his attention mainly to them.

(*b*) In xii. 14, xiii. 1 St Paul definitely states his purpose of coming to the Corinthians for the third time. On the other view this was explained to mean 'I may be obliged to come to you, but I shrink from it, and will not do so if this sorrowful letter that I am writing, and Titus' exhortations, prove successful.' But if 2 *Corinthians* is a unity, these passages are given their straightforward natural sense. St Paul *was* about to come to Corinth from Macedonia.

(*c*) In the passages printed above in parallel columns, the echoes of language are not in themselves a proof that the passages in the first column were written earlier than those in the second. The former may look forward to the visit which St Paul did in fact pay when he went South from Macedonia (Acts xx. 2, 3, 'He came to Greece; and when he had spent three months etc'); the latter may look back to the visit which he had refrained from paying, and had substituted for it the sorrowful letter.

(*d*) The more natural explanation of xii. 17, 18, quoted above, is that St Paul is referring to the conduct of Titus when he carried the sorrowful letter.

(*e*) In iii. 1, v. 12 St Paul deprecates the necessity of commending himself afresh to the Corinthians. This is in opposition to some of his opponents who armed themselves with commendatory letters, whom he attacks in *both* parts of the epistle (iii. 1, x. 12, 18). The meaning of iii. 1 is explained in *v*. 2: the only recommendation that the Corinthians ought to need is the work that he had done among them; they were themselves his letter of recommendation, written not with ink but with the Spirit of the living God.

To these considerations two more must be added:

(*f*) The apostle's description of the writing of his sorrowful letter is as follows: 'Out of much affliction and anguish of heart I wrote unto you with many tears; not that ye should be made sorry, but that ye might know the love which I have more abundantly unto you' (ii. 4). This does not really apply very well to chs. x.-xiii. It is difficult to find in them the trace of tears of one who longed to exhibit his love. They are composed for the most part of three ingredients—burning indignation, scathing satire, and vehement self-defence. It is not the letter of one humiliated by failure, and yet writing more in sorrow and heart-ache than in anger.

(*g*) His words in ii. 5-10 shew that the sorrowful letter had been chiefly concerned with the wrong-doing of an individual offender, 'he that did the wrong,' and the attitude of the Corinthian Church towards him. But of this offender, or this attitude, there is not one word in chs. x.-xiii. The supporters of the opposite view are compelled to suppose that those chapters are only the latter portion of the sorrowful letter, and that the former portion (containing that which is most crucial to the theory) is lost.

They urge that the Corinthians probably did not take the trouble to preserve with much care a letter of that nature, or may even have suppressed the portion dealing with the offender; but at a later time, when the offender and most of his contemporaries were dead, and when anything that St Paul wrote was considered valuable simply because he wrote it, all available fragments of his letters were combined.

This is not, in itself, impossible. We have already seen the probability that 2 Cor. vi. 14–vii. 1 is a fragment of the earliest of all the apostle's letters to Corinth of which we have any knowledge. That in neither case do our MSS or versions afford any textual evidence to support the conjecture is not a difficulty, since the collection of Pauline material must have taken place much earlier than any of our documents. But a careful study of the points noted above will shew that the arguments are by no means conclusive for the theory that chs. x.–xiii. contain a mutilated fragment of the sorrowful letter, which has lost its most important part. A large number of scholars is found on both sides of the question, and complete certainty will perhaps never be reached

CHAPTER IV

I CORINTHIANS

1. CAUSES OF WRITING. The epistle was written solely to meet the needs of the moment in the Corinthian Church. St Paul deals (1) with matters for blame of which he has received reports from 'them of Chloe' and perhaps from other sources; (2) with questions addressed to him by the Corinthians in a letter he had just received from them; (3) with matters reported to him probably by the bearers of their letter, Stephanas, Fortunatus, and Achaicus. The questions asked by the Corinthians seem to be indicated by a recurring formula, as follows:

'Now concerning what you wrote'   vii. 1.
  ,,   ,,   virgins'   vii. 25.
  ,,   ,,   idol-foods'   viii. 1.
  ,,   ,,   Spirit-filled persons' xii. 1.
  ,,   ,,   the collection' xvi. 1.
  ,,   ,,   Apollos'   xvi. 12.

The remainder, therefore, of chs. vii.–xvi. (except xvi. 5–11, 13–24) will have been due to the reports brought by the three bearers of their letter.

(*a*) The Corinthians remembered St Paul, and were faithful to the traditions which he had taught them (xi. 2); but some women were committing an irregularity with regard to dress at public worship (xi. 3–16).

(*b*) Some of the richer Christians were guilty of an abuse in their manner of eating food at the Eucharistic feasts (xi. 17–34).

(*c*) Some Christians, probably Gentiles only, denied that there would be a Resurrection of the dead, because the material body could not inherit the divine Kingdom (ch. xv.; see *v.* 50).

2. ANALYSIS.
   i. 1–3. Salutation.
   i. 4–9. Thanksgiving.
A. i.–vi Matters for blame of which the apostle has heard.
   i. 10–iv. 21. Party divisions.
   v. 1–13. A case of gross immorality.
   vi. 1–11. Litigation in heathen courts.
   vi 12–20. Fornication.
B. vii. 1–xvi. 12. Matters on which the Corinthians had asked for advice, and others of which he had heard from the bearers of their letter.
   vii. 1–24. Concerning Marriage.

vii. 25–40. Concerning Virgins.
viii. 1–xi. 1. Concerning Idol-foods.
  (a) viii. The Higher Expediency.
  (b) ix. The Higher Expediency illustrated in the apostle's own manner of life.
  (c) x. 1–22. The peril of presuming upon Christian privileges by partaking in Idol-feasts.
  (d) x. 23–xi. 1. Advice in three other cases connected with Idol-foods.
xi. 2–16. The covering of the head in public worship.
xi. 17–34. The Holy Eucharist.
xii.–xiv. Concerning Spirit-filled persons.
xv. Resurrection.
xvi. 1–11. The Collection (with some Personal Matters).
xvi. 12 Apollos
xvi. 13–18. Personal Matters.
xvi. 19–24. Salutations and Autographic Conclusion.

3. CONTENTS.

i 1–3. Salutation, in which 'Sosthenes the brother' joins.

i. 4–9. Thanksgiving for the spiritual condition of the readers.

A. i.–vi. Matters for blame of which the apostle has heard.

i. 10–iv. 21. *Party Divisions.*

Party divisions condemned. St Paul expresses his thankfulness that he had never made a practice of baptizing, which might have encouraged them (i. 10–17). Worldly wisdom is not divine wisdom (*vv.* 18–25). It is not the worldly wise whom God has chosen to be Christians (*vv.* 26–31). The apostle did not preach among them worldly wisdom (ii 1–5); and yet he does preach divine wisdom, taught by the Spirit of God (*vv.* 6–16). Party spirit shews that they are like babes, spiritually immature, and incapable of understanding that he and Apollos are only God's ministers, each doing his appointed work in God's husbandry (iii. 1–9). Or to use another metaphor, the work is that of a builder, the permanence of whose work will be tried by fire at the Last Day (*vv.* 10–17). Worldly wisdom, as he said before, is not God's wisdom (*vv.* 18–21). Apollos' preaching and his are to be reckoned only as a fraction of the infinite privileges bestowed upon the readers as Christians (*vv.* 22, 23). He and Apollos are only God's ministers and stewards to dispense His mysteries. No test of their work is of any value except the divine test at the Last Day (iv. 1–5). He has spoken of himself and Apollos as illustrative instances, but he means it equally of them all, that they may not be proud of their individual gifts and personal importance,—they who are so gifted and rich, while the apostles are subject to every imaginable hardship and indignity¹ (*vv.* 6–13). An earnest appeal to his spiritual children, with a statement that he has sent Timothy, and will probably come shortly himself to deal with the trouble (*vv.* 14–21).

v. 1–13. *A case of gross immorality.*

The apostle hears that one of their number has committed a sin which unconverted pagans would not tolerate, and they are not even grieved about it enough to expel him (v. 1, 2). As though present with their whole Christian community, he solemnly condemns him to excommunication in hope that the fearful consequences may be effectual to the saving of his spirit (*vv.* 3–5). They boast that such a sin is an expression of Christian 'liberty'; but evil spreads like leaven, and must be purged out as leaven is purged out at the Passover; for since Christ our Victim was sacrificed, Christians must keep a perpetual Passover (*vv.* 6–8). When he speaks of purging out, he does not mean, as they seem to have thought from his first letter, that they must entirely avoid all immoral persons; if they did that, they would have to leave the world altogether. But they must avoid the company of any *Christian* who is guilty of immorality (*vv.* 9–11). It is only Christians, not heathen, that they can judge (*vv.* 12, 13)[1].

vi. 1–11. *Litigation in heathen courts.*

How can they so degrade themselves as to take one another up before heathen judges, when they know that very soon Christians will be the judges of men and angels! (vi. 1–6). Christians ought not to have lawsuits against one another at all, better suffer injury than that (*v.* 7). Nay, but they injure other Christians, although they know that those who lead evil lives shall not inherit the coming Kingdom. Some of them were once of their number, but having been washed, sanctified, and justified, they ought no longer to behave like them (*vv.* 8–11).

vi. 12–20. *Fornication.*

Christian liberty does not mean slavery to fleshly lust (vi. 12). Five reasons against fornication: 1st. Man's

[1] Archbp. Bernard (*Studia Sacra*, ch. ix.), with some earlier writers, sees in this a link between chs. v. and vi., and thinks that the injured father (v. 1) brought the matter ($\pi\rho\hat{a}\gamma\mu a$) before a heathen court.

body in its true inner nature is made for the Lord, and will share in the Resurrection (*vv.* 13, 14). *2nd.* Man's body in its true inner nature is made to be united with Christ as one of His members, not with the body of a harlot (*vv.* 15–17). *3rd.* Other sins are external to the body, but fornication is an offence against the true inner nature of the body (*v.* 18). *4th* Their body is the temple of the Holy Spirit (*v.* 19) *5th.* They are not their own property to do what they like with, since they were bought with a price (*v.* 20).

B. vii.–xvi. 12 Matters on which the Corinthians had asked for advice, and others of which he had heard from the bearers of their letter.

vii. 1–24. *Concerning Marriage.*

The best condition is to remain unmarried. But the demands of natural instincts make marriage imperative for some; and husband and wife must accordingly fulfil to each other their functions God's will is different for different people (vii 1–7). The principle in the last words is applicable to a variety of cases: The unmarried men, and widows, had better remain, the apostle says, as he is. But marriage may be necessary for some (*vv.* 8, 9). The married must not leave one another by divorce. If they do, the wife must not marry anyone else (*vv.* 10, 11). If a Christian man has a heathen wife, or a Christian woman a heathen husband, St Paul's private opinion is that they need not separate. The Christianity of either makes their children Christian (*vv.* 12–14). But if the heathen partner wishes separation, let it be done; for in calling men to be Christians, God intended them to live in peace. It is far from certain that the Christian man or wife will be able to convert the other (*vv.* 15,

16). Everyone must follow his God-given opportunities and vocation (*v.* 17).

There are quite other cases in which the principle applies. Some were circumcised before they became Christians, some were not. Let them remain as they were; neither condition is of any value in itself[1] (*vv.* 18-20). Some were slaves before they became Christians. Some of these may have the opportunity of gaining their freedom, in which case they had better take it[2] (*v.* 21) But earthly slavery is a matter of no moment, and among Christians the relationship of master and slave is virtually done away, in view of the fact that Christ has bought us all to His bond-service (*vv.* 22, 23). Let everyone follow his God-given vocation (*v.* 24).

vii. 25-40. *Concerning Virgins*[3].

St Paul says he has no divine command, but gives his personal opinion (*v.* 25).

Because the distress accompanying the Last Day is so near, it is better for a man to remain single[4] (*v.* 26). A married man must not, indeed, cancel his marriage; but a widower should not seek a wife. It is not sinful for him to marry, but only unadvisable. Similarly it is not sinful for a virgin to marry (*vv.* 27, 28 a). But married people will have more trouble in the last days than the unmarried (*v.* 28 b). The Last Day being so near, life

1 Cf. Gal. v. 6, vi. 15.
2 This is probably the meaning of the words, though grammatically they could also mean that the slave, even if he has the chance of being free, should 'rather make use of' his slavery. See Lightfoot, *Coloss and Philem* p 322, footnote
3 This section is loosely strung together, virgins as a class are dealt with only in the last three verses, though they are mentioned in *vv.* 28, 34
4 Lit. 'to be so' i e. unmarried, in reference to the word παρθενῶν, 'virgins,' in the preceding verse, which can apply to men as well as women.

in all respects should be treated as about to pass away (*vv.* 29–31). The unmarried, whether man or woman, can [in the terrible circumstances that are soon to come] wait upon the Lord without distraction, while the married are torn asunder between attending upon the Lord and attending upon their wives and husbands (*vv.* 32–35).

A parent or guardian in charge of a virgin had better allow her to marry if she feels the necessity for it. But if he can adhere to his determination that she shall remain a virgin, he does well. The former action is right, but the latter is preferable (*vv.* 36–38)[1].

A woman is bound by the marriage tie while her husband is alive. When she has become a widow she can be married again, provided she is married to a Christian; but she will be happier if she remain a widow (*vv.* 39, 40).

viii –xi. 1. *Concerning Idol-foods.*

(*a*) viii. 1–13. The Higher Expediency.

Enlightened knowledge [of the nothingness of idols] must yield place to Christian love (*vv.* 1–3). The enlightened Christian knows, of course, that an idol is a mere nothing; he acknowledges only one God and one Christ (*vv.* 4–6). But this knowledge is not shared by all. Some, in eating idol-foods, are conscientiously convinced that the foods have been consecrated to real beings. Christian liberty must not be allowed to wound the conscience of others (*vv.* 7–12). Rather than do that, St Paul says, he would renounce meat for the rest of his life (*v.* 13).

---

1 Another explanation of this difficult passage is that some Christians at that period were adopting the custom of 'spiritual marriage' with virgins, and the apostle says that a man and his virgin (not 'virgin *daughter*' as R.V.) may marry if necessity demands it, but if he can adhere to his spiritual attitude towards her it is preferable. See Lake, *The Earlier Epistles of St Paul*, pp 188–191.

(*b*) ix. 1–27. The Higher Expediency illustrated in the apostle's own manner of life

He holds the position of an apostle, at least to the Corinthians whose conversion is the seal of his work (*vv.* 1–3). He can therefore claim the right of an apostle to receive maintenance (*vv.* 4–12 a). All ministers in sacred things have the same right, but he forbears to insist on it (*vv.* 12 b–18): firstly, that he may win as many as possible to Christianity by being 'all things to all men' (*vv.* 19–23); secondly, that he may gain the heavenly prize, for which he must keep his bodily desires in control as an athlete in a race or a boxing match (*vv.* 24–27).

(*c*) x. 1–22. The peril of presuming upon Christian privileges by partaking in Idol-feasts. The Israelites had received a foretaste of Christian Baptism in the cloud and the crossing of the sea, and a foretaste of the Eucharist in the manna and the water from the rock (*vv.* 1–4); and yet they fell (*v.* 5). The Corinthian Christians are in a similar danger (*vv.* 6–11). If they think they are strong and enlightened enough to run spiritual risks, they will probably fall, and it will be their own fault (*v.* 12); for otherwise, God has never, and will never, let a temptation assail them that is too hard for them (*v.* 13)[1]. Therefore they must shun idolatry, for it is idolatry to partake of idol-feasts, in spite of their enlightened knowledge (*vv* 14, 15, 19–22), just as to partake of the Christian cup and bread is to share in the Blood and the Body of Christ (*vv.* 16, 17), and to partake of Jewish sacrificial feasts is to share in the altar (*v.* 18).

---

[1] This line of thought, which leads naturally to *v.* 14, is drawn out by Godet Other less satisfactory explanations will be found mentioned in commentaries.

(d) x. 23–xi. 1. *Advice in other cases connected with Idol-foods.*

No eating of food can be wrong in itself, but it may sometimes be unadvisable (vv. 23, 24). All meat sold in the shops may be eaten freely, for the whole world belongs to God (vv. 25, 26). A Christian at dinner with a heathen may eat his meat if nothing is said about its being idol-food (v. 27). But if anyone draws attention to the fact that it is idol-food, it should be declined, for the sake of the conscience of others, and to prevent Christian liberty from being misunderstood (vv. 28–30). They should aim, therefore, at the higher expediency, as the apostle does himself (v. 31–xi. 1).

xi. 2–16. *The covering of the head in public worship.*

He is glad that they preserve the traditions which he taught them; but they must not lose sight of woman's status in the divine order (vv. 2, 3). In public worship men dishonour their heads if they veil them, and women if they do not (vv. 4–6). Woman is by nature in subjection to man (vv. 7–9). Man's authority over her ought, therefore, to be symbolized by a veil, 'because of the angels[1]' (v. 10). It should be remembered, however, that in their union with the Lord neither man nor woman is complete without the other (vv. 11, 12). Common decency, if nothing else, requires the veiling of woman (v. 13). And nature itself teaches the same, by the instinctive feeling that long hair is a dishonour to a man but a glory to a woman (vv 14, 15). If anyone disputes the advice here given, he must simply submit to the universal custom in the Church (v. 16)

---

[1] The meaning of this verse, which is much disputed, must be studied in commentaries.

xi 17–34. *The Holy Eucharist.*

(*a*) The apostle has heard of abuses. They come together in a wrong spirit (*v.* 17) Unity is destroyed, firstly by their party divisions (*vv.* 18, 19), secondly by their habit of each one eating the food that he has brought, instead of waiting till all are present, so that rich and poor can share alike (*vv.* 20–22).

(*b*) The origin of the feast was in the commands of the Lord Jesus (*vv.* 23–25), so that it is a perpetual declaration of His death until His Advent (*v.* 26).

(*c*) In view, then, of the nature of the feast, they should test their practice and their attitude towards it, because unworthy participation is perilous (*vv.* 27–32). Let them wait till all are assembled, if they are too hungry to wait, let them eat at home (*vv.* 33, 34 a) Other matters he will put right when he visits them (*v.* 34 b)

xii.–xiv. *Concerning Spirit-filled persons*[1].

(*a*) He is anxious that they should understand this matter rightly (xii. 1). Before their conversion they used to be carried away by the obsession of idol-demons (*v.* 2) The test to distinguish divine from demoniacal inspiration is that with the former none can say 'Jesus is anathema,' and without it none can say 'Jesus is Lord' (*v.* 3).

(*b*) The several *charismata* possessed by inspired persons are many and various; but the variety is due to the action of the one and self-same Spirit, Lord, and

---

[1] περὶ τῶν πνευματικῶν. This may be either masculine (cf. ii. 15, iii 1, xiv 37, Gal vi. 1) or neuter, 'spiritual things, or charismata' (cf. xiv. 1) Elsewhere, however, the neuter has a different force (cf. ii. 13, ix. 11, Rom. xv. 27).

God (*vv.* 4–6), *for the advantage of the community* (*vv.* 7–11). The nature of the community as the Body of Christ is illustrated by the human body and its members, shewing what should be the attitude of individuals with their respective *charismata* (*vv.* 12–30).

(*c*) But the readers are eager[1] to know which are the greatest *charismata* (*v.* 31 a). There is one thing which far excels any ordinary *charisma* (*v.* 31 b), i.e. *Love* (ch. xiii.):

All *charismata* are worthless without Love (*vv.* 1–3). The value of Love (*vv* 4–7). The permanence of Love (*vv.* 8–13).

(*d*) If, and only if, they follow this supreme principle of corporate life, it will be right for them to desire the spiritual *charismata*, especially that of Prophesying (xiv. 1). For prophecy [ecstatic utterance that is intelligible] is preferable to 'tongue-speaking,' *glōssolalia* [ecstatic utterance that is unintelligible]: the former edifies all who hear it, the latter only the speaker (*vv.* 2–6). Tongues are as useless to others as music with no tune (*vv.* 7–9), or a foreign language unknown to the hearer (*vv.* 10, 11). Tongue-speaking must therefore be regulated for public edification (*vv.* 12–19). It is right to be childlike in spirit, but that must not mean to be lacking in common-sense (*v.* 20). As the Old Testament suggests (*v* 21), tongues are a sign to unbelievers; prophecy to believers. The former looks like madness, the latter can be a means of conversion (*vv.* 22–25). Practical regulations that *charismata* may be used for public edification (*vv.* 26–33). Women must not speak at all in church (*vv.* 34–36).

[1] Or imperative, as in xiv. 1: By all means be eager for the greatest *charismata*.

Conclusion: The genuinely Spirit-filled person will realise that the advice here given is good (*vv.* 37, 38). Prophecy is to be eagerly desired, but tongues are not to be forbidden (*v.* 39), provided seemliness and order are preserved (*v.* 40).

xv. *Resurrection.*

vv. 1–34. The Fact. Christian development of Jewish belief.

(*a*) Christ's Resurrection is a fundamental article of apostolic preaching: The fundamentals which the apostle delivered to the Corinthians (*vv.* 1–4). The witnesses of Christ's Resurrection (*vv* 5–9). The preaching of St Paul and all the apostles (*vv.* 10, 11).

(*b*) The Resurrection of Christ and that of Christians are complementary aspects of one truth: to deny either is to deny the other (*vv.* 12, 13), a denial which does away with a life after death, and therefore makes apostolic preaching false, and Christian faith and hope futile (*vv.* 14–19). But if Christ has been raised, dead Christians will be brought to life in Him as all men are brought to death in Adam (*vv.* 20–22).

(*c*) The course of final events from Christ's Resurrection till His ultimate subjection to the Father (*vv.* 23–28).

(*d*) Further considerations. If there is no Resurrection [and therefore no life after death], why baptize living persons for the benefit of the dead? (*v.* 29), and why does the apostle endure daily perils and persecutions, instead of enjoying himself while he can? (*vv.* 31, 32). They must not be led astray from their faith by bad influence (*vv.* 33, 34).

vv. 35–58. The Nature of the risen body. A reply to Gentile objections.

(a) Analogies from Nature (*vv.* 35-42) offer illustrations of the truth that the 'spiritual' body differs from the 'psychic' body as the Second Adam from the First (*vv.* 43-49).

(b) It is true [as Gentiles in Corinth had probably objected] that material flesh and blood cannot inherit the divine Kingdom (*v.* 50); but the Christian mystery is that a change of the material flesh and blood will take place at the moment of the last trump (*vv.* 51-53), and the final victory will be won in Christ over sin and death (*vv.* 54-57). Concluding exhortation (*v.* 58).

xvi. *Personal matters.*

The Collection (*vv.* 1-4). Intended movements, of himself[1] (*vv.* 5-9), of Timothy[2] (*vv.* 10, 11), of Apollos[3] (*v.* 12). Exhortation to stedfastness and love (*vv.* 13, 14). Commendation of the household of Stephanas (*vv.* 15, 16), his mission to the apostle at Ephesus, with the other bearers of the letter from the Corinthians (*vv.* 17, 18) Salutations (*vv.* 19, 20), and Conclusion (*vv.* 21-24).

CHAPTER V

II CORINTHIANS

This letter, though addressed not only to the Church at Corinth but also to 'all the saints which are in the whole of Achaia,' was called forth, as 1 *Corinthians* was,

[1] See p. 140.   [2] See p. 139.
[3] The words 'Now concerning (R.V. 'But as touching') Apollos' suggest that the Corinthians in their letter had asked that Apollos might visit them again. This was probably the wish chiefly of the Apollos-party. But at any rate his presence would only have intensified the party spirit; and in complete loyalty to St Paul he refused to go, which the apostle states with incisive brevity.

entirely by the circumstances of the moment. These have been discussed on pp. 136–9. As regards its teaching in detail it has less bearing on the subsequent life of the Christian Church than any other of St Paul's epistles. But on the other hand, far more than any other it affords a living picture of the man himself. It is his character that here speaks to us, rather than his doctrine or advice.

1. ANALYSIS

    i. 1, 2. Salutation.
    i. 3–11 Thanksgiving.
    i. 12–14. The ground of his confidence.

A. i. 15–vii. 16. Self-vindication
    i. 15–ii. 13. Of his dealings with them.
    ii. 14–vii. 4. Of his apostleship.
      (*a*) ii. 14–iv. 6. His office.
      (*b*) iv. 7–v. 10. His sufferings.
      (*c*) v. 11–vi. 10. His life.
      (*d*) vi. 11–13 and vii. 2–4. His personal feelings for them.
        [vi. 14–vii. 1. Warning to separate themselves from the uncleanness of heathen idolatries[1].]
    vii. 5–16. Of his dealings with them.

B. viii., ix. The Collection.
    viii. 1–15. An appeal to their liberality.
    viii. 16–24. The mission of Titus and two other brethren.
    ix. 1–5. The same.
    ix. 6–15. An appeal to their liberality.

[1] On this passage, which is probably a fragment of an earlier letter, see pp. 137 f.

C. x.–xiii. 10. Rebukes to opponents.
   x. 1–11. He can act as sternly as he writes.
   x. 12–xi. 15. A comparison of himself with his opponents.
   xi. 16–xii. 12. His right to boast.
   xii. 13–18. He has not been, and will not be, burdensome.
   xii 19–xiii. 10 He will act sternly if necessary.
      xiii. 11–13. Conclusion.

2. CONTENTS.
   i. 1, 2. Salutation, in which Timothy joins.
   i. 3–11. Thanksgiving for the comfort which God has given him in his recent tribulations.
   i. 12–14. The ground of his confidence is his behaviour when he was at Corinth, to which both his own conscience and their acknowledgement bear witness.

A. i. 15–vii. 16. Self-vindication.

i. 15–ii. 13. *Of his dealings with them.*

His change of plan did not involve fickleness (*vv.* 15–17 a). His Yea and Nay in earthly matters, like his teaching in spiritual matters, were in accordance with the Truth which exists in the divine Nature (*vv.* 17 b–22). His change of plan was in order to spare them (*v.* 23–ii. 1). That he might be gladdened by the penitence of the offender (*v.* 2), and that he might have joy and not sorrow from them, he wrote his sorrowful letter (*vv.* 3, 4). Having punished the offender adequately, they must not be over-severe, but must forgive him as the apostle himself does (*vv.* 5–11). His agony of mind at Troas, and his relief and joy when Titus met him in Macedonia (*vv.* 12, 13).

ii. 14–vii. 4. *Of his apostleship*.

(*a*) ii. 14–iv. 6. His office. His work is like a sacrificial odour rising to God, life-giving to those who are being saved, death-bringing to the perishing (*vv.* 14–16). The sincerity of his teaching (*v.* 17). His independence of human commendation, since the Corinthians by their conversion are his true commendation (iii. 1–4). His ministry is that of the New Covenant, which is incomparably greater in glory than the Old, although the Old, being of divine origin, had a temporary glory (*vv.* 5–18). The high character of his ministry is in keeping with this (iv. 1–6).

(*b*) iv. 7–v. 10. His sufferings. They are necessary to the spiritual efficiency of his ministry (*vv.* 7–15). They are a preliminary stage in the stripping off of the tent or garment of this earthly body, that he may be clothed with heavenly life (*v.* 16–v. 5). They therefore free him from all preference for earthly life, and help to prepare him for the coming Judgment (*vv.* 6–10).

(*c*) v. 11–vi. 10. His life. The *motive* of his life is not self-commendation, but the fear of the Lord[1], and the love of Christ because He died for us (*vv.* 11–15). The *nature* of his life is that of a newly created being in Christ, through whom God reconciles the world to Himself; and He commits to the apostle the office of proclaiming this, so that he intreats the Corinthians as an ambassador of Christ and of God (*v.* 16–vi. 2). The *earthly marks* that his life is of this nature are sufferings (*vv.* 3–5), character (*vv.* 6, 7), and a spiritual independence of circumstances (*vv.* 8–10).

(*d*) vi. 11–13, vii. 2–4. His personal feelings for the Corinthians. His heart was wide open to them, and he

[1] *Sc* because of the coming Judgment.

longs that they should open their hearts to him (*vv.* 11–13, vii. 2 a). He had wronged none of them because he loved them (*vv.* 2 b, 3). And now he was full of glorying and joy about them (*v.* 4).

[vi. 14–vii. 1. For a Christian to be in close relation with idolatrous non-Christians is incongruous and impossible. They must therefore separate themselves from this defilement, as Israel was commanded to do.]

vii. 5–16. *Of his dealings with them.*

After reaching Macedonia in intense anxiety, he was comforted by the arrival of Titus (*vv.* 5, 6). His joyful relief at the report of the effect of his sorrowful letter as shewn in their treatment of the offender (*vv.* 7–12). His joy was increased by the joy which Titus felt about them (*vv.* 13–16).

B. viii., ix. The Collection

May the example of the Macedonian churches stir them to a like liberality (viii. 1–7). Inspired by Christ's example of self-sacrifice may they be liberal, that they and other churches may contribute in just proportions (*vv.* 8–15). He is sending Titus and two other brethren whom they can safely trust (*vv.* 16–24). He is sending them to bring their collection to a successful issue, that his boast of them to the Macedonians may not be disappointed (ix. 1–5). He asks them to give liberally, not only for the relief of the poor, but as a thankoffering to God for all His goodness to them (*vv.* 6–15).

C. x.–xiii. 10. Rebukes to opponents.

x. 1–11. *He can act as sternly as he writes.*

He hopes that he will not have to act sternly, when he comes, against some who treat him as an ordinary man not filled with the Spirit (*vv.* 1, 2). For his warfare is spiritual, and therefore powerful (*vv.* 3–6). To anyone who self-confidently boasts that he belongs to Christ, the apostle replies that he also belongs to Christ (*v.* 7). But he will not boast of it in writing, for fear of appearing to support those who scoffed at him as being stern on paper but weak when present in person (*vv.* 8–10). Let such a scoffer take note that he can act as sternly as he writes (*v.* 11).

x. 12–xi. 15. *A comparison of himself with his opponents.*

They must not imagine that his estimate of himself—like that of some—is exaggerated, or that he oversteps rightful limits in the area of his authority (*vv.* 12–18). There are those who would lead them astray from Christ to whom he had married them; and when this occurs they put up with it remarkably well! (xi. 1–6). Or perhaps it was the apostle himself that wronged them by accepting help from Macedonia, and refusing to make his maintenance a burden upon them! (*vv.* 7–10). His reason was that if, in his love for them, he had accepted their help, false apostles among them, doing Satan's work, would have made it an opportunity of misrepresenting his motives (*vv.* 11–15).

xi. 16–xii. 12. *His right to boast.*

They put up with it remarkably well when other people injure and enslave them, make gain of them, and insult them; so he asks them to put up with him also, while for a moment he speaks like a fool, and indulges in a little boasting! (*vv.* 16–21). He can boast of as good a Jewish pedigree as they (*v.* 22), of far more labours and sufferings in Christ's ministry (*vv.* 23–33), and of visions and revelations, though here it is of another self that he speaks (xii. 1–7 a). To prevent his being over-elated by the revelations, a stake in the flesh was sent him, which God, for his spiritual good, would not remove; gladly therefore will he confine his boasting to his infirmities and sufferings for Christ (*vv.* 7 b–10). They must forgive him this folly! It was they who forced him to shew that he is at least up to the level of those 'apostles' who think so much of themselves; his work among them proves it (*vv.* 11, 12).

xii. 13–18. *He has not been, and will not be, burdensome.*

They must forgive him for wronging them more than other churches by not making his maintenance a burden upon them! (*v.* 13). When he now comes he will be no more burdensome than before, or than Titus was, or anyone else whom he had sent to them (*vv.* 14–18).

xii. 19–xiii. 10. *He will act sternly if necessary.*

He is afraid that when he comes he will find many abuses among them (*vv.* 19–21); and if so, he warns them that he will act unsparingly (xiii. 1–6). But he prays that they may shew themselves approved, not for his credit but for their own (*vv.* 7–9). That is why he writes thus, that he may not be obliged to use the authority which the Lord has given him (*v.* 10)

xiii. 11–13. Conclusion.

CHAPTER VI

GALATIANS

1. TIME AND PLACE OF WRITING. We are here met by complicated difficulties. The two views on the locality of 'Galatia' (p. 51 f.) should be carefully read at this point. It will then be clear to the reader that if, as may be assumed, St Luke means by 'Galatia' the same dis-

trict as St Paul (1 Cor. xvi 1, Gal. 1 2, 2 Tim. iv. 10), the epistle must, on the North-Galatian view, have been written later than the visit of Acts xvi 6; on the South-Galatian view it must have been written later than the double journey of Acts xiii. 14–xiv. 24. In favour of the South-Galatian view is the fact that St Paul habitually uses the names of Roman provinces in geographical statements: cf. Achaia (Rom. xv. 26 and elsewhere), Macedonia (*ibid.*, and elsewhere), Judaea (1 Thes. ii. 14, 2 Cor. i. 16, Rom. xv. 31), Arabia (Gal. i. 17, iv. 25), Syria and Cilicia (Gal. i. 21), Asia (1 Cor. xvi. 19, 2 Cor. i. 8, Rom. xvi. 5). It may also be noted that Barnabas, who accompanied St Paul on his first tour but not afterwards, is mentioned as though known to the readers of the epistle (ii. 13)[1].

In iv. 13 St Paul says that because of an infirmity of the flesh he preached to the Galatians 'the first time' (R.V.),—'at the first' (A.V.). The word[2] would, in strictly classical Greek, mean 'the former of two times.' If this is the meaning, St Paul had paid *two* visits to the Galatians before he wrote. On the North-Galatian view, this would date the epistle after the visit of Acts xviii. 23 on the third tour; on the South-Galatian view, after the visit of Acts xvi. 6 on the second tour. The former is adopted by Lightfoot, who thinks that it was written at Corinth during the third tour, the latter by Zahn and Rendall, who think that it was written at Corinth during the second tour, and by Ramsay, who prefers Antioch between the second and the third tour. But in the Greek

1 Zahn ingeniously suggests a connexion between iv. 14 ('ye received me as an angel (*or* messenger) of God') and Acts xiv. 12 ('they called...Paul, Hermes,' i.e the messenger of the gods).
2 τὸ πρότερον.

of the Empire the meaning was often nearer to that in the A.V., 'formerly,' 'originally,' a meaning found elsewhere in the New Testament[1]. In this case the expression gives us no help in fixing the date, and we are thrown back on our previous pair of alternatives.

Of these the North-Galatian alternative need not be further discussed[2]. Accepting the South-Galatian view, we can enter upon the study of the date of the epistle, starting with the single fact that it was written after the first tour, to those churches in Asia Minor which the apostle had evangelized during that tour (Acts xiii. 14–xiv. 24).

The first important event recorded in the *Acts* after the first tour is the Council of Jerusalem (Acts xv. 6–29). Kirsopp Lake[3], Emmet[4], Bartlet[5] and others would date the epistle just before the Council, which would make it the earliest of all St Paul's letters of which we have any knowledge. In that case the Judaizers who troubled the Christians in Antioch (xv. 1) must—though there is no evidence of it—have travelled on further and acted similarly in Galatia; and St Paul, receiving news of it, wrote off at once. There is no chronological difficulty in this. The length of the first tour is not told us in the *Acts*, nor of the 'no little time' that they stayed at Antioch after their return (xiv. 28). But if the first tour began in the spring or early summer, and ended, say, in the early autumn of the next year, some nine

[1] Cf. John vi. 62, ix. 8, 1 Tim. i. 13, and πρότερον (without the article), 2 Cor. i. 15, Heb. iv. 6; see also Heb. x. 32, 1 Pet. i. 14
[2] Most of the necessary material will be found in Askwith, *The Ep. to the Galatians: an Essay on its Destination and Date.*
[3] *The Earlier Epistles of St Paul*, pp. 297–302.
[4] *Epistle to the Galatians*
[5] *The Apostolic Age*, pp. 84, 85.

months may have elapsed before the Council. And if the Judaizers went to Galatia before St Paul reached the end of his tour, as they may very likely have done, they would have a full year in which to 'pervert the Gospel of Christ.'

The student should here recall what was said about St Paul's visits to Jerusalem (pp. 23-25). In the epistle he does not, according to the most probable view, mention the Council visit. And that is the strongest argument adduced for this early date. St Paul is thought to be enumerating the events in his career, either which occurred up to the time of his writing, or 'which played a part in the campaign between him and the Judaizers, either for attack or defence' (Lake). In either case his silence as to the apostolic decrees formulated at the Council is inexplicable. Lake suggests that he wrote the epistle after leaving Antioch, *en route* for the Council, and that 'all the brethren who are with me' (Gal. i. 2) are his travelling companions[1]. Antioch itself is also possible; but the words 'when Kephas came to Antioch' do not make this certain.

This view has much in its favour. But it cannot be considered conclusively proved, for two reasons:

(1) St Paul's object in writing Gal. i.-ii. 14 may not have been quite as Lake describes it. The apostle was concerned to meet the attacks which his opponents made upon him. He wanted to prove (*a*) that he was not an unauthorised upstart, and (*b*) that he did not seek to 'persuade' and 'please men' (i. 10). The former (*a*) he proves by enumerating the events of his career,

---

[1] If so, Barnabas was among them, but the apostle is unlikely to have shewn him the letter he was writing, in view of ii. 13.

not up to the time of writing but, up to the point at which the apostles pledged themselves to recognise his mission to the Gentiles; the latter (*b*) he illustrates by the boldness with which he rebuked Kephas himself when he made a mistake. If this is the right point of view, his silence as to the apostolic decrees is not inexplicable.

(2) *Galatians* is linked in language and thought with *Romans* almost as closely as 1 *Thessalonians* with 2 *Thessalonians*, or as *Ephesians* with *Colossians*. The Galatian and the Roman Christians both needed the apostle's teaching in opposition to Judaizers *Romans* was written at Corinth during the third tour (p. 181 f.). If, then, *Galatians* was written before the Council, the Judaistic controversy must have broken out at a later date at Rome. But, as Lake says, there is no other evidence that the controversy had first a lull and afterwards a recrudescence; and he concludes that 'the choice seems to be between Lightfoot's date [i.e. shortly before *Romans*], which satisfies the literary problem caused by the resemblance of *Galatians* to *Romans*, but fails to meet the historical difficulties raised by St Paul's silence as to the Council and its decrees, and the theory placing *Galatians* before the Council, which satisfies these historical difficulties, but fails to meet the literary problem[1].' If, however, as suggested above, the historical difficulties connected with the Council are by no means insuperable, Lightfoot's date gains in probability. And this date in no way depends on his North-Galatian view. On the contrary, if Acts xvi. 4 is trustworthy (which,

---

[1] On Lake's conjecture that Rom. 1.-xiv. was originally a circular letter written at the same early date that he claims for *Galatians*, see p. 187.

however, is doubtful), St Paul, according to the South-Galatian view, had published in Galatia the decrees of the Council before he wrote the epistle, which rendered it still less incumbent upon him to mention them when writing. Other minor considerations can be urged on both sides, which cannot be discussed here. In a problem so complex certainty is perhaps impossible. But no other dates which have been suggested can be so well supported as these two. Any intermediate date fails, no less than the early one, to account for the close affinity which the epistle bears to *Romans*. We conclude, therefore, that *Galatians* was written either immediately before the Council, between the first and the second tour, or shortly before *Romans* in the course of the third tour, and that the latter is on the whole the more probable.

If the latter date is correct, Ephesus[1] can hardly have been the place of writing, as several scholars have held, since in iv. 20 he implies that it is impossible for him to visit the Galatians in person, which, in his anxiety about them, he would like to do, but from Ephesus he could have gone to Galatia as easily as he did to Corinth (see p. 140). The epistle may have been written *en route* from Macedonia, in which case 'all the brethren that are with me' (i. 2) were probably the travelling companions named in Acts xx. 4 as journeying with him back from Corinth. Or he may have written soon after his arrival at Corinth, and the brethren may have been the Christians in that city. He does not give salutations

[1] Barton, *Journal of Biblical Lit* June 1915, revives the theory of Wieseler that 'years' in Gal. iv. 10 refers to the observance of a Sabbatical year. From some references to Sabbatical years in 1 Macc. and Josephus he reckons that a Sabbatical year began in the autumn of 53 A.D, and that *Galatians* was written in 54, when he thinks that St Paul was at Ephesus. But the argument is very precarious.

from particular persons, perhaps because no individual Christians in Galatia were known to the brethren that were with him.

2. CAUSES OF WRITING. There is no epistle of St Paul in the study of which we have more need to remember that it was a *letter*, called forth by the circumstances of the moment. It contains much that was clear to his readers, but obscure to us. Fortunately his main object in writing, which is the chief thing that we want to know, is clear.

He had himself founded the churches of Galatia. In iv. 19 he compares himself with a mother who has, with pangs of travail, brought to birth the Christ that is in them; and in i. 8, 9, iv. 13 he speaks of his preaching in Galatia. In i. 8 'we preached' perhaps refers to the fact that Silas was with him when he first visited them. The Galatians were, for the most part, Gentiles, and St Paul the Apostle of the Gentiles had taught them the Gospel, which included the great truth that men are saved, not by their obedience to the Jewish or any other law, but through the Spirit, by faith in Jesus Christ. But though they had received him enthusiastically, 'as an angel of God, as Jesus Christ' (iv. 14, 15), they had since begun to be led astray by false teachers (i. 7), who troubled and unsettled them (i. 7, v. 10, 12). This they did in two ways: (1) by trying to undermine his influence and reputation, (2) by persuading them that they could not rightly become Christians without also accepting Judaism.

(1) They seem to have told the Galatians that St Paul, after his conversion, had held a position in the Church quite subordinate to that of the apostles in Jerusalem; that he was an unauthorised upstart, who took too much

upon him; and that in order to 'please men' (i. 10), he made religion easier by omitting some of its essential elements.

(2) They tried to curry favour with them by flattery and fair speech (iv. 17), so that they 'bewitched' them (iii. 1), and hindered them when they were 'running well' (v. 7) on their Christian course. Their chief object had been to persuade them to be circumcised (v. 2–12, vi. 12, 13, 15). They had, in fact, 'perverted the Gospel of Christ' (1. 7). The Galatians had turned to a different Gospel, which could not really be called a second Gospel because it was not a Gospel at all (*ib.*). So that St Paul is afraid that when he tells them the unpalatable truth, it will make him their enemy (iv. 16). They had already begun to observe Jewish festivals (iv. 9, 10), and some of them wanted to be 'under the Law' altogether (iv. 21).

These two dangers roused St Paul to a white heat of indignation and sorrow. He wished he could come to them in person (iv. 20), but that being impossible he wrote them a letter. The attacks on himself he meets in i.–ii. 14, with a final vehement exclamation in vi. 17; the false teaching by which they had been bewitched is dealt with in ii. 15-v. 26.

3. ANALYSIS. It is natural that a letter thus born of indignation and sorrow should shew no deliberate articulation or arrangement. Their very absence contributes to its force and fire. But it may be regarded as falling into five parts, as follows:

A. i.–ii. 14. Self-defence.

B. ii. 15–iv. 7. Doctrinal Instruction.

C. iv 8–v. 24. Appeal to the Galatians on the basis of this instruction.

D. v. 25–vi. 10. Further pieces of advice.

E. vi. 11–18. Vehement Conclusion.

4. CONTENTS.

A. i.–ii. 14. *Self-defence.*

i. 1–5. Salutation, introducing at the outset the self-defence (*v.* 1 a, His apostleship was given him neither from a human origin nor by human agency, but through Jesus Christ and God the Father), and the doctrinal instruction (*v.* 1 b, Christ's Resurrection, *v.* 4, His atoning Death).

i. 6–10. He is amazed at their rapid abandonment of the Gospel which he had preached to them (*vv.* 6, 7). Cursed is anyone who preaches to them any other Gospel, which in fact cannot be a Gospel at all (*vv.* 8, 9). He asks if that sounds as though he wants to 'please men'! (*v.* 10).

i. 11, 12. He received his Gospel not by any human authorisation or teaching, but direct from Jesus Christ.

i. 13, 14. They know how he used, as a strict Jew, to persecute Christians.

i. 15–17. But when God's revelation of His Son in him, for which He had destined him from birth, came to him, he sought no human authorisation, even from the apostles, but went away into Arabia.

i. 18–20. Then three years after his conversion he paid Kephas a fortnight's visit in Jerusalem, where he saw also James the Lord's brother; but no other apostles were there.

i. 21–24. Then he went to Syria and Cilicia. He was still unknown to the Christians in Judaea; only they heard of his conversion, and glorified God in him.

ii. 1–10. Then fourteen years afterwards[1] he went to Jerusalem with Barnabas and Titus, and had a private conversation with the leading Christians there, to see whether they agreed with his work among Gentiles. Even then he refused to allow Titus, although a Gentile, to be circumcised[2]. James, Kephas, and John, realising that God had been working in him no less than in Peter, pledged their agreement that he and Barnabas should preach to Gentiles, and they to Jews, only asking him to remember the needs of the poorer Christians, which, of course, he was eager to do.

ii. 11–14. But Kephas, on a visit to Antioch, shewed cowardice in the matter of Christian liberty, under the influence of some Jewish Christians from Jerusalem, and even Barnabas was carried away by them. When Kephas made this mistake, he did not hesitate to rebuke him publicly.

B. ii. 15–iv. 7. *Doctrinal Instruction.*

ii. 15–21. St Paul and other Jews who had believed in Jesus Christ, and had been crucified with Him, had thereby acknowledged that they could not be saved by obedience to Law. For them to turn back, therefore, to the Law would be to nullify the death of Christ.

iii. 1–5. The Galatians, to whom he had vividly taught the meaning of Christ's crucifixion, were bewitched. When they became Christians they received the Spirit through faith, not through obedience to Law. Did they now expect to be perfected through obedience to Law?

iii. 6–9. Even Abraham (the great representative of all Jews) received righteousness through faith (not works); and it is those who do that who are his true sons.

[1] See p. xiv.   [2] See p. 25 f.

iii. 10–14. Scripture (Deut. xxvii. 26) proves that those who are under the Law are subject to a curse, since none can keep its requirements perfectly, and (Habak. ii. 4) that it is faith that gives life. Christ redeemed us from this curse by becoming a curse on our behalf in that He hung on a tree, in order that Gentiles and Jews alike might, as true sons of Abraham, receive the blessing that comes from faith.

iii. 15–18. This was promised to Abraham in language which by its wording pointed to Christ; and the promise was not annulled by the Law which was not given till 430 years later.

iii. 19–24. What, then, was the Law for? It was a temporary arrangement added on because of sins—not opposed, but inferior, to the promise—an arrangement by which Jews were guarded and kept under control as children, until their time of tutelage was past.

iii. 25–29. This tutelage was to fit them for the freedom of sonship, which every man and woman alike, of all races and classes, can now receive by union with Christ.

iv. 1–3. The tutelage is like that of a child, who possesses nothing until he comes of age.

iv. 4–7. But by the Incarnation are received all the potentialities involved in sonship; and by the Holy Spirit is received that which makes this sonship real and actual.

C. iv. 8–v. 24. *Appeal to the Galatians based on this instruction.*

iv. 8–12. They used to be in bondage to gods which were no gods, and yet now that they are free they want to enslave themselves again, this time to the bondage of Law! They had already begun to observe some of its ordinances, so that the apostle is afraid that his work among them was in vain. He had made himself virtually a Gentile as they were, by giving up Judaism; and he beseeches them to make themselves free as he is, by doing the same.

iv. 13–20. They had received his preaching originally with enthusiasm; but now they treat him as their enemy because he tells them the truth. They have been cajoled by the flatteries of false teachers. The pangs by which he brought them to their spiritual birth need to be repeated, and he is at a loss to know what to think about them.

iv. 21–28. But the very Law, to which they want to submit, proclaims its own inferiority by relating the story of Isaac the son of the free woman and Ishmael the son of the slave. Now Hagar with her son Ishmael, Mt Sinai where the Law was given[1], and the earthly Jerusalem (i.e. the Jewish nation), which is bondage to the Law, all stand in the same category, and are opposed to Sarah with her son Isaac, and the heavenly Jerusalem (i.e. the Christian Church).

iv. 29–v. 1. But the former, in accordance with the Scripture story, must give place to the latter. Christians, therefore, are free, and the Galatians ought to stand firm in their freedom, and refuse to be again enslaved.

v. 2–6. They will be throwing away that freedom, and Christ's work will avail them nothing, if they submit to circumcision.

v. 7–12. It is not God (who called them to be Christians) who had led them to this step, but they had been

---

[1] The difficult clause 'For Sinai is a mountain in Arabia' (as read by Lightfoot and in R V. margin) is perhaps a marginal gloss by a scribe.

persuaded by their false teachers. The apostle's persecutions shew that he does not preach the necessity of circumcision; those that do, might just as well go the whole length and mutilate themselves (as do heathen devotees)!

v. 13–15. At the same time freedom is not selfish licence. They are not free from the law of love to their neighbour.

v. 16–24. If they live in the Spirit, which frees them from the Law, it will produce in them not the works of the flesh but the fruits of the Spirit.

D. v. 25–vi. 10. *Further pieces of advice.*

v. 25–vi. 5. Life in the Spirit does not free them from the necessity of humility and gentleness. They must shew forbearance and sympathy to an erring brother, bearing the burdens of others, remembering their own worthlessness; for everyone shall be held individually responsible for his own load of obligations.

vi. 6–10. One way of bearing the burden of others is that the Galatians should supply liberally the earthly needs of those who teach them. Since everyone shall reap what he sows, whether fleshly corruption or eternal spiritual life, let us do all the good we can to others, especially to Christians, while we still have the opportunity.

E. vi. 11–18. *Vehement Conclusion.*

vi. 11. He is writing[1] to them with his own hand, to press the importance of his words.

[1] It is doubtful if the epistolary aorist ἔγραψα refers to the whole letter or only to the postscript. But the use of large handwriting in an autograph conclusion finds analogies in Egyptian papyri (see Kenyon, *Handbook to the Textual Criticism of the N.T.* p. 26; ed. 2, p. 30).

vi. 12, 13. Those who try to persuade them to be circumcised are insincere in their attempts; they only want to boast over them.

vi. 14-16. He will boast of nothing but the Cross of Christ, through which the world is dead to him and he to it; for nothing matters except to live the life of a new creation. Peace be to all Gentiles and Jews alike who follow this rule.

vi. 17. Let no-one henceforth cause trouble by opposing his authority. The scars of persecution mark him as the slave of Jesus.

vi. 18. The Grace.

CHAPTER VII

ROMANS

1. TIME AND PLACE OF WRITING. The problems here raised are different in kind from those which we have studied in connexion with the preceding epistles. The indications seem clear, at first sight, that the epistle was written from Corinth, during the visit of Acts xx. 3, in the third missionary tour, just before St Paul started on his last fateful journey to Jerusalem. In xv 25–27 he states that he is just starting for Jerusalem with the contributions for the poor from the Christians of Macedonia and Achaia. In xvi. 1 he commends to his readers Phoebe the 'ministress' of the Church at Cenchreae, the eastern harbour of Corinth. And some of the names of those who join him in greetings are in harmony with this: (1) Gaius (xvi. 23); St Paul had baptized a Gaius at Corinth (1 Cor. i. 14). (2) Erastus the treasurer of the city (xvi. 23); in 2 Tim. iv. 20 an Erastus is mentioned as having stayed behind at Corinth, which he might

naturally do if it was his home. (3) Timothy and Sosipater or Sopater (xvi. 21); in Acts xx. 4 they are named among the apostle's companions on his departure from Corinth.

It must be noticed that all these indications occur in chs. xv., xvi. But there are reasons for doubting whether ch. xvi. was originally written to Rome at all; and there is MS evidence, though much less convincing, which has led some to think that ch. xv. as well as ch. xvi. was absent from the original epistle (see next section). The only safe conclusions, therefore, are: (*a*) Ch. xvi. was written from Corinth at a time when Timothy and Sosipater were with him, and when Prisca and Aquila (to whom he sends greeting, *v.* 3) were not with him, i.e. later than the visit of Acts xviii., and probably during the visit of Acts xx. 3, just before he started for Jerusalem. (*b*) Ch. xv. (*probably* with chs. i.–xiv.) was written either at Corinth just before he started for Jerusalem, or in the course of the journey to Jerusalem

2. INTEGRITY. (*a*) Ch. xvi. Some think that this chapter was originally addressed not to Rome but to *Ephesus*, and that it was combined with *Romans* when St Paul's letters were formed into a collection. The principal reasons for this view are as follows:

(1) Seeing that St Paul had never visited Rome before he wrote, it is unlikely that he knew personally so many Christians there as the salutations would suggest, whereas he had stayed over two years at Ephesus. Moreover in the letters which he afterwards wrote from Rome, not one of these Christians who are saluted in *Romans* is mentioned.

(2) A salutation is sent to Prisca and Aquila (*v.* 3) They had come from Rome to Corinth, where St Paul

joined them (Acts xviii. 1–3). They had accompanied him thence to Ephesus, where they stayed (*vv.* 18, 19), not only till Apollos went thither (*v* 26), but till St Paul paid his long visit there and wrote 1 Cor. xvi. 19 in which he sent greeting from them 'with the Church that is in their house.' But in Rom. xvi. 5 the greeting to them is followed by a greeting to 'the Church that is in their house.' If, then, ch. xvi. is really part of the original letter to Rome, Prisca and Aquila, after making their house a Christian centre at Ephesus, must have left that city and returned to Rome, and so established themselves there that their house became a Christian centre, between the writing of 1 *Corinthians* and *Romans*, i.e. within two years at the outside, very possibly within twelve months (see pp. 135–7).

(3) Epaenetus is described (*v.* 5) as 'the firstfruits of Asia unto Christ,' i.e. the first convert to Christianity who had been won in the province of Asia. St Paul would be more likely to mention this fact if Epaenetus were then in Asia Minor than if he were at Rome.

(4) St Paul would be more likely to commend Phoebe (*vv.* 1, 2) to a Church which he knew, and where his commendation would have special weight, than to a Church which he had never visited.

(5) The evils which he rebukes in *vv.* 17, 18 were rife at Ephesus, but there is no evidence that they were to be found, at that time, in Rome.

(6) xv. 33 sounds like the final conclusion of a letter.

None of these amounts to actual proof, but their combined force is strong, and gives to the conjecture a high degree of probability. If it is correct, the letter may be practically complete as it stands, its main purpose being to commend Phoebe and to send greetings to friends. The closing Grace or Benediction is probably lost, for *v.* 24[1] is absent from the best MSS, and the Doxology (*vv.* 25–27) does not seem originally to have belonged to the chapter.

(*b*) Chs. xv., xvi. Difficult questions relating to the last two chapters as a whole are occasioned by the Doxology. The following are the principal elements in the problem.

(1) In some MSS xvi. 25–27 is placed at the end of ch. xiv.[2] The chapter headings in two of the most important[3], and in several other, MSS of the Vulgate seem to imply that the epistle was sometimes found without chs. xv., xvi. Origen, in Rufinus' Latin translation, says of the heretic Marcion that he omitted (*abstulit*) the Doxology, and *dissecuit* chs. xv., xvi.; but the meaning of the latter verb is disputed[4] And it is not improbable

---

[1] 'The grace of our Lord Jesus Christ be with you all. Amen'

[2] In ALP, many minuscules, Syr[hcl], arm. *codd.* Chrys. Of these AP 5 17 arm. *codd* have it also at the end of the epistle. It stands at the end of the epistle in ℵBCDE, a few minuscules, codd. known to Origen[lat], vulg. syr. memph. aeth. Orig[lat], Ambst. It is omitted in FG, but the scribe of G leaves a space at xiv. 23, shewing that he knew a MS or MSS in which it stood there.

[3] Amiatinus and Fuldensis. The Amiatine chapter headings were based on a Latin text earlier than Jerome.

[4] The ordinary meaning 'cut up,' 'mutilated' (so Zahn) can hardly be intended. It seems to mean either 'cut away,' 'removed,' being used for the sake of variety with the same force as *abstulit* (Lake), or 'separated off' (Hort). It probably represents διέτεμεν. The two chapters contain so much that was opposed to Marcion's doctrine that Sanday and Headlam (*Romans*, p. xcvi f.) and Corssen (*ZNW.* 1909, pp. 1, 97) think that he was first responsible for their omission. But it is more probable that he adopted the shorter form of the epistle which he already found to hand.

that the early Latin writers Cyprian and Tertullian used the shorter form of the epistle[1].

(2) There is evidence that in a number of early MSS, including those from which the text of Origen was derived, the words 'in Rome' in i 7, and 'who are in Rome[2]' in i. 15, were omitted. Without these words, and without chs. xv., xvi., there would be nothing whatever to shew that the epistle was addressed to Rome at all.

(3) Apart from the textual evidence, many have doubted whether the Doxology was written by St Paul. The style and language are unlike those of *Romans*, and approximate to those of *Ephesians* and the Pastoral Epistles. It is questioned whether St Paul would have spoken of 'the mystery which hath been *kept in silence* through times eternal' (R.V.); his usual thought is that it was proclaimed in the Old Testament, but not understood till Christ's coming made it clear.

(4) A consideration to which too little weight is given is that xv. 1–13 continues the thought of ch. xiv., so that their separation is strange. It is also strange that xiv. 23, with no Grace or Benediction, should have formed the end of a letter.

The following are some of the suggestions which have been made.

LIGHTFOOT (*Biblical Essays*, pp. 287 ff.) thought that the original epistle contained all that is in the present one except the Doxology. At some later date St Paul himself altered it into a circular letter for general use by omitting chs. xv., xvi., which contain personal matter, and the mention of Rome in i. 7, 15, and then wrote

---

[1] The significance of their silence as to the last two chapters is pointed out by Lake, pp. 337–9.
[2] τοῖς ἐν Ῥώμῃ.

the Doxology to form a fitting close to the shortened letter. Editors afterwards transferred the Doxology to the end of the original, longer, letter.

This is beset by two difficulties, apart from the style and language of the Doxology. (1) It is not easy to see why St Paul, in shortening the letter for general use, omitted xv. 1–13, which, as said above, forms a continuation of ch. xiv. The personal matter does not begin till xv. 14, and $v.$ 13 would have made an excellent ending. (2) In omitting personal matter, why did he not omit the personal references to his intended visit, and his desire to see his readers, in i. 10–13?

SANDAY and HEADLAM (*Romans*, p. xcvii f.) avoid the difficulty of the separation of xv. 1–13 from ch. xiv. by St Paul himself They think that Marcion omitted xv. 1–13 for the same reason that made him omit the Doxology, because it contained material at variance with his heretical views, e.g. the Old Testament quotations, the statement in $v.$ 4 that the Old Testament was 'written for our learning,' and in $v.$ 8 that 'Christ hath been made a minister of the circumcision on behalf of the truth of God.' He also omitted the remainder of chs. xv., xvi., because the personal matter was useless for the definite dogmatic purposes which he had in view, and therewith also the mention of Rome in i 7, 15. This shortened form became current, and was afterwards adopted in the Church as useful for ecclesiastical purposes.

But this explanation, though attractively simple, falls to the ground if the evidence, as is probable, points to the fact that Marcion did not shorten the epistle himself, but found it already shortened, and merely perpetuated that form of it because it suited his purpose.

KIRSOPP LAKE (*The Earlier Epistles of St Paul*, p. 362) proposes an inversion of Lightfoot's theory. The short form of the letter was the original, 'written by St Paul at the same time as Galatians, in connection with the question of Jewish and Gentile Christians, for the general instruction of mixed Churches which he had not visited.' 'Later on he sent a copy to Rome, with the addition of the other chapters to serve, as we should say, as a covering letter.' As it was originally a circular letter, he left a blank space where the name 'Rome' now stands in i. 7, as is done in the best MSS at Eph. i. 1. Lake explains xv. 1–13 as an addition 'continuing the thoughts of his original writing, probably because Aquila had told him that this would be desirable.'

The date of *Galatians* does not affect the theory. But there are difficulties. It is not easy to imagine why the general remarks of xv. 1–13 (especially of *vv.* 1–7) were desirable after the particular injunctions on the same subject in ch. xiv. Details might have been desirable after generalities, but not *vice-versa*. It is still harder to explain i. 8–15. A blank space might be left in i. 7, in the opening salutation, as some think was done in *Ephesians*, but it is much more awkward in i. 15, where the theory also requires it, though Lake does not mention it. And it is impossible to suppose that to each of the Churches to which the circular letter was to be carried St Paul wrote that he was always praying that he might at last be able to come to them (*v.* 10), and that he had frequently purposed to do so but had been prevented (*v.* 13). The contents of *vv.* 8–15 as a whole seem to point to a particular Church, and are out of place in a circular letter.

MOFFATT (*Introd to the Lit. of the N.T.* p. 142) arrives

at the conclusion that the epistle originally consisted of chs. i.–xv., to which xvi. 1–23, a letter to Ephesus, was added when the Pauline epistles were collected. An editor composed the Doxology and placed it in its present position at the end. But the desire arose to adapt the epistle for general use to be read in Church; so chs. xv., xvi. were omitted, together with the mention of Rome in i. 7, 15, and the Doxology was transferred to the end of the shortened epistle, i.e. to follow xiv. 23.

But the difficulty of the separation of xv. 1–13 from ch. xiv. still remains. In those days the epistle was not divided into chapters; and there is no discernible reason why these verses should not have been included, to form a natural ending to the epistle for general Church use.

None of these solutions, then, are free from objections; and the tantalizing combination of difficulties invites another attempt at explanation. The phenomena may have arisen as follows. The epistle may originally have contained chs i.–xvi. without the Doxology, or more probably chs. i.–xv., to which xvi. 1–23, a letter to Ephesus, was added in a collection of Pauline epistles. Someone, probably not St Paul, at an early date composed the Doxology, placing it either after xv. 13 or somewhere in connexion with xv. 8–12, as a comment upon the Old Testament quotations about the Gentiles. But he placed it in such a position in his manuscript (in the margin or otherwise) as to lead to its *accidental* transference by a copyist to the end of ch. xiv. Thus xv. 1–13 was separated from ch. xiv., and chs. xv., xvi. received the appearance of being a separate whole, the bulk of which was of a personal character, and was therefore omitted, with the mention of Rome in i. 7, 15, in copies made for general Church purposes. This shortened form was adopted by Marcion. If either he or St Paul himself had been responsible for the shortening of the epistle, they would not have scrupled to go further, and omit the personal matter in i. 8–13, which ecclesiastical editors did not venture to do. Finally, later editors of the epistle in its longer form transferred the Doxology to the end.

3. CAUSES OF WRITING. St Paul must have received, no doubt from Aquila and Priscilla, who had recently left Rome, and had been with him at Corinth and Ephesus (Acts xviii. 2, 18 f., 26, xix. 1), a full account of the Christian Church at Rome, its composition and condition, and its spiritual and doctrinal needs. His evangelizing work had hitherto prevented him from visiting Rome, and even now, though he intended soon to do so if possible, he did not know what might be the outcome of his visit to Jerusalem, in view of the hostility of the Jews (Rom. xv. 31). He must, therefore, have seized the first opportunity that occurred of writing fully to the Christians at the all-important centre of the Empire. Since his practice was to refrain from evangelizing places where Christianity was already established (xv. 20), he would not go to Rome as a missionary, but intended only to pay a passing visit. And meantime it would be an advantage to have the Roman Christians in harmony with his general doctrinal position before he extended his missionary labours further westward, as he hoped to do. He had learnt a good deal about them, but at the same time few of them can have been personally known to him. He could, therefore, write them a long letter, much calmer and more deliberate in tone than those which he had felt compelled to write to Corinth or Galatia. But that does not mean that he composed a general treatise on Christian doctrine. Some of the

fundamental things of Christianity, e.g. the Holy Communion, the Church, the nature of Christ, His Resurrection, and His future Advent, receive no definite treatment. As in his other letters, it is of great interest to note the truths which he takes for granted. The contents of the letter were no doubt determined, as elsewhere, by the immediate needs of his readers. They seem to indicate that the majority of the Roman Christians were Gentile, and the minority Jewish. And the former needed the guidance of a master mind, not so much in meeting particular local difficulties as in framing a comprehensive *apologia* for the principle of a universal religion as set over against Jewish nationalism. He therefore spends the greater part of the epistle on two subjects: (1) the contrast between the Jewish and the Christian methods of obtaining 'righteousness[1]'; (2) the problem of the failure of the Jews in view of their divine election

It is not always easy to trace with exact precision his line of thought from sentence to sentence. 'We must try to comprehend the position of such a man when, perhaps in the midst of his handicraft, he dictated on difficult matters in which his thoughts pressed one upon another, in order to judge truly to what degree he would be likely to fail in good connexion and orderly progress of thought[2].' Nevertheless in general outline the course of argument is clear and well maintained.

4. ANALYSIS.

    i. 1–7. Salutation.
    i. 8–15. Thanksgiving, and Personal matter.

[1] On this fundamental conception see p. 293. A study of it is essential for an understanding of the epistle
[2] P. W. Schmiedel, *Hibbert Journal*, 1903, p. 549.

A. i. 16–v. 21. Justification.
  i. 16, 17. Thesis.
   1. 18–iii. 20. Universal failure of Gentile and Jew to attain to Righteousness.
      (a) i. 18–ii. 29. Statement of their failure.
      (b) iii. 1–8. Three objections answered[1].
      (c) iii. 9–20. The failure proved from Scripture.
   iii. 21–31. The New System of attaining to Righteousness is explained.
   iv. 1–25. The New System corroborated by the case of Abraham.
   v. 1–21. The glorious effects of the New System.
      (a) vv. 1–4. The effects enumerated
      (b) vv. 5–11 The consideration of God's love gives confidence of final salvation.
      (c) vv. 12–21. Adam and Christ. vv. 12–17, Their similarities and difference vv. 18–21, Summary.
B. vi.–viii. Sanctification.
  vi., vii. Four objections answered.
      (a) vi 1–14. If more sin on man's part means more grace on God's, why not go on sinning?
      (b) vi. 15–vii. 6. If we are released from Law, are we not free to sin if we like?
      (c) vii. 7–12. If release from Law means release from sin, are not Law and sin identical?

[1] These and other objections in the epistle seem to be merely rhetorical, introduced in order to lead up to the answers; it is not probable that St Paul thought they would actually be brought forward by any of the Roman Christians.

(*d*) vii. 13–25. Did the good Law, then, cause death?

viii. The working out of the Christian's salvation by the indwelling of the Spirit.

C. ix.–xi. The Rejection of Israel.

    ix. 1–5. Introduction.

    ix. 6–29. The Justice of the Rejection.

        (*a*) *vv.* 6–13. It is not inconsistent with God's promises.

        (*b*) *vv.* 14–29. It is not inconsistent with God's justice.

    ix. 30–x. 13. Causes of the Rejection.

    x 14–21. The Jews had no excuse from want of warning.

    xi. Facts which lessen the difficulty.

        (*a*) *vv.* 1–10. The rejection is not that of *all* Israel.

        (*b*) *vv.* 11–24. The rejection is not final.

        (*c*) *vv.* 25–36. God's ultimate purpose is mercy to all.

D. xii.–xv. 13. Practical Exhortations based on the foregoing teaching

    xv. 14–33. Personal matter.

    xvi. 1, 2. Commendation of Phoebe.

    3–16. Salutations.

    17–20. A warning against false teachers.

    21–23. Greetings.

    25–27. Doxology.

5. CONTENTS.

i. 1–7. Salutation. St Paul says that he was set apart to preach the Gospel of Jesus Christ, who was foretold in the Old Testament, a descendant of David, marked out as Son of God by the Resurrection. And his apostleship was in order to bring to the obedience of faith all nations, among whom are his readers.

i. 8–15. He gives thanks for their widely known faith. He constantly prays that he may be able to visit them, that he and they may be mutually helped, but hitherto he has been prevented. He owes much to Gentiles of all sorts, and is therefore eager to preach in Rome also.

A. i. 16–v. 21. JUSTIFICATION, or the attaining to 'Righteousness.'

i. 16, 17. Thesis. He is proud of the Gospel which he preaches, for it consists of the saving truth that a new kind of righteousness is revealed by God, attainable by Jew and Gentile alike.

i. 18–iii. 20. *Universal failure of Gentile and Jew alike under the old system.*

(*a*) i. 18–ii. 29. Statement of their failure. Gentile (i. 18–32); Gentile and Jew (ii. 1–16); Jew (ii. 17–29).

(*b*) iii. 1–8. Three objections answered.

(1) *vv.* 1, 2. What advantage, then, have the Jews from their privileged position? *Answer.* A great deal. First of all they were entrusted with Messianic prophecies. [St Paul breaks off, and does not speak of their other privileges till ix. 4, 5.]

(2) *vv.* 3, 4. If disobedience forfeits God's promises, does it annul God's faithful adherence to His word? *Answer.* Far from it. Let man be as bad as you like, but at all costs maintain the character of God.

(3) *vv.* 5–8. If, then, our unrighteousness only shews up God's righteousness in a clearer light, what right has He to be angry with us? *Answer.* Because

He must be Judge of the world; and because, if the objection were sound, it would be right to do evil that good may come (which some people falsely charged St Paul with teaching), which is in fact utterly bad.

(c) iii. 9–20. The failure proved from Scripture[1].

iii. 21–31. *The New System is therefore explained.*

vv. 21–25 a. Its nature is that of a free gift, a righteousness to which the Old Testament witnesses, obtainable by all alike through faith, and resulting from the death of Christ.

vv. 25 b, 26. God formerly overlooked men's sins, but it was with a view to vindicating His righteousness by His new system.

vv. 27–30. Two corollaries. Personal merit is excluded (*vv.* 27, 28); Jew and Gentile are on the same footing *vv.* 29, 30).

v. 31. Objection: Does not this annul Law? *Answer.* On the contrary, it brings to fulfilment the deepest principle of Law.

iv. 1–25. *The New System corroborated by the case of Abraham.*

vv. 1–8. Abraham attained to righteousness, not by works but by faith. Scripture itself says 'Abraham *believed* God etc.' (Gen. xv. 6). And a righteousness apart from works is clearly implied in Ps. xxxii. 1 f.

vv. 9–12. Faith and Circumcision. Abraham's faith

---

[1] St Paul gives a catena of passages from Ps. xiv. 1 ff, v. 9, cxl. 3, x. 7, Is lix 7 f, Ps xxxvi 1. All these, after the first, were inserted by Christian scribes into MSS of the LXX in Ps. xiv., and thus found their way through the Vulgate, and the translations of it by Coverdale, Matthew, and Cranmer, into the Prayer Book Psalter of the English Church.

was earlier than his circumcision; the latter was added afterwards as a seal, ratifying his possession of the righteousness which he had already gained. And his true descendants are all who imitate his faith, whether they are circumcised or not.

vv. 13–17 a. Promise and Law   The promise to Abraham and his descendants was no more dependent upon Law than it was on Circumcision. Law only makes sin to be sinful, since transgression implies a Law to be transgressed. God's New System, therefore, was made to turn on faith, which is possible for all, whether they are under the Law or not.

vv. 17 b–25. Abraham's faith that God could bring Isaac to birth, as it were from the dead (Abraham and his wife being both of great age), is a type of the Christian's faith in God who raised Jesus from the dead

v. 1–21. *The glorious effects of the New System.*

(*a*) *vv.* 1–4. The effects enumerated. Peace with God, access into our present state of grace, hope of the glory of God, also boasting in our tribulations, since they result in patience, approved worth, and hope.

(*b*) *vv.* 5–8. And we shall not be disappointed in this hope, because God's love, poured into our hearts by the Holy Spirit which was given to us when we became Christians, makes us confident of final salvation, through the death of Christ which He suffered for us when we were yet sinners

vv. 9–11. [The first step having been accomplished, i.e. a *potential* righteousness having been provided for all by Christ's death] *a priori* the second and easier step will be accomplished, i.e. our *actual* salvation by appropriating what He has done for us.

(c) *vv.* 12–21. *Adam and Christ.* *v.* 12. Adam is a type of Christ[1], in that the effects of his act were transmitted to his descendants. *vv.* 13, 14. That the effects of Adam's sin were transmitted is clear from the fact that, though sin is not reckoned as such when there is no law to be transgressed, yet real sin was in the world before the Mosaic Law was given, as is shewn by the universal reign of death in the period between Adam and Moses, even though men did not sin in the same sense that Adam did, i.e. by transgressing a definite command.

But Adam and Christ are unlike in three ways: (1) *v.* 15, In the quality of their act. Adam's fall brought death to the many; God's action in Christ was free kindness to the many. (2) *v.* 16, In the order of working. In Adam's case, one sin was followed by universal condemnation; in Christ's case, the sins of many were followed by one act of acquittal for all. (3) *v* 17, In the consequences. In the one case, death reigned; in the other, Christians shall reign in life.

vv. 18–21. *Summary.* The Old and the New System, then, present a series of opposites. On the one hand one trespass bringing condemnation because it made men sinners: on the other, one act of righteousness bringing life because it constitutes men righteous. Law came in later, to make sin more sinful, that God's free kindness might be enhanced; so that a contrast again offers itself—sin reigning in the realm of death, free kindness reigning through righteousness resulting in eternal life

---

[1] This is not stated till the last clause of *v* 14, but St Paul is about to lead up to it in *v* 12 when he breaks off with the parenthesis.

B. vi.–viii. SANCTIFICATION. (This is the making actual, in the individual, of the righteousness which is potentially his in Christ.)

vi., vii. *Four objections answered.*

(*a*) vi. 1–14. If more sin on man's part means more grace on God's, why not go on sinning? *Answer.* It is unthinkable. The baptized Christian, in his true ideal nature, cannot sin, for he has been killed, buried, and risen, with Christ. As having reached this condition he must present himself to God, free from Law and therefore from sin.

(*b*) vi. 15–vii. 6. If we are released from Law, are we not free to sin if we like? *Answer.* Far from it. We are released, only to belong to another Master, like a transferred slave (vi. 15–23), or a re-married woman (vii. 1–6).

(*c*) vii. 7–12. If release from Law means release from sin, are not Law and sin identical? *Answer.* Far from it. Law, by forbidding sin, stirs it to action so that it leads to death.

(*d*) vii. 13–25. Did the good Law, then, cause death? *Answer.* Far from it. It only shewed how terrible sin was. My better self is powerless to prevent me from doing wrong (*vv.* 14–17), and to make me do right (*vv.* 18–21). Thus a conflict is always raging within me, from which Christ alone can deliver me (*vv.* 22–25).

viii. *The working out of the Christian's salvation by the indwelling of the Spirit.*

vv. 1–4. The result of the Incarnation and Death of Christ is a life according to the Spirit, in Him, which gives freedom from condemnation because it gives freedom from the law of sin and death.

vv. 5–11 The old and the new life, the fleshly and the spiritual, compared.

vv. 12–17. Those who live the spiritual life are God's sons, and the divine Spirit in union with theirs witnesses to the certainty of it. And as sons, they are heirs, who will obtain their inheritance with Christ if they are united with Him by suffering.

vv. 18–22. For suffering is the path to glory, not only in man but also in the whole of creation, which is waiting in sorrow and pain like a woman in childbirth, till it shares the glorious existence destined for the sons of God.

vv. 23–25. And Christians feel the same pain and longing, though they already experience, in their partial possession of the Spirit, a foretaste of that for which they long; they yearn for the possession of full sonship and the final deliverance of their bodies. Hope is the Christian's necessary attitude while the things for which he hopes are still out of sight.

vv. 26, 27. And when we try to express our hopes in prayer we are capable only of inarticulate groanings, but these are uttered by the divine Spirit within us interceding for us with perfect success because God knows that His intercessions are in complete accord with His will.

vv. 28–30. Moreover the Christians' salvation proceeds along the lines of God's eternal plan working for their good; He planned that they should receive a share in the life of his Son; for this purpose He planned their call, then their acquittal, and finally their participation in His glorious perfection

vv. 31–34 From all this we can gain the confident assurance that God who spared not His Son from death will give us all things necessary for our salvation. Since He, the Judge, is on our side, none can prevent our acquittal, and the ascended Christ intercedes for us.

vv. 35–39. Nothing—not persecution, nor anything else in heaven or earth—can come between us and the great love of God in Christ Jesus.

C. ix.–xi. THE REJECTION OF ISRAEL.

ix. 1–5. *Introduction*, emphasizing the difficulty of the problem (which St Paul, as a Jew, feels intensely, *vv.* 2, 3)[1] by enlarging upon the privileges given to the Jews.

ix. 6–29. *The Justice of the Rejection.*

(*a*) *vv.* 6–13. The rejection is not inconsistent with God's promises. The possibility of some Jews being rejected is illustrated by the fact that the promises were originally given not to all Abraham's descendants but only to the line of Isaac.

(*b*) *vv.* 14–29. Nor is it inconsistent with God's justice.

vv. 14–18. Does this choice of Isaac's line to the exclusion of Esau's mean that God can commit injustice? *Answer.* Far from it. Scripture shews that He has the right to confer favours as He wills, both by His words to Moses (Ex. xxxiii. 19) and by His treatment of Pharaoh.

vv. 19–29. If God has willed that some persons shall be rejected because of their sins, why should they be blamed if they fulfil His will by sinning? *Answer.* A mere man has no more right to find fault with God than

[1] 'His religious philosophy of history is suddenly shot across by a strong personal emotion...and this passage shews how his religious patriotism flickered up inside his Christian outlook, even in spite of the treatment which he received from Jews and Gentiles alike' (Moffatt).

a vessel to find fault with the potter who made it. Still less when he realises that God's ultimate purpose is to shew mercy both to the Jewish nation is spite of their sins, and also to all men, Jew and Gentile alike, whom He has chosen for glory.

ix. 30–x. 13. *Causes of the Rejection.*

ix. 30–33. The solution must be that Israel was rejected because they sought righteousness in their own way, by works, and not in God's way, by faith. So that when the Messiah came, they stumbled, as Scripture foretold.

x. 1–4. They refused to give up the Law, though the Law had come to an end in Christ.

x. 5–13. And this although the old system of obtaining righteousness was impossible, while the new one was easy, within reach of all (as Scripture indeed declared, Deut. xxx. 12 ff.) because Christ is in the world available for all, and universal in its scope.

x. 14–21. *The Jews had no excuse from want of warning.* They would have had if the Gospel message had not been proclaimed; but it was proclaimed as widely as the stretch of the firmament of heaven. And Scripture[1] shews that they had every opportunity of knowing about it, and failed solely by their own fault.

xi. *Facts which lessen the difficulty*

(a) *vv.* 1–10. The Rejection is not that of *all* Israel.

It is not true to say that God has entirely rejected His people. (St Paul speaks feelingly, because he is a devoted Jew himself, *v.* 2.) God's answer to Elijah's complaint expresses the truth that a Remnant was

---

[1] Ps. xix 4, Deut. xxxii. 21, Is. lxv. 1, 2.

preserved, not by works but by grace The rest of Israel, who sought salvation in the wrong way, were punished with spiritual obtuseness and blindness.

(b) *vv.* 11–24. The Rejection is not final.

Its result having been the extension of God's blessings to the Gentiles, the Jews in turn will be stirred to jealousy (*vv.* 11–15). The guarantee of this is that the stock from which Israel sprang (i.e. the patriarchs) was sacred (*v.* 16). If God, against the usual order of nature, grafted the Gentiles into it, they must not be proud, for sin will exclude them no less surely than it excluded the Jews; and on the other hand, the Jews can much more easily be re-grafted into their own stock (*vv* 17–24).

(c) *vv.* 25–36. God's ultimate purpose is mercy to all.

The saving of Israel will take place when the saving of the Gentiles is accomplished (*vv.* 25–27). They are at present rejected for the sake of the Gentiles, but God's promises to the patriarchs cannot fail (*vv.* 28, 29). The conversion of Israel will be parallel with the conversion of the Gentiles, that God's mercy may be extended to all (*vv.* 28–32).

Conclusion: an exclamation of praise and wonder at God's wisdom (*vv.* 33–36).

D. xii–xv. 13. PRACTICAL EXHORTATIONS based on the foregoing teaching.

xii. 1, 2. Therefore the readers must apply these truths to their life by self-dedication to God.

xii. 3–21. Ways in which self-dedication will shew itself in the behaviour of members of a Body to the other members.

xiii. 1–7. It will shew itself in the behaviour of members of a civil state to its rulers.

xiii. 8–10. Love is to be the all-pervading principle of action.

xiii. 11–14. The nearness of the Last Day supplies a strong additional motive.

xiv. 1–23. A particular way in which Love must shew itself, i.e. in regard to foods. Christian liberty must give place to Christian charity towards the scruples of weak consciences.

xv. 1–7. The same thought in more general language. *vv.* 8–13. The exhortation 'receive one another etc.' [*sc.* in the matter of foods, and in other respects] is enforced by reminding the Gentiles that Christ submitted to circumcision in order to save them and to fulfil thereby the promises made to the ancestors of the Jews, and by reminding the Jews that those promises included the saving of the Gentiles[1] (*vv.* 8, 9 a). Four Old Testament passages[2] are quoted in support of this (*vv.* 9 b–12) Concluding prayer for the readers (*v.* 13).

In the *personal matter* with which St Paul closes, he refers (*a*) to his work in the past, (*b*) to his proposed movements in the future.

(*a*) xv. 14–17. He writes this advice, not because he has any doubt of the readers' goodness and knowledge, but because he is the apostle of the Gentiles, offering them to God as His priest. *vv.* 18–21. He makes bold to do this, because God has so wonderfully used him in his mission work to Gentiles over a wide sphere.

(*b*) xv. 22–33. His proposed visit to Rome, on the way to Spain, after taking the alms to Jerusalem.

---
[1] I e. in the words 'all the families of the earth.'
[2] Ps xviii. 49, Deut xxxii. 43, Ps. cxvii. 1, Is xi 10.

Ch. xvi.

vv. 1, 2 The readers are asked to give a cordial Christian reception to Phoebe, a 'ministress' of the Church at Cenchreae, and to afford her any help she needs.

vv. 3–16. Salutations to individuals and to groups of Christians.

vv. 17–20. A warning not to be led away into divisions and mistakes by false teachers, who for purely selfish ends delude the simple by their plausibility and flattery. The obedience (to the faith) of the readers is widely known, and St Paul rejoices at it, but he wants them to be careful. The Last Day is near at hand, when God will beat down Satan under their feet.

vv. 21–23. Greetings from eight Christians at Corinth

vv. 25–27. Doxology.

EPISTLES WRITTEN IN CAPTIVITY

CHAPTER VIII

COLOSSIANS

1. COLOSSAE. This epistle is like *Romans* in being written to a church which St Paul had not founded, or even visited (i. 4, 9, ii. 1). It had been founded, and probably also Laodicea and Hierapolis, by Epaphras[1] (i. 7, iv. 12 f.), who was himself a Colossian (iv. 12), and a Gentile, as his name suggests, and as St Paul implies by separating him from 'those who are of the circumcision' (*v.* 11).

Colossae and Laodicea lay some 10 miles apart, on

---

[1] A shorter form of Epaphroditus But he must be distinguished from the Christian of that name mentioned in Phil. ii. 25, iv. 18. It was a common Greek name.

the high road from Ephesus to the East, in the valley of the river Lycus, a southern tributary of the Maeander. Hierapolis was about 6 miles north of Colossae, on high ground on the other side of the river. St Paul on his third tour would have passed through the first two towns if he had kept to the main road; but he had travelled by 'the higher parts' (Acts xix. 1), i.e. probably by a smaller road which ran further North than Hierapolis (see p. 79). St Luke states that through St Paul's long activity at Ephesus 'all they which dwelt in [the Roman province of] Asia heard the word of the Lord' (Acts xix. 10). This must have been through the agency of St Paul's converts, of whom Epaphras was no doubt one. St Paul speaks of him as 'a faithful minister of Christ *on our behalf*' (Col. i. 7), which probably means that the apostle had sent him as his substitute to evangelize Colossae.

2. TIME AND PLACE OF WRITING. St Paul when he wrote was a prisoner in bonds (iv 3, 18). This must have been the imprisonment related in Acts xxviii., since it is fairly certain that Rome was the place of writing. The epistle is connected by obvious links with *Philemon*, which was written from Rome (see p. 211): Onesimus accompanies both epistles (iv. 9, Philem. 10–12), in both Archippus is greeted (iv. 17, Ph 2), Timotheus joins in the opening salutation, and Epaphras, Mark, Aristarchus, Demas, and Luke are named (iv. 7–14, Ph. 23, 24). The suggestion that the apostle wrote in prison at Caesarea has nothing to recommend it. At Caesarea he had recently stayed with Philip the evangelist (Acts xxi. 8), and since his friends were allowed access to him in prison (xxiv. 23), he would probably have mentioned Philip had the epistle been written there.

3. CAUSE OF WRITING. The cause which drew forth the letter was a report, brought to the apostle by Epaphras, of the spiritual condition of the Colossians. St Paul tactfully speaks (1. 3–8) of this report as having acquainted him with their 'faith in Christ Jesus,' and the 'love which they have toward all the saints' (*v.* 4), and their 'love in spirit' (*v.* 8). They were still keen and true-hearted. But the simple strength of their first faith, as Epaphras must also have told him, was in danger of being affected by the intellectual atmosphere of the district in which they lived. The Laodicean Church was similarly affected, and St Paul's letter was intended for both (iv. 16).

4. THE COLOSSIAN DANGER. There were many Jews in the neighbourhood who had become Christians. But they were different in character from the Judaizers who had troubled the Gentile Christians in Galatia. The Jews in and around the Lycus valley were affected by the variety of foreign tendencies which went to form the popular ideas of the surrounding Phrygian paganism, including Greek philosophical speculations, and mystical theosophy from the East. The Colossian heresy cannot be described as purely Jewish, though its authors were Jews by race. There can hardly have been a single Jew in the district whose religious and intellectual ideas were unaffected by foreign influences. The Jewish false teachers tried to persuade the Gentile Christians, not that Judaism with its circumcision and other ordinances was a necessary step towards Christianity, but that Christianity, as Epaphras had taught it when he evangelized Colossae, was only a preliminary step towards a deeper, vaster, and therefore humbler 'philosophy' (ii. 8).

There appear to have been two main aspects in their teaching, *angel-worship* and *asceticism*.

(*a*) It was not enough, they said, to be simple believers in Christ; they ought to go further and be 'perfected' (cf. i. 28, 'perfect in Christ') by being initiated into the greater mystery that the Fulness of the Godhead (cf. ii. 9) is brought into relationship with men by the agency of Angels[1] (ii. 18), who must therefore be worshipped with a 'self-imposed service' and 'abasement' (*vv.* 18, 23).

(*b*) To reach this intenser, more exalted, religious condition, man must purge himself from the malign influence exercised upon his soul by his material body. For this purpose a rigid and ascetic rule of life was necessary, involving obedience to man-made ordinances, commands, and teachings (ii. 21, 22), which include circumcision (*vv.* 11–13), the observance of festivals, new moons, and sabbaths, and restrictions in the matter of food and drink (*v.* 16), and other things, which must not be handled, tasted, or touched (*v.* 21).

These are the two *foci* round which their mistaken ideas revolved—the 'treasures of wisdom and knowledge hid' (cf. ii. 3) in the mystery of an angelic theosophy, and the asceticism, containing elements of the Jewish rules of life, by which those who are initiated into the mystery advance towards perfection. This was not the developed Gnosticism which a little later ran riot in the Church; but some of its theosophical and dualistic features are beginning to appear.

St Paul, in opposing them, steadily refuses to admit

[1] According to one interpretation of ii 8, 20 the 'elements (R.V. rudiments) of the world' are the Angels, i e. personifications of cosmic powers (cf. 1. 15, 11 10, 15), especially of the stars. Jewish thought had begun to assimilate such ideas from the East.

the two *foci* He points instead to the true mystery, the Person of Christ Jesus, as the *centre* and the *whole* of the circle of all things that are. Each several mistake that the Colossians are in danger of making arises from the loosening of their grip of the fundamental truth of Christ.

5. ANALYSIS.

    i. 1, 2. Salutation.
    i 3–8. Thanksgiving for the readers.
    i. 9–14. Prayer for the readers.

A. i. 15–20. The true Mystery: the Person of Christ.
    i. 15 a. Christ in relation to God.
    i. 15 b–17. Christ in relation to the Universe
    i. 18. Christ in relation to the Church.
    i. 19, 20 The divine intention which necessitated this three-fold relation.

B. i. 21–ii. 3. In this Mystery the Colossians have a share.
    i 21–23. The Colossians were Gentile sinners reconciled to God.
    i. 24–29. The apostle is appointed to teach men of the Mystery.
    ii 1–3. His eager desire that his readers may learn it.

C. ii. 4–iii. 4. Warnings against those who would initiate them into a false mystery.

D. iii. 5–iv. 6. Exhortations based on the above teaching.
    iv. 7–9 Personal matter.
    iv. 10–15. Salutations.
    iv. 16, 17. Two injunctions
    iv. 18. Autographic conclusion.

6. CONTENTS.

i. 1, 2. Salutation from St Paul and Timotheus.

i. 3–8. Thanksgiving for the readers' faith in Christ and love to other Christians. The Gospel which taught them of their heavenly hope has borne fruit in them through the preaching of Epaphras, who has brought a report of them to the apostle.

i. 9–14. Prayer for the readers that they may go on advancing in knowledge and wisdom, pleasing God in their daily lives, divinely strengthened for joyful patience and longsuffering, and giving thanks to the Father for what He has done for men in Jesus Christ. [A transition is thus made to the doctrinal portion of the epistle.]

A. i. 15–20. The true Mystery: the Person of Christ.

i. 15 a. Christ in relation to God He is the Image, the exact 'Replica,' of the invisible God.

i. 15 b–17. Christ in relation to the Universe. He is, eternally, prior to and supreme over the Universe, as its unifying Principle.

i. 18. Christ in relation to the Church. He is, in time, prior to and supreme over the Church, as its Head, so that He might become supreme over everything.

i. 19, 20. Christ has this three-fold relationship because it was God's will

(a) that the divine Pleroma should dwell in Him (v. 19).

(b) that by His death all things in the entire Universe might be brought back into union with God (v. 20)

B. i. 21–ii. 3. In this Mystery the Colossians have a share.

i. 21–23. They were once aliens and enemies, but were

reconciled to God by Christ's death, that He may present them faultless before God, if they remain faithful to the universal Gospel.

i. 24–29. Of this Gospel the apostle is a minister. By sufferings he does his part to complete the work of Christ's Passion; by preaching to fulfil the work of God's word, striving hard to dispense to all men the knowledge of the Mystery.

ii. 1–3. He strives in particular for the Colossians and their neighbours, that they may be encouraged, and in close Christian unity may learn the true and all-embracing Mystery of God, i.e. Christ.

C ii. 4–iii. 4. Warnings against those who would initiate them into a false mystery.

ii 4–7. He says this to warn them against being misled (*v.* 4), at the same time rejoicing in their spiritual state (*v.* 5); and he exhorts them to go on to further progress (*vv.* 6, 7)

ii. 8–10 They must let none mislead them to follow anything lower than Christ, for it is He in whom the divine 'Fulness' dwells 'bodily-wise' (i e. in the Church, His Body), and in Him they are 'fulfilled.'

ii. 11–15. It is not by Jewish circumcision that they can be perfected, but by the spiritual circumcision, i.e. union with Christ's death by baptism, the death by which He did away with human ordinances, and triumphed over all angelic powers.

ii. 16–19. Therefore they must not be misled to trust in human ordinances such as the Jewish rules of foods or festivals, or in the self-imposed abasement in the worship of angelic powers, instead of holding fast to Christ the Head, from whom the whole Body receives its life.

ii. 20–23. If they died with Christ from their pagan life, it is a relapse into their old condition to trust in human ordinances of asceticism and voluntary abasement.

iii. 1–4. If they were raised with Christ, they must set their minds on heavenly things in union with Him, and then in union with Him they will be finally glorified.

D. iii. 5–iv. 6. Exhortations based on the above teaching.

iii. 5–11. Because by their death with Christ they have potentially put off their old self and put on the new self, they must make this actual in their lives by killing all fleshly passions and putting off all sins of the heart and tongue.

iii. 12–17. Conversely they must put on all Christian graces both in their dealings with one another, and in their attitude of mind towards God.

iii. 18–iv. 6. Particular graces:
    iii. 18, 19. Of wives and husbands.
    iii. 20, 21. Of children and parents.
    iii. 22–iv. 1. Of slaves and masters.
    iv. 2–4. Prayer and thanksgiving to God, including prayer for the apostle and his work.
    iv. 5, 6. Right behaviour and language towards non-Christians.

iv. 7–9. The apostle is sending Tychicus, and also Onesimus a faithful and beloved fellow-Christian, to bring news of himself.

iv. 10–15. Salutations from three Jews, Aristarchus, Mark, and Jesus Justus, also from Epaphras who always prays for them and has laboured hard in preaching to them, Luke the beloved physician, and Demas. Salutations to the Laodicean Church, and to Nympha

(? Nymphas) and the Christians who meet at her (*v.l.* their) house.

iv. 16, 17 The Colossians and Laodiceans are to interchange the letters that the apostle is sending to them. Archippus is exhorted to fulfil his Christian ministry.

iv. 18. Final greeting in the apostle's own handwriting.

CHAPTER IX

PHILEMON

1. INTRODUCTION. This is the only complete letter of St Paul that we possess written to an individual. It must have owed its place in the Canon to the zealous care with which the early Church collected all known letters of the apostle. It is an affectionate note to a Christian named Philemon about his runaway slave Onesimus whom St Paul had converted, and was sending back to him. Philemon probably lived at Colossae, since Onesimus is mentioned as accompanying Tychicus thither, and is described as 'one of you,' i.e. a Colossian (Col. iv. 9). On the points of connexion between this letter and *Colossians* see p. 204.

St Paul wrote it in captivity (*vv.* 9, 13), at Rome. That it was Rome, where the narrative of the *Acts* leaves him, and not Caesarea (Acts xxiii. 33), is clear from the fact that he hoped soon to be released and to visit Colossae (*v.* 22). When he was imprisoned at Caesarea he claimed and expected to be sent to Rome, and could have had no thought of going to Colossae. Moreover Onesimus the runaway slave would be likely to escape to Rome, and very unlikely to escape to Caesarea.

The letter is important, partly as giving an insight into St Paul's character, as revealed in his warmhearted affection for the slave his convert, and delicate tact towards Philemon, and partly as shewing his *attitude towards slavery*. He did not attempt to raise his voice against it. With all its unspeakable horrors it was a universal practice deeply engrained in Greek and Roman life, as it had been in the life of all ancient races. To attempt to do away with it in that age would have produced a revolution with horrors even worse than those of the institution itself. The apostle took the same line that our Lord had taken with regard to many points: instead of laying down definite injunctions, he penetrated to principles. He taught that in God's sight there were no distinctions of master and slave (1 Cor. xii. 13, Gal. iii. 28, Eph. vi. 8, 9, Col. iii. 11); all alike were 'bought' by Christ for His service (1 Cor. vii. 22, 23). Therefore Philemon must, not release Onesimus but, *love* him[1]. This principle was in the long run bound to put an end to slavery, and has in fact done so in all modern communities influenced by Christian ideals.

2. CONTENTS.

vv. 1–3. Salutation from Paul and Timothy to Philemon, Apphia his sister, and Archippus and the Christians who met at Philemon's house.

vv. 4–7. Thanksgiving for Philemon's spiritual condition and his loving helpfulness to other Christians.

---

[1] Cf Ignat *ad Polyc.* 4, 'Despise not slaves, whether men or women. But neither let them be puffed up, but let them do their duty as slaves the more (diligently) to God's glory, that they may obtain a better freedom from God. Let them not desire to be redeemed (by money) from the public fund (of the Church), lest they be found slaves of lust.'

vv. 8–12 For this reason the apostle affectionately pleads with him on behalf of the slave Onesimus whom he had, while a prisoner, converted, and was now sending back to him.

vv. 13, 14. He would have liked to keep him as his attendant, but would not do so without Philemon's permission.

vv. 15–17. He begs him to receive him back, no longer as a mere slave, but as a Christian slave, 'a brother beloved.'

vv. 18, 19. He promises to make good anything in which Onesimus has wronged him or any debt that he owes him. At the same time he tenderly reminds Philemon that he can claim from him a far greater debt, his own self.

vv. 20, 21. He pleads, but also expresses confidence, that Philemon will do what he asks, and more.

v. 22. He asks him to prepare a lodging for him, as he hopes to visit him shortly.

vv. 23–25. Greetings from five[1] Christians The Grace.

CHAPTER X

EPHESIANS

1. OBJECT OF WRITING. This epistle stands alone among the Pauline writings in that it was not called forth by the external circumstances or immediate needs of any particular Church or person. It deals with the theme treated in *Colossians*, 'Christ in relation to God, the Universe, and the Church,' but not, however, in opposition to false views, but as a means of defining *God's eternal purpose* for the human race Consequently

[1] Or perhaps six; see p. 254 n.

it presents close parallels of language with the non-polemical portions of *Colossians*. But because the apostle was not attacking opponents, he was free to work out his great theme in the highest heights and deepest depths of thought. Christian writers have vied with one another in their praise of the sublimity and massiveness of his teaching.

2. TIME AND PLACE OF WRITING. The epistle was written in captivity (iii. 1, iv. 1, vi. 20), at the same time as *Colossians*, and therefore at Rome This is shewn by the close similarity of the language, and by the mention of Tychicus (vi. 21, 22) in words almost identical with Col. iv. 7, 8. (Onesimus is not, as there, named as his companion, because he was going straight back to Colossae to his master Philemon, and would not accompany Tychicus when he went on to deliver this letter.) And Rome, the head of the Empire, with its wonderful organization by which it controlled its vast dominions, probably helped the apostle, in both letters, in forming his vivid conception of the one Body controlled by the Head (i. 22, ii. 16, iii. 6, iv. 4, 12 f , 15 f., v. 23, 30). Perhaps also the constant presence of the soldiers to whom he was chained suggested to him the thought of the Christian armour (vi. 10–17), though the wording of the passage is borrowed from the Old Testament.

3. DESTINATION. According to the Received Text of i. 1 the salutation is addressed 'to the saints which are in Ephesus, and the faithful in Christ Jesus.' But some very ancient authorities omit *in Ephesus*[1], as noted in R.V. margin, i e the important uncials ℵB, a corrector of 67 who often preserves ancient readings, 184 a late

---

[1] Westcott and Hort mark the fact by printing the passage thus: τοῖς ἁγίοις τοῖς οὖσιν [ἐν Ἐφέσῳ] καὶ πιστοῖς ἐν Χριστῷ Ἰησοῦ.

minuscule closely allied to the text of Origen's commentaries, Origen himself who fancifully explains the words 'the saints which are' by referring to the divine title I AM in Exodus, and by Marcion who styles the epistle 'to the Laodiceans.' Basil knew early MSS which omitted the words, and it is possible, though not certain, that Jerome's remarks (*Comm in Eph.*) imply that his text omitted them.

If they are omitted, the only grammatical rendering of the sentence is 'to the saints which are also faithful in Christ Jesus.' But (1) this puts an impossible emphasis on 'faithful,' as though the apostle meant that he did not intend to write to those saints who were not faithful. (2) It is forbidden by the parallel expressions in other epistles. Rom. i. 7 'to all who are *in Rome*, God's beloved, called as saints[1].' 1 Cor. i. 2 'To the Church of God which is *in Corinth*, sanctified in Christ Jesus, called as saints.' 2 Cor i. 1 'To the Church of God which is *in Corinth*, with all the saints who are *in the whole of Achaia*' Phil. i. 1 'To all the saints in Christ Jesus who are *in Philippi*.' And in Col. i 2, to which the present epistle is closely allied, the words are 'to the saints and faithful brethren in Christ *in Colossae.*'

The explanation now widely accepted is that St Paul wished to write a circular letter to the series of Churches which Tychicus would visit in turn, and that he left a blank space which could be filled in with the name of the Church in the copy intended for each. This would also account for the absence of any greetings to individuals, which would be very surprising if the epistle were

[1] In the shorter form of *Romans* (see p. 185) the omission of 'in Rome' produced much the same phenomenon as in *Ephesians*, though the omission there does not make the sentence grammatically quite so difficult as here.

addressed only to the Ephesian Church whose members St Paul knew intimately.

Many writers also think it probable that when St Paul bade the Colossians (iv. 16) read 'the letter [which will reach you] from Laodicea,' he was referring to this circular letter. As he was sending them a special letter of their own, he would not be likely to send them also a copy of the circular letter with 'in Colossae' inserted in the blank space, though he might think it would be good for them to read it. This conjecture, however, does not affect the main question of the circular letter, though it depends upon it. If *Ephesians* was a circular letter, it is not impossible that the words in *Colossians* referred to it. But on the other hand St Paul may have written a letter to Laodicea which is now lost.

But the theory of the circular letter is not free from difficulty If a place name was inserted in each copy delivered by Tychicus as he travelled from town to town, one must have been inserted in the archetype of ℵ and B. Why was it omitted by subsequent scribes between the archetype and ℵB? It is difficult to suppose that that archetype happened to be a spare copy that was never delivered by Tychicus, and therefore contained no place name. It is even more improbable that the original place name to which St Paul addressed the letter dropped out accidentally, and not only the place name but also the preposition. If, however, it was a circular letter, and if it was the letter that the Colossians were to receive from Laodicea, we can only conjecture that the Laodiceans, not liking to send away their own letter, sent to Colossae a copy omitting the place name; and that this was the copy used when the collection of Pauline epistles was made. Some think that 'in Ephesus' was inserted at that time, because the collection was probably made at Ephesus, which was the chief city of the district and the place where St Paul resided for the longest period in his missionary work.

Another possibility must not be lost sight of, that the epistle was originally written to a single Church, and concluded with salutations to individuals, but that the place name and the salutations were omitted when the desire arose to adapt it for general Church use. The case would then be parallel with that of *Romans* (see pp. 185–9); and as the ecclesiastical editors did not go so far as to omit the personal allusions in Rom. i. 8–15, so here they refrained from omitting those in vi. 21, 22. If the epistle was written to a single Church that was not Ephesus, Marcion and other heretics[1] may have been right after all in calling it the Epistle to the Laodiceans, and it may have been the letter which the Colossians were to receive from Laodicea in return for their own epistle which they were to send thither[2].

If this theory is right, no MSS of the original epistle were preserved. But the awkwardness of i. 1 without a place name was felt, and when the Pauline collection was made, 'in Ephesus' may have been inserted.

4. GENUINENESS. Much more important than the textual difficulty, which will perhaps never be solved, is the contention of many writers that *Ephesians* is not

---

[1] Tert *Adv Marc.* v 11 'Praetereo hic et de alia epistola, quam nos "ad Ephesios" perscriptam habemus, haeretici vero "ad Laodicenos"'

[2] This reason for omitting the original ἐν Λαοδικίᾳ is at least as probable as that suggested by Harnack (*Sitzungsber. d. kon preuss Akad d. Wiss.* xxxvii), that it was omitted when Laodicea had become a name of ignominy as in Rev. iii 14–16. And see Bacon, *Expos.* March 1915, pp. 239–241.

a genuine letter of St Paul. This view is based upon its language, style, and doctrine.

(*a*) *Language.* This differs in many words, phrases, and constructions from the language of the epistles which are certainly by St Paul. But difference in subject matter involves some difference of language. And where the subject matter is similar, as in the portions which find parallels in *Colossians*, it is unsafe to suppose that a mind such as St Paul's could not vary his forms of expression. In particular, the expression 'His holy apostles and prophets' (iii. 5; cf. ii. 20, iv. 11) is thought to be unsuitable from St Paul's pen, and to be the work of one who could not claim to be either apostle or prophet. But apart from the fact that the author, if he was not St Paul, was writing in his name, and did not consider it unsuitable to represent him as using the expression, it must be remembered that St Paul speaks elsewhere of 'apostles and prophets' in the Christian Church (1 Cor. xii 28, 29, a passage closely allied with Eph. iv. 11), and that the word rendered 'holy,' 'saints' is that which he frequently employs in the sense of 'Christians.' It represents the ideal for all, though none reach it.

(*b*) *Style.* This has undeniably a literary stamp of its own. In other epistles St Paul frequently appears as a spiritual father burning with eagerness for the correction and building up of his converts by dealing with their particular needs and failings; or as a combatant, striving to ward off the attacks of opponents. And his pen is a rapier, which with all its quickness is often too slow for the rush of his thoughts. But here his pen and his thoughts are at one, moving forward with the flow of a deep river. But as in the case of the language the difference can be accounted for by the difference of subject matter. His style is the natural result of the temper of mind in which his high themes were written, a rapt contemplation of the cosmic mystery of Christianity.

(c) *Doctrine.* It is on this that the denial of the Pauline authorship is chiefly based. The doctrine is said to represent a more developed state of thought regarding the nature of Christ and of the Church than St Paul is likely to have reached. In some respects it approximates to that in the Pastoral Epistles (the genuineness of which is open to considerable doubt), 1 *Peter* (which the author of *Ephesians* is thought to have used), *Hebrews*, and the Gospel and First Epistle of St John. The teaching of the epistle is described as 'a set of variations played by a master hand upon one or two themes suggested by *Colossians*'; 'a catholicized version of *Colossians* written in Paul's name to Gentile Christendom (ii. 11, iii. 1); the solitary reference to concrete conditions (vi. 21, 22) is adapted from *Colossians* in order to lend *vraisemblance*[1] to the writing, and the general traits of the homily rank it among the catholic epistles or pastorals of the early Church' (Moffatt). If it was known to Clement of Rome (96 A.D.), who has what appear to be echoes of its language in two or three passages[2], the unknown author must have written it

[1] If so, i. 1 with its place name must have been written with the same purpose It is impossible to suppose that St Paul or anyone else originally wrote that verse as it stands in אB

[2] 'Through Him the eyes of our hearts were opened; through Him our foolish and darkened mind springeth up unto the light' (xxxvii.); cf. Eph. 1 18. 'Let the whole Body be saved in Christ Jesus, and let each man be subject unto his neighbour' (xxxviii.); cf. Eph v. 23, 21. 'Have we not one God and one Christ and one Spirit of grace that was shed upon us? And is there not one calling in Christ?' (xlvi.); cf. Eph. iv. 4–6.

some years before that date. Those who deny its genuineness suggest 75–85 A.D. as the earliest date at which it can have been written.

That the work is that of a master hand none has ever denied. And that a great spiritual genius might write in St Paul's name instead of his own is far from impossible. The practice of pseudonymity, i.e. of writing under the name of some great teacher of the past, was common enough in ancient literature. 2 *Peter* is a well known instance, though it does not even distantly approach the depth and spiritual power of *Ephesians*.

The fact must, indeed, be faced that the Christology of the epistle does mark a stage of thought somewhat more developed than that in earlier epistles. But development is to be expected in a genius, whether in the spiritual or in other spheres of thought. It must not be supposed that the epistle is lacking in numerous, close points of contact with St Paul's epistles earlier than *Colossians* They are very numerous and close. The author, if he was not St Paul, was fully steeped in his spirit and language, and if he was not St Paul the value of his teaching is in no way lessened. The question that has to be decided is whether the *extent* of the development in doctrine can be adequately accounted for by the fact that the epistle was of the nature of a treatise or meditation, the serene depths of which were not disturbed by controversy with opponents It is not a matter on which we can be entirely confident. The epistle *may* be Pauline but not by St Paul; but it is doubtful if the reasons adduced are strong enough to force us to abandon the traditional view that it contains the sublime outpouring of the maturest thoughts of the apostle of the Gentiles.

5. ANALYSIS.
        i. 1, 2. Salutation.
A. i. 3–iii. 21. Doctrine.
1 1. 3–14. *The divine Aim*, and *the divine Medium*.
        i. 15–19. Prayer, leading to
2. i. 20–ii. 10. *The divine Method*.
    (*a*) i. 20–23. The performance of a three-fold act upon Christ.
    (*b*) ii. 1–10. The potential performance of the same upon Gentile and Jew alike.
3. ii. 11–22. *The Effect*: the Unity of Gentile and Jew.
4. iii. 1–13. *St Paul's part in the divine plan*.
       iii. 14–19. Concluding Prayer.
       iii. 20, 21. Doxology.
B. iv.–vi. 20. Exhortation based on the above teaching.
    vi 21, 22. Personal matter.
    vi 23, 24. Greeting to the brethren. Grace.

6. CONTENTS.

i. 1, 2. Salutation from the apostle alone to the saints which are [in Ephesus], and the faithful in Christ Jesus.

A. i. 3–iii. 21. Doctrine.

1. i. 3–14. The divine Aim, and the divine Medium.

(*a*) i. 3–6. God chose us eternally to be holy, having marked us out beforehand unto adoption as sons, *to the praise of the glory of His grace*.

i. 11, 12. St Paul and his fellow Jews, who became Christians first, were made God's heritage, having been marked out beforehand in order to be *to the praise of His glory*.

i. 13, 14. The Gentiles also, to whom he was writing, were sealed with the Holy Spirit, the pledge of the Christian inheritance, for the redemption of God's possession, *to the praise of His glory*.

(*b*) Inseparable from the divine Aim is the divine Medium. [This is not a system of ethics, an institution, a legal process, a philosophy, or even the entire hierarchy of angelic powers.] The Medium is a Mediator[1], the Eternal Person, Christ Jesus, in whom God has eternally purposed to sum up the universe (i. 7–10). The section, *vv*. 3–14, is permeated with the thought: *v*. 3 'in Christ'; *v*. 4 'in Him'; *v*. 5 'through Jesus Christ'; *v*. 6 'in the Beloved'; *v*. 7 'in whom'; *v*. 10 'in Him'; 'in Christ'; *v*. 11 'in Him, in whom'; *v* 12 'in Christ'; *v*. 13 'in whom'; 'in whom.' (It also appears in the rest of the epistle, as shewn below by the italicised words.)

After a prayer (1. 15–19) that the readers may be given the spirit of wisdom and enlightenment to comprehend the vast truths, the apostle states

2. i. 20–ii. 10. The divine Method by which the Aim is reached in Christ.

(*a*) i. 20–23. A three-fold act was performed upon Christ:

He was raised from the dead (*v*. 20 a),
    exalted to God's right hand (*v*. 20 b),
        given supremacy over every conceivable power in the universe, and thus made the head of the Church, His Body (*vv*. 21–23).

(*b*) ii. 1–10. By that same three-fold act, Gentiles

[1] Though St Paul does not in this epistle use the word itself to describe Christ's work.

and Jews alike, when dead in sins (*vv.* 1–4), were (potentially)

> given new life *with Christ* (*v.* 5),
> lifted up *with Him* (*v.* 6 a),
> made to sit [in royalty] with God *in Christ Jesus* (*v.* 6 b),

in order that hereafter God's free kindness might be shewn in our actual salvation *in Christ Jesus* (*vv* 7–9), since He has created us anew *in Christ Jesus* to do the good works which He eternally prepared for us (*v.* 10).

3. ii. 11–22. The Effect.

vv. 11–13. The uncircumcised Gentiles who used to live apart from God, and aliens from the divinely given privileges of Israel, have *in Christ* been 'brought near' *in the Blood of Christ*.

vv. 14–16. For He has broken down the impassable barrier between Jew and Gentile, that He might create *in Himself* one new man, one Body through the Cross.

vv. 17, 18. He proclaimed peace both to Jew and Gentile, for *through Him* both have access in one Spirit to the Father.

vv. 19–22. So that Gentiles form part of one city, one household, one building founded upon the apostles and prophets, Christ being the Corner-stone, a building which *in Him* grows into a holy temple *in the Lord*, *in whom* the Gentiles are being builded together as God's spiritual dwelling-place.

4. iii. 1–13. St Paul's part in the divine Plan.

(In the opening verse the apostle is about to say that he prays for his readers; but he does not do so till *v.* 14. After naming himself he throws in a fine parenthesis.)

vv. 3–6. The apostle has been entrusted with the duty of dispensing, teaching, this mystery of God's eternal purpose, i.e. that Gentiles are joint heirs, joint members of the Body, joint partakers of the promise *in Christ Jesus.*

vv. 7–10. The apostle, in spite of all his past sins, was given this marvellous privilege of throwing light upon the working out of the mystery hidden through all past ages, that now through the Church the angelic powers might learn God's wisdom, according to the eternal plan purposed *in Christ Jesus* our Lord—*vv.* 12, 13, *in whom* we can approach God boldly with a confident faith So that the apostle's sufferings do not mean the failure of his cause; they are the glory of his Gentile readers.

iii. 14–19. Therefore he prays that they may be strengthened by the Spirit of the Father of all, that Christ may dwell in their hearts, that firmly rooted in love they may have strength to grasp the immeasurable, and to know the unknowable love of Christ, which is finally to result in the 'fulfilment' of God Himself.

iii. 20, 21. Doxology.

B iv.–vi. 20. Exhortation based on the above teaching.

iv. 1–6. Therefore [because God's eternal purpose is such as has been explained] the apostle beseeches his readers to live as that purpose requires, i.e. in the corporate unity which God has given and done so much to secure.

iv. 7–16. It is a living and growing unity developing into the perfect Man, just because of the wide diversity of gifts and functions of individuals in the one Body, which receives its vital force from Christ the Head.

iv. 17–v. 21. Therefore they must put off their old Gentile vices, and put on the New Man (iv. 17–24). They must put off falsehood, anger, dishonesty, corrupt speech, and everything unkind and unloving (iv. 25–32). They must imitate God, and love others as Christ loved them, and sacrificed Himself for them (v. 1, 2). They must put off many grievous sins, which exclude from the divine Kingdom and incur God's wrath (v. 3–6). They used to live in Gentile darkness, but now that they 'are light in the Lord' they must 'walk as children of light,' refusing things of darkness (v. 7–14) They must be careful, therefore, to live not as Gentiles but as Christians (v. 15–21).

v. 22–vi. 9. Particular graces: Wives and Husbands must in their union be a reproduction of the loving union of Christ and His Church (v. 22–33). Children and Parents (vi. 1–4). Slaves and Masters (vi. 5–9).

vi. 10–20. To live thus, they need the whole spiritual armour of God (vi. 10–17), to which are added prayer, and intercession for all Christians, including the apostle himself, that he may teach the divine mystery boldly (vi. 18–20).

vi. 21, 22. Tychicus would give them all news about him.

vi. 23, 24. Greeting to the brethren. Grace.

CHAPTER XI

PHILIPPIANS

1. TIME AND PLACE OF WRITING. St Paul when he wrote was a prisoner (i. 7, 13, 17) This cannot have been at Caesarea, since he hoped soon to visit his readers (ii. 24; cf. i. 26). To Philemon he expressed the same

hope (see p. 211), and, as there, he could not have done so at Caesarea after appealing to Caesar, and when he was therefore expecting to be sent at once to Rome. There are two possibilities as to the place of writing: (1) Rome, either before or after the other epistles of the captivity, *Colossians*, *Philemon*, and *Ephesians*. (2) Ephesus, during the apostle's long stay there in the course of the third tour. The former has long been the prevailing theory, and the discussion of the epistle is therefore placed at this point. But, as will be seen, the latter is far from being an improbable alternative.

(1) *Rome.* For this there are three arguments.

(*a*) In i. 13 St Paul says 'my bonds have become manifest in the whole *praetorium.*' It is generally agreed that the *praetorium* is not a place, either the Emperor's 'palace' (A.V), or the barracks attached to it, or the military camp outside the walls, but a body of men, either the 'praetorian guard' (R.V., so Lightfoot), or possibly the imperial court, 'the whole body of persons connected with the sitting in judgment' (Ramsay) That the word is applied to a body of men is rendered probable by St Paul's next words, 'and to all the rest.' There is no clear evidence for Ramsay's meaning of the word, and yet Lightfoot's explanation is open to the difficulty that the praetorian guard numbered some 9000 men But if the epistle was written in Rome Lightfoot's is the best explanation.

(*b*) In iv. 22 'they that are of Caesar's household' send greetings Caesar's household included slaves of every sort and rank, as well as courtiers. The enormous number of slaves owned by wealthy Romans is noted by Lightfoot (*Philemon*, p 319), and the Emperor would probably own a larger number than anyone else. Some of those of lower ranks were no doubt Christians See Sanday-Headlam on the 'household of Aristobulus' and 'of Narcissus' (Rom. xvi. 10, 11).

(c) In i. 1 Timothy joins St Paul in the opening salutation, as in *Colossians* and *Philemon*.

Those who accept Rome as the place of writing differ as to whether the epistle should be dated before or after the other epistles of the captivity.

The Earlier Date. Lightfoot argues for the earlier date on account of the close resemblance of language with *Romans*. He gives the following parallels (*Philippians*, pp. 43, 44)

Phil	Rom	Phil.	Rom.
i. 3, 4, 7, 8	i 8–11	iii. 4, 5	xi. 1
i. 10	ii 18	iii. 9	x. 3, ix. 31, 32
ii. 8, 9, 10, 11	xiv 9, 11	iii 10, 11, 21	vi. 5
ii. 2–4	xii 16–19, 10	iii 19	vi. 21, xvi 18
iii 3	ii. 28, 1 9, v. 11	iv. 18	xii 1

If the student will look these up in the New Testament or in Lightfoot who quotes them he will see that they contain several strikingly close parallels, while the language of *Colossians* and *Ephesians* is markedly different. But this might be accounted for by the fact that the Philippians and the Romans needed similar teaching, while the Asiatic churches needed something different. Lightfoot further writes that 'if these resemblances suggest as early a date for the Epistle to the Philippians as circumstances will allow, there are yet more cogent reasons for placing the others as late as possible The letters to the Colossians and Ephesians—the latter more especially—exhibit an advanced stage in the development of the Church. The heresies, which the Apostle here combats, are no longer the crude, materialistic errors of the early childhood of Christianity, but the more subtle speculations of its maturer age.' This is, of course, true. But it has very little bearing on the order in which the four epistles of the captivity are to be placed; the 'early childhood' and the 'maturer age' of the Church cannot both fall within the two years or so of St Paul's imprisonment at Rome.

The Later Date. Those who place *Philippians* last of the Roman epistles argue as follows:

(a) Time must be allowed for St Paul's bonds to become known in the whole *praetorium* (i. 13) if it means the praetorian guard. If it means the Emperor's court, St Paul's trial had actually begun.

(b) His 'defence (*apologia*) of the gospel' (i. 16) is his self-defence at the trial against the charges brought against him by the Jews; and the 'salvation' which he expected to obtain through his readers' 'prayer, and the supply of the spirit of Jesus Christ' (i. 19) was the acquittal of which he felt confident (i. 25), though he still recognises the possibility of being 'poured out as a libation' (ii. 17; cf 2 Tim. iv. 6), i.e. put to death.

(c) Some time is needed for the communications between St Paul and Philippi. The Philippians had heard, from some quarter, that he had arrived at Rome; they collected money, and sent it by Epaphroditus; he fell ill with strenuous service to St Paul; news of his illness reached the Philippians, and news that they had heard of it reached him in turn. Lightfoot reckons that a month would be a fair average time for the journey between Rome and Philippi; and he ingeniously minimises the period required by the events to the length of two journeys. But whether his suggestions are right or not, the point is not important. If there were four journeys, all that is required is four months *plus* the time for the

Philippians to contribute money, and for Epaphroditus at Rome to fall ill and to recover sufficiently to return to Philippi with the letter.

The first of these three arguments is the strongest; and if the epistle was written from Rome, it was probably the latest of the four.

(2) *Ephesus*. The indications, however, adduced in favour of Rome point with equal force to Ephesus.

(*a*) Even if the *praetorium* of which St Paul speaks were a building, it could be explained as the official residence in Ephesus of the Roman governor of Asia. But, as we have seen, he probably refers to a body of soldiers; and an inscription found at Ephesus[1] shews that there were *praetoriani* there. Compared with those at Rome, their number would be small, so that the apostle might easily come into contact with all of them, making the most of the opportunities afforded by his bonds.

(*b*) An inscription[2] also shews that members of Caesar's household were to be found in Ephesus, in numbers large enough for them to form burial clubs.

(*c*) Timothy's name in conjunction with St Paul's would be as natural at Ephesus as at Rome, since he was there with the apostle until sent by him with Erastus to Macedonia (Acts xix. 22). And therefore just before Timothy went, it was natural that St Paul, in writing to the Philippians, should tell them that he hoped to send him to them 'shortly' (Phil. ii. 19), 'immediately' (*v*. 23).

---

[1] J. T Wood, *Discoveries at Ephesus*, Append 7, p 4: 'T. Valerio T F. Secundo Militis Cohortis VII Praetoriae Centuriae Severi.'

[2] *ib* Append. 7, p. 18: 'Quorum [a monument and sarcophagus] Curam Agunt Collegia Libertorum Et Servorum Domini Nostri Augusti.'

But further. (*d*) If the similarities between *Philippians* and *Romans* are to have weight on the question of the order of the epistles, they can be used in favour of Ephesus, for if the epistle was written there, it can be dated shortly before St Paul went *via* Macedonia to Corinth (Acts xix. 21, 22, xx. 1, 2), where he wrote *Romans*.

(*e*) And since he would certainly visit Philippi when he was in Macedonia, his words in Phil. ii. 24, 'I trust in the Lord that I myself also shall come shortly,' are explained.

(*f*) In iv 10 he tells the Philippians that he quite understands how it was that they had not sent him a contribution for so long; it was not want of thought for him, but it was because they 'lacked opportunity.' Now, if he wrote from Rome, he had been for three months in Corinth after leaving Ephesus (Acts xx. 3); and since they had sent him supplies to Corinth on his second tour, they could have sent him supplies again to the same town on his third tour; indeed they could have given them to him in person when he was in Macedonia on his way to Corinth. Consequently, if the epistle was written at Rome, 'ye lacked opportunity' must be understood as a graceful way of giving a mild rebuke, by assuming that they felt themselves too poor to give him anything. But this is surprising after their previous liberality, to which he bears grateful record in iv. 15, 16. But all difficulty is removed if he wrote from Ephesus, since in that case he had been, ever since he left Corinth (Acts xviii. 18), far away in Palestine and Galatia, and they really had 'lacked opportunity.'

Probably none would hesitate to accept these indications as pointing to Ephesus rather than Rome, were it not for the lack of definite evidence that St Paul was imprisoned at Ephesus This is not related in the *Acts*; but neither are many of the sufferings which he enumerates in 2 Cor. vi 4, 5, xi. 23–27. In both passages he speaks of 'imprisonments,' 'prisons,' in the plural, though St Luke up to that point relates only the one imprisonment at Philippi (Acts xvi. 23 ff.). Clement of Rome (*Cor* v), on the other hand, speaks of the apostle as having been in bonds seven times. It is not unnatural to suppose that he may have been imprisoned, at any rate for a time, in connexion with the riot at Ephesus. He speaks himself of some definite trouble from which he personally suffered: 'our affliction which befell in Asia,' 'we were excessively burdened beyond our power, so that we despaired even of life' (2 Cor. i. 8). And in 1 Cor. iv 9–13, 2 Cor iv. 8–12 (the former written in Ephesus, the latter shortly afterwards) he makes it clear that he passed through a period of anguish both of mind and body. Further, in 1 Cor. xv. 32 he writes 'If after the manner of men I fought with beasts at Ephesus etc.' He cannot actually have fought with beasts, if the authorities recognised his Roman citizenship, for no Roman citizen could be condemned to the arena. If the words are metaphorical, the arena supplied him with a vivid metaphor for the wild unreasoning opposition of men that he encountered[1], which may have included imprisonment. But the words can be rendered 'If...I *had fought* with beasts at Ephesus, what advantage would it have been to me etc.?' In that case he may actually have been

[1] Ignatius on his way to Rome, expecting to be martyred in the arena, writes 'I fight with wild beasts' metaphorically of the soldiers who guarded him on the journey (*Rom.* v.). He probably borrowed the word from St Paul, but that does not make it certain that the latter used it in a metaphorical sense.

condemned to the arena, but managed to escape by convincing them of his Roman citizenship. And if so, it is very likely that he was for a short time in prison.

2. CAUSES OF WRITING. These were mainly two—(a) to correct what was amiss in the Philippian Church, and (b) to thank them for a contribution which they had sent to him by Epaphroditus.

(a) St Paul is writing to his closest friends, who since his first visit to them had preserved the warmest affection for him, as he for them. And yet he hints that all was not quite right with them. He prays that their love may increasingly abound in knowledge and discernment, to approve the things that really matter, that they may be sincere and without offence (i. 9, 10). He had heard, no doubt from Epaphroditus, that they were suffering from a not uncommon complaint—squabbles between Church workers. They were in danger of *disunion*, when a united front was needed against their adversaries (i. 27, 28), of *party spirit* and *vainglory* (ii. 3), which were the very reverse of the humility shewn by Christ, in His Incarnation, life of obedience, and death (*vv.* 5–11), and of *murmurings and disputings* which set a bad example to the world (*vv.* 14–16). And after saying what he wanted to say, he cannot refrain from bringing up the matter once more, this time mentioning two Church workers, certain ladies named Euodia and Syntyche, who seem to have been chiefly responsible for the disagreements (iv. 2). And he goes on to exhort the readers to let all men see their forbearance[1], i.e. their readiness not to assert their individual rights and wishes, because the Lord is soon coming (*v.* 5). They must keep their

---

1 τὸ ἐπιεικές, a word for which there is no exact English equivalent.

thoughts on the highest plane (*v.* 8), and follow St Paul's example, and the God of peace will be with them (*v.* 9).

These words of gently expressed advice and warning do not point to serious religious factions such as had been rife at Corinth, and there is no trace of heretical beliefs or of heathen crimes by which some of the Gentile churches were endangered. But Lightfoot goes too far when he says 'to them [the Philippians] alone he writes in language unclouded by any shadow of displeasure or disappointment.' Though their mistake was small in comparison with the blots to be found elsewhere, St Paul was not one to let it go unnoticed. He felt it so much that he thought it necessary to deal with it before turning to the happier duty of thanking them for their contribution.

(*b*) A marked feature of their Christian character was their liberality. They must have been one of the Macedonian churches of whom St Paul says (2 Cor. viii. 2), referring to the collection for the poor in Jerusalem, 'in much testing of affliction the abundance of their joy and their deep poverty abounded unto the wealth of their liberality.' Not only so, but they also sent contributions to St Paul for his personal use. When he was in Thessalonica, immediately after his first visit to them, they, and they only, sent him supplies more than once (Phil. iv. 16), and when he went on to Corinth they, and perhaps some other Macedonian churches, did so again (*v.* 15, 2 Cor. xi. 8, 9). To the Corinthians (*l c.*) he explains why he had not accepted anything from them, i.e. because he would not be burdensome to them. The Macedonian churches were bound to him by so close a friendship that he felt sure that no-one there would charge him with being burdensome, or preaching the Gospel for his own profit. And now, when he was a prisoner, the Philippians sent him supplies once more by Epaphroditus (Phil. ii 25). They would doubtless, as St Paul readily acknowledges (iv. 10, 11), not have waited so long to do so if they had had the opportunity (see p. 230). Epaphroditus, since joining St Paul, had made up for the deficiency of their service to him (i e. probably the smallness of their contribution, due to their poverty, which they had very likely lamented in an accompanying letter, or a message by Epaphroditus) by a personal devotion so strenuous that his health failed and he almost died (ii. 27, 30). On recovery, he was anxious to return to Philippi, because he feared that they would be greatly distressed at the news which they had received of his illness (v. 26). So St Paul let him go back, sending by him the letter of affectionate advice, and grateful thanks for their gift.

3. UNITY OF THE EPISTLE The first part of the epistle deals with the disagreements within the circle of the Philippian Christians, and, as has been said, the apostle cannot refrain from bringing up the matter once more, in iv. 2 ff. He also speaks of the relations of himself and Epaphroditus with the Philippians (ii 19–30 and iv 10–19) iii. 1 is a new departure But the passage iii. 2–iv. 1 stands by itself. It breaks in unexpectedly, deals with a danger much more serious than the disagreements between individual Christians, and is altogether different in tone. Instead of the quiet, tactful language of friendly advice, the passage sounds the note of battle against the Judaizers. St Paul is suddenly the stern and fiery combatant, as in *Galatians* and 2 *Corinthians*

Lightfoot suggests that St Paul happened to be inter-

rupted in his letter, and that before returning to it he
heard of some fresh activity against him of his Judaizing
opponents in Rome, which made him fear lest they
might try to tamper with the Philippians; this made
him write the warnings in iii. 2–iv. 1 before resuming
his subject. Some such artificial explanation is necessary
if the unity of the epistle is to be maintained. But it is
more probable that this is a portion of another letter,
which was combined with the present one when a collection of Pauline writings was made. This theory is
not impaired by the uncertainty that exists as to whether
iii. 1 b ('To write the same things[1] etc.') belongs to the
interpolated passage or not. That St Paul wrote more
than one letter to his best-loved converts is itself probable[2]. But the epistle of which the interpolated passage
was a fragment was not necessarily an epistle to the
Philippians. The warning against libertines (iii 18, 19)
seems to point to some Church in which the Christians
were more in danger of pagan influence than the Philippians. Some interchange of letters between the several
Christian communities must have taken place when the
collection of Pauline writings was formed. And other

[1] Lightfoot explains the words as meaning 'to bring up
the subject of your dissensions again,' which the apostle does
in iv 2. Lipsius *al.* think that they referred to previous warnings against Judaizers, which do not occur in our epistle
before this point, but were contained in a lost portion of the
interpolated epistle.

[2] It is unsafe to support this by Polycarp's words to the
Philippians (§ 3), 'the blessed and glorious Paul...who also
when absent wrote letters (ἐπιστολάς) unto you,' since instances are known of the use of the plural in classical and
later Greek for a single letter. See Lightfoot, *Phil.* pp. 140–2.
It should be noted, however, that Polycarp in § 13 expressly
distinguishes the plural and the singular. But on the other
hand the plural may refer to the Macedonian epistles, 1, 2
Thessalonians and *Philippians*.

instances have already been noted in which fragments of letters have been incorporated in the same way[1]. The complete incongruity of the position in which the passage is inserted causes no difficulty, since it may well have been due to purely mechanical reasons. If a sheet of St Paul's manuscript ended at iii. 1, or iii. 1 a, a stray sheet (or sheets) of Pauline material may have been accidentally placed next to it, and a scribe might easily copy it (or them) unthinkingly, and then proceed with the sheet beginning at iv. 2.

4. ANALYSIS.
  i. 1, 2. Salutation.
  i. 3–11. Thanksgiving and Prayer.
(1) i 12–26. St Paul's account of himself.
  i. 12–18. The result of his imprisonment.
  i 19–26. His confidence for the future.
(2) i. 27–ii. 18. Exhortations relating to the dissensions at Philippi.
  i. 27–ii. 4. Exhortations to unity and humility.
  ii 5–11. The example of Christ.
  ii. 12–18. Further exhortations.
(3) ii. 19–30. Personal matters.
  ii. 19–24. Timothy.
  ii. 25–30. Epaphroditus.
  iii. 1. Closing remarks begun but postponed.
[(4) iii. 2–iv. 1. Warning against Judaizers and Libertines.
  iii. 2, 3. Judaizers.
  iii. 4–14. St Paul's example.

[1] 2 Cor. vi. 14–vii 1 (see p. 137 f.) and Rom. xvi. 1–23 (see p. 182 f.). Some would add 2 Cor. x.–xiii. (see pp. 144–9).

iii. 15, 16.   Exhortation.
iii. 17–21.   Libertines.
iv. 1.   Exhortation.]
(5) iv. 2–9.   Continuation of (2).
(6) iv. 10–20. Thanks for the Philippians' contribution.
iv. 21–23.   Salutations. Grace.

5. CONTENTS.

i. 1, 2. Salutation, in which Timothy joins, to the Philippian Christians with their 'bishops and deacons.'

i. 3–11. Thanksgiving for his readers, his confidence in them and love for them, and a Prayer for their further spiritual progress.

(1) i. 12–26. St Paul's account of himself.

i. 12–18. His imprisonment has helped forward the cause of the Gospel, and so has the preaching of others, even of those who preach in the spirit of envy and party strife.

i. 19–26. He is confident that the final result will be his 'salvation,' and his earnest hope is that Christ may be magnified whether he lives or dies. He would prefer to die for his own sake, but to live for the sake of his readers, and he feels sure that he will live, and visit them again.

(2) i. 27–ii. 18. Exhortations relating to the dissensions at Philippi.

i. 27–30. He longs to hear that they are shewing a united front in their fight on behalf of the Gospel, for they have been granted the privilege of waging the conflict not only by their faith in Christ, but also by their sufferings for His sake.

ii. 1–4. Therefore they should be united, shewing not vainglory but humility.

ii. 5–11 They should follow the example of Christ's humility, who, though existing eternally in the essential form of God, humbled Himself in His Incarnation by an act of self-emptying, and in His human life humbly rendered obedience to God to the full extent of dying on the Cross. Wherefore God has exalted Him, and invested Him with the divine Name which is invoked in worship by the whole universe, and confessed by every tongue.

ii. 12–18. Let them, then, work out their own salvation, for it is God that worketh in them. Let them avoid murmurings and disputings, thus setting a good example to the world around them, that the apostle may be able to boast that his work among them was not in vain. Nay, if his blood is to be a libation poured over the sacrificial offering of their faith, he and they can mutually rejoice.

(3) ii. 19–30. Personal matters.

ii. 19–24 He hopes soon to send Timothy to them, for he has none at hand who will care for them with the same natural devotion, inherited from the apostle his spiritual father[1]. And they know how he has laboured with him, as a son with a father, in the service of the Gospel. He will send him as soon as he knows how his own affairs will turn out, and he hopes soon to come himself.

ii. 25–30. Meanwhile he is sending Epaphroditus to them, whom they made the bearer of their gift. Epa-

---

[1] Some such expansion is needed to represent the force of γνησίως, 'truly' (R V), 'genuinely' (R V marg.), 'naturally' (A.V.)

phroditus was greatly troubled because they had heard of his illness. He was, indeed, seriously ill, but God mercifully restored him. They must receive him joyfully, and hold him in high esteem, for he staked his very life in his strenuous service to the apostle to supply what they were unable to give

iii. 1. Finally, he bids them rejoice in the Lord — But he cannot help, for their good, referring once more to the subject of which he has already spoken.

[(4) iii. 2–iv. 1. Warning against Judaizers and Libertines.

iii. 2, 3. Judaizers. The readers are bidden to beware of those who are themselves—though they apply the words to the Gentiles—the 'dogs,' the 'evil workers,' the 'mutilation[1].' Christians have the true spiritual circumcision

iii. 4–14. St Paul's example. As regards earthly considerations he can say at least as much for himself as the Judaizers· he is a thorough Israelite of unmixed descent, and was a zealous and blameless Pharisee. But he willingly renounces it all that he may gain Christ, and all that that means of union with His righteousness, passion, death, and resurrection. He does not claim to have fully gained it yet, but he follows after it as for a heavenly prize.

iii. 15, 16. Let those, then, who are spiritually mature, fully initiated into the Christian mystery[2], be thus minded. If anyone is not, God can reveal it to him;

1 κατατομή A play on περιτομή, 'circumcision,' which cannot be represented in English He ironically describes the physical circumcision as no better than pagan self-mutilation Cf Gal. v 12
2 This is the force of τέλειοι (see p. 305).

only the straight rule of life hitherto followed must not be abandoned.

iii. 17–21. Libertines. The apostle begs them to imitate him, and those who follow his example. For many do not; they repudiate the Cross to their ruin, make bodily self-indulgence their God and glory in it. Christians are citizens of heaven, from which Christ will come to transform our earthly bodies into the glorious condition of His own spiritual Body.

iv. 1. He exhorts them, therefore, to stand fast against these dangers.]

(5) iv. 2–9. He exhorts Euodia and Syntyche to be in Christian harmony; and he asks him who is, in spiritual affinity[1] with himself, his 'yokefellow,' to help them and other women, together with Clement and other Christians who laboured with him in the Gospel.

iv. 4. 'Rejoice in the Lord always!'; again he says it, 'Rejoice!'

iv. 5–7. They must let their selfless yielding of their own rights and wishes be known to all. Christ is soon coming and will put everything right. There is, therefore, no need to worry, but simply to pray and give thanks, and divine peace, which is beyond the grasp or comprehension of mere human thought, will guard their hearts and thoughts, as in a safe fortress, in Christ Jesus.

iv. 8, 9. Let them concentrate their thoughts on all subjects that will keep them on a high plane; let them follow the apostle's example, and the God of peace will heal their dissensions and be with them.

(6) iv. 10–20. Thanks for their contribution The apostle expresses his gladness that they have again been

[1] γνήσιε. Cf. ii. 20.

able to shew their care for him. He quite understands that till now they have not had the opportunity. Not that he speaks from a feeling of want; his experience has taught him to be content in any condition; but their kindness is in itself a good thing. They know that when he left them after his visit to them, he accepted gifts from them and from no other Church. What he wants is not their gifts, but the proof that his work among them is bearing fruit. And their gift, sent by Epaphroditus, is like a sacrifice of sweet odour to God. God will, in turn, supply every need of theirs.

iv 21–23. Salutations. Grace.

CHAPTER XII

THE PASTORAL EPISTLES

1. GENUINENESS. The three epistles 1 *Timothy*, *Titus*, and 2 *Timothy* are usually known as the Pastoral Epistles, because in them advice is given to Timothy and Titus on the pastoral care which they are to exercise in the communities under their charge. In 2 *Timothy*, however, this is not very prominent. They are so closely allied in language and tone that they must be studied together. As in all the epistles, the religious teaching is the matter of primary importance, and can be studied independently of critical problems. But the latter, which arise chiefly in connexion with the question whether or not the three epistles are genuine writings of St Paul, are interesting and complex. They are mainly of four kinds, connected with (*a*) the personal allusions to people and events, (*b*) the ecclesiastical organization presupposed, (*c*) the style and language, (*d*) the doctrine.

(a) *Personal Allusions.* Even if St Paul was not the author of the three epistles, it is probable that the personal allusions are based upon real traditions as to the movements and plans of the apostle and others. A later writer would be unlikely to invent them all; but if he did, he would take care not to invent such as were difficult to harmonize, as some of them are, with St Paul's history as it was known in the *Acts*. He would be unlikely also to invent such trivial details as the apostle's need of his cloak, and books, especially the parchments (2 Tim. iv. 13). And he would hardly have dared to invent weaknesses in the character of Timothy (1 Tim. iv. 7, 12, 14, v. 21, 22, vi. 20, 2 Tim. i. 6-8, ii. 1-3, 16, 22), a shrinking from opposition and hardship, a want of strength in the exercise of his authority (cf. also Tit. ii. 15), a need of warning against youthful lusts, and perhaps a tendency to pay to erroneous doctrines and ideas more attention than they deserved. Julicher (*Introd. to the New Test.* p 187) follows the line taken by several modern writers in holding that it is not really Timothy and Titus who are being blamed: 'the world at large is being addressed, not the addressees'; 'the unpleasing traits in the picture of Timothy and Titus are demanded by the parts assigned to them'; 'the untrustworthiness, the weakmindedness, the lack of clearness of those who wished to be leaders and examples appeared to him [the unknown author] as the canker gnawing at the roots of the Christianity of his time.' But an objection to this view is the difficulty of supposing that a 'pseudo-Paul' would venture to single out as his lay figures two of the apostle's best loved and most strenuous fellow-workers.

The place occupied by the personal allusions in

relation to the narrative in the *Acts* will be studied later.

(b) *Ecclesiastical Organization* It is held that this is more advanced than would be possible in St Paul's lifetime. In earlier days, when the intense spiritual enthusiasm of the Church shewed itself in the form of *charismata*—gifts such as ecstasy, prophecy, and tongues —the government and organization of the Church were, of course, in the hands of the apostles or their delegates. But from the first, for the oversight (ἐπισκοπεῖν) of local matters they had appointed presbyters in each local Church (Acts xi. 30, xiv. 23, xv. 2, 4, 6, 22 f., xvi. 4, xx. 17 [cf. 28], xxi 18, and see 1 Thes. v. 12 f.), selected, no doubt, partly for preeminence in the possession of *charismata*. As the Church rapidly grew, and the local communities could not be so frequently visited by apostles or their delegates, the range of functions included in the ἐπισκοπή of the presbyters was necessarily enlarged, and details of government and organization began to play a larger part in men's thought. This is the condition of things reflected in the Pastoral Epistles

(i) Beside the primary office of 'oversight,' and the ministry of 'deacons,' some sort of official status held by women is perhaps implied in 1 Tim. iii. 11, analogous to that which St Paul recognised as having been won by Phoebe in Cenchreae (Rom. xvi. 1, 'deaconess'). 'Widows' also, under certain conditions of age and character, have definite functions (1 Tim. v. 3–16), and their names are registered (v. 9), service to the Church being probably expected from them in return for their maintenance from the public funds, in cases where their relatives were unable to help them. The passage, however, does not make it quite clear that widows formed a definite ecclesiastical *order*. But they must, from early days, have busied themselves in charitable works (cf. Acts ix. 39, 41), and the writer's intention here seems to be to lay down new and fixed rules regarding a loosely defined body which was already in existence.

(ii) The later idea, however, that the 'bishop' is one who holds monarchical authority in a town or district has not yet appeared. It is unsafe to see in either Timothy or Titus an instance of such a bishop; their ministry in Ephesus and in Crete appears to have been temporary, though of course during the period of their charge they possessed apostolic authority of an 'episcopal' nature (e.g. compare Tit. i. 5 with Acts xiv. 23). Moreover, although 'bishop' is always used in the singular (contrast Phil. i 1), while 'deacons' are always spoken of in the plural, and the 'presbytery' is referred to as a body (1 Tim. iv. 14), the distinction between 'bishop' and 'presbyter' is not yet quite explicit[1], as it became at the end of the 1st century, when, by a natural and universally accepted development, there was a shrinkage of the recently enlarged ἐπισκοπή of the whole body of presbyters, each local group recognising one of their number as the ἐπίσκοπος *par excellence,* who summed up in his own person, as the apostles had done, the function of oversight possessed

---

[1] Nor is it in Clem. Rom. (*c*. 96 A.D), *Cor* §§ 21, 42, 44, 47, 54, 57 , see, however, Archbp Bernard, *Studia Sacra,* ch. xii. But less than 20 years later, Ignatius with repeated emphasis ascribes to the 'bishop' a supreme monarchical position, with 'presbyters' under him and 'deacons' inferior to them.

by them all, so that they now exercised it only as delegated by him.

(iii) A regulation was still needed against public speaking by women (1 Tim. ii. 11, 12), as it was when St Paul wrote 1 Cor. xiv. 34, 35.

The ecclesiastical organization, then, does not necessarily 'carry us beyond the possible conditions of a flourishing community in a large city which may have been established at least ten years, at a time of quick development such as is stamped on every page of the New Testament' (Lock, in Hastings' *DB*. iv. 773 a).

(c) *Style and Language*. (1) Un-Pauline expressions — It is not denied that some Pauline traits have been seized by the writer, but it is pointed out that he uses many phrases and expressions not found in the other Pauline epistles, some of which sound as though they had already become technical and stereotyped. 'There is an articulated fixity about them which seems to mark a late date, and to be unlike the freshness of the earlier style' (Lock). E.g 'the healthy teaching' or 'words' (1 Tim. i. 10, vi 3, 2 Tim. i 13, iv. 3, Tit. i. 9, ii 1; cf. i. 13, ii. 2, 'healthy in faith'); 'the teaching' (1 Tim. iv. 13, 16, vi. 1; cf. iv. 6, vi. 3, 2 Tim iii. 10, Tit. ii. 10); 'faithful is the saying,' perhaps referring to current sayings in the Church at the time (1 Tim. i. 15, iii. 1, iv. 9, 2 Tim. ii. 11, Tit. iii. 8), to which may be added what appears to be a Christian hymn about Christ (1 Tim. iii. 16), 'the Faith,' almost equivalent to the body of truths which are, or ought to be, believed (1 Tim. i. 19, iii. 9, iv. 1, 6, v. 8, vi. 10, 21, 2 Tim. iii. 8, iv. 7); 'the commandment' (1 Tim. vi. 14); 'the charge' (1 Tim. i. 5); 'the (my) deposit' (1 Tim. vi. 20, 2 Tim. i. 12, 14); 'the truth' (1 Tim. iii. 15, iv. 3,

vi. 5, 2 Tim. ii 15, 18, iii 8, iv. 4, Tit i. 14), 'knowledge of (the) truth' (1 Tim ii. 4, 2 Tim. ii. 25, iii. 7, Tit. i. 1); 'our Saviour,' applied to God or to Jesus Christ (1 Tim. i. 1, ii. 3 (cf. iv. 10), 2 Tim. i. 10, Tit. i. 3, 4, ii. 10, 13, iii. 4, 6); 'the present age¹' (1 Tim. vi. 17, 2 Tim. iv. 10, Tit. ii. 12).

The proportion of *hapax legomena* is much larger than in any other Pauline epistle, one for every verse and a half. Lock, however, notes that while the proportion is 1 for 1·55 verses in the Pastoral Epistles, it is 1 for 3·66 verses in 2 *Corinthians*, and 1 for 5·53 in 1 *Corinthians*, the difference between 2 and 1 *Corinthians* being thus practically as great as between 2 *Corinthians* and the Pastoral Epistles. Nevertheless the difference between 2 and 1 *Corinthians* is not of the same kind as between the Pastoral and the other Epistles. 'The author has a favourite vocabulary of his own, full of compounds and Latinisms², with new groups of words³, and an unwonted predilection for others⁴. As compared with Paul, he employs the definite article more frequently.... The differences in the use of the particles⁵ is one of the most decisive proofs of the difference between Paul and this

1 ὁ νῦν αἰών. In other epistles St Paul always writes 'this age' (eight times), except in Gal. 1. 4 ἐκ τοῦ αἰῶνος τοῦ ἐνεστῶτος πονηροῦ

2 The latter is an overstatement The only certain Latinisms are φελόνη and μεμβράναι (2 Tim. iv. 13).

3 E.g. those in ἀ privative, διδασκ-, εὐσεβ-, οἰκο-, σωφρ-, φιλο-, etc

4 E.g those in καλο-. 'Καλός, which Paul uses only as a predicate or a neuter substantive, is employed repeatedly by this author as an attribute Δεσπότης supplants the Pauline κύριος as a human term, and ἐπιφάνεια replaces the Pauline παρουσία.'

5 'Unlike the apostle, he uses μήποτε and δι' ἣν αἰτίαν (thrice), and eschews ἀντί, ἄρα, ἄχρι, διό, διότι, ἔμπροσθεν, ἔπειτα, ἔτι, ἰδού, παρά (with accus.), σύν, and ὥστε.'

Paulinist' (Moffatt, *Introd. to the Lit. of the N.T.* pp. 406, 407). And to this must be added the absence of many of the most characteristic of St Paul's words and expressions.

(ii) Quality of the style.—As compared with St Paul's impetuous fervour and eager home-thrusts the style is correct and diffuse, somewhat lacking in warmth and colour. 'The syntax is stiffer and more regular' (Lightfoot, *Biblical Essays*, p. 402). 'The comparative absence of rugged fervour, the smoother flow of words, and the heaping up of epithets, all point to another sign-manual than that of Paul' (Moffatt, *l.c.*).

It cannot be denied that this is a strong argument against the Pauline authorship. If the historical allusions clearly pictured St Paul as being in the first Roman imprisonment, it would be practically impossible to maintain that the three epistles as a whole came from his pen. The difference of style and language from those of *Colossians, Philemon, Ephesians*[1] [and *Philippians*] is too great. But if he wrote in a later imprisonment, different readers will think differently about it None can decide with exactness the extent to which psychological changes will affect a writer's tone and vocabulary with the lapse of a few years, and in altered circumstances.

(*d*) *Doctrine.* A later writer could of course echo St Paul's teaching; but if the three epistles shew a marked advance, and still more any clear disagreement, then the Pauline authorship of the doctrinal and didactic portions cannot stand.

In Christian doctrine, as such, the Pastoral Epistles

[1] *Ephesians*, however, stands in this respect nearer to the Pastoral Epistles than to the others.

are in entire agreement with St Paul,—'life eternal, won by Christ's death, which has brought salvation to all mankind; and this life must show itself by a high Christian morality, and be ready to face the appearing of Jesus Christ' (Lock). But some objections have been raised:

(i) St Paul, who expected *the Last Day* to come in the immediate future, would be unlikely, it is said, to take so much care about the organization of Christian communities for an indefinite future. But he had, from early days, 'appointed elders in every Church' (Acts xiv. 23), and had spent much trouble upon a host of practical details in the conduct and arrangement of the Churches which he had founded (2 Cor. xi. 28), notably Corinth. And even in the Pastoral Epistles the references to the Last Day (1 Tim. vi. 14, 2 Tim. i. 18, iv. 1, 8, Tit. ii. 13) are expressed in language which at least does not imply the giving up of all hope of its near approach. He always felt that he was living in the dawn of the last days, and he declares that the abuses belonging to that period were already rife (1 Tim iv. 1, 2 Tim. iii. 1), or soon to appear (2 Tim. iv. 3).

(ii) In other Pauline epistles stress is not, as here, laid on *good* [i.e. attractive] *works* (1 Tim. iii. 1, v. 10, 25, vi. 18, Tit. ii. 7, 14, iii. 8, 14), *piety*[1] (1 Tim [8 times], 2 Tim. iii. 5, Tit. i. 1; not elsewhere in Pauline writings), and *safe* or *sane mindedness*[2], or verb, adj., or adv. (1 Tim. ii. 9, 15, iii. 2, 2 Tim. i. 7, Tit. i. 8, ii. 2, 4, 5, 6, 12).

[1] εὐσέβεια. This and cognate words occur elsewhere only in the *Acts* (4 times, but not of distinctively Christian piety), and in the late writing 2 *Peter* (5 times)

[2] σωφροσύνη. Elsewhere only Acts xxvi 25. The verb -νεῖν is used twice by St Paul, Rom. xii. 3, 2 Cor. v. 13.

(iii) St Paul does not elsewhere urge, in the same way, the importance of *orthodoxy*. He fights, indeed, vehemently in other epistles against false teachers, but here 'the Faith[1]' tends to be considered as a definite body of beliefs, almost a creed. And when St Paul fights against false teachers he does it by argument, by confronting error with truth, by demolishing with a master hand his opponents' defences But here there is little more than authoritative denunciation.

(iv) This tendency to formularise beliefs has not helped the writer to preserve in their depth and fulness some of the greatest of St Paul's inspired conceptions. 'No possible change of circumstances or rise of fresh problems could have made Paul thus indifferent to such cardinal truths of his gospel as the fatherhood of God, the believing man's union with Jesus Christ, the power and witness of the Spirit, the spiritual resurrection from the death of sin, the freedom from the law, and reconciliation' (Moffatt, *Introd.* p 412).

(v) The *false teaching* dealt with in the Pastoral Epistles is said to belong to a later date than St Paul. It is not necessary to suppose that any individual false teacher held all the mistaken ideas which are here attacked; but the same general tendency was observable both at Ephesus and Crete. It is not impossible that it affected even some who held office in the Church; hence the careful injunctions as to their character and behaviour (1 Tim. iii. 1–13, v. 17–21, Tit i. 5–9, iii 1, 2), and the discrimination needed in ordaining them (1 Tim v. 22) Some of the false teachers, but not all, were 'of the circumcision,' i.e Jewish Christians (Tit. i 10). They aspired to be 'law-teachers,' though they misunderstood

---

[1] See p. 245

the true purpose of the law (1 Tim. i. 7–10). But their false teaching was not the old Judaism against which St Paul fought in 1, 2 *Corinthians, Galatians, Romans,* and *Philippians*.

A study of it, however, will shew that it contains no features which are quite certainly later than St Paul. The following points should be noticed:

(1) The writer's insistence that 'the law is good if one treats it as law,' i.e. as a prohibition of grievous sins (1 Tim. i. 8–10), and that every passage in the Old Testament, given by inspiration of God, is intended to be spiritually and morally profitable (2 Tim. iii. 16, 17), suggests that some of the false teachers, or their dupes, held Christians to be above law, and free to behave as they liked. But the beginnings of such antinomian tendencies can be seen already in Gal. v. 13, Rom. vi. 15.

(2) Some, on the other hand, went to the opposite extreme, and taught a rigid asceticism (1 Tim. iv. 8, E.V. 'bodily exercise'), prohibiting marriage, and requiring abstention from certain foods (*v.* 3), apparently holding that matter was in itself evil. This the writer contradicts (*vv.* 4, 5; cf. v. 23). Perhaps the idea, not mentioned as heretical elsewhere in the New Testament, that 'the Resurrection is past already' (2 Tim. ii. 18) was connected with the depreciation of matter: the truly religious man, they thought, is living in the spiritual sphere, independent of the body. Thus the Christian ideal for the future is claimed as having been already reached by the false teachers[1]. These ascetic and

---

[1] A travesty of the thought expressed in John v. 21, 24, 1 John iii. 14; the former is safeguarded from misunderstanding by *vv.* 28, 29.

XII] THE PASTORAL EPISTLES 251

dualistic tendencies, however, had already formed an element in the Colossian heresy (see p. 206).

(3) The false teachers laid claim to special 'knowledge'—'falsely so called' as the writer says (1 Tim. vi. 20)—and complacently prided themselves on the 'oppositions' (*antitheses*) between ordinary Christian teaching and their profounder esoteric doctrines. This is the simplest explanation of the word; and if it is right the claim is not different from that made by the Colossian heretics. Or the word may have been used in the early stages of Jewish Gnosticism in Asia with a somewhat more technical force unknown to us. It is doubtful if it should be explained, as a purely rabbinic product, of 'the endless contrasts of decisions founded on endless distinctions which played so large a part in the casuistry of the scribes as interpreters of the law' (Hort, *Judaistic Christianity*, pp. 138-140), for these were not a novelty such as the passage seems to imply.

(4) The false teachers made use of 'myths [R V. 'fables'] and endless genealogies' (1 Tim. i. 4), 'old-womanish myths' (iv. 7), 'Jewish myths' (Tit. i. 14). These are probably not specifically Gnostic speculations about the aeons and emanations which were thought of as intervening between the supreme God and created matter. They may refer to myths and legends in apocryphal works in which Jewish and other elements were mingled, and which appeared in great numbers in the 1st century A.D. and later. Even if some of the elements in the false teaching here attacked were Gnostic[1], it is not improbable that they had already

[1] The combination of Jewish and Gnostic elements can be seen, e.g., in the Naassenes, an early form of the Ophites (see Lightfoot, *Biblical Essays*, p 411 f.; Legge, *Forerunners and Rivals of Christianity*, ch. viii.).

begun to appear among Jewish Christians in Asia in St Paul's day.

2. CONCLUSION AS TO AUTHORSHIP. It will be seen that the Pastoral Epistles present many and various difficulties, some of which it has been necessary, in this short sketch, to dismiss very briefly. But enough has been said to enable the reader to arrive at a general impression. The subject has been dealt with, as far as possible, from the point of view of those who still uphold the Pauline authorship, and in this way it has been shewn possible to maintain, with regard to almost every difficulty in turn, that it does not quite certainly require an author later than St Paul. But when they are surveyed as a whole, it is difficult not to feel their cumulative force. If St Paul had really written the three letters as they stand, would they have differed so widely from his other letters as to present this array of varied problems which need, one after the other, to be explained, or explained away? Several different attempts have been made to distinguish portions written by St Paul from those by a later writer. The variety of these attempts shews how difficult the task is[1]. To some extent it is a matter of personal feeling and impression. And yet it is along those lines that the true explanation is probably to be sought. Some portions, certainly most of the personal allusions (1 Tim. i. 3 a, 20, iii. 14, iv. 12 a, 2 Tim. i. 3–5, 15–18, iv. 7, 8, 9–22 a, Tit. i. 5 a, iii. 12, 13), shew every indication of being from the apostle's pen; but the three epistles as wholes have probably been built up as general treatises for the guidance of the Church by some devoted disciple of his, who has breathed in his spirit and teaches his Gospel. The voice

[1] See Moffatt, *op. cit.* pp. 402–6.

is St Paul's voice, but the hand is the hand of a Christian teacher in the generation which followed him[1].

3. THE PERSONAL ALLUSIONS IN RELATION TO THE ACTS According to 2 Tim. i 8 St Paul was a prisoner, and *vv.* 15, 16 shew that it was at Rome. In 1 *Timothy* and *Titus* there is no indication of imprisonment, while certain passages suggest the reverse: 1 Tim iii. 14, '...hoping to come unto thee shortly; but if I delay etc.' iv. 13, 'Till I come, give heed to reading etc.' Tit. iii. 12, 'Give diligence to come unto me to Nicopolis[2], for there I have decided to winter.' The words 'if I delay' do not naturally suggest the meaning 'if I am kept a prisoner longer than I expect'; and 'there I have decided to winter' is hardly the language of a prisoner, even if he felt considerable confidence of release. If these passages imply that St Paul was at liberty, they must refer to a time earlier than that of 2 Tim. iv 6–8 in which his expectation of imminent death is expressed, and of i. 8, 15, 16 in which his imprisonment is spoken of. And this must have been either the imprisonment recorded in Acts xxviii., or a later one.

Many of those who maintain that the three Pastoral Epistles as wholes are the work of St Paul find a solution of the problems presented by the personal allusions in

[1] If so, the order in which the epistles were written was probably not that suggested by the personal allusions taken alone. If 1 *Timothy* was already in circulation as a general treatise, the same writer is unlikely to have written *Titus* at all. 1 *Timothy* is the most, and 2 *Timothy* the least, advanced in its teaching on ecclesiastical and doctrinal matters The order, therefore, is probably 2 *Timothy*, *Titus*, 1 *Timothy*. Some writers would even accept the genuineness of the first or of the greater part of it and not of the others, but the three epistles are so closely akin that as wholes they must stand or fall together.

[2] Of the various cities of that name this was probably the Nicopolis near Actium in Epirus.

the theory that the apostle was released from the imprisonment of Acts xxviii., and that after visiting Ephesus and Macedonia (1 Tim. i. 3), Troas (2 Tim. iv. 13), Crete (Tit. i. 5), perhaps Nicopolis (Tit. iii. 12), and possibly Spain (see below), he was again imprisoned, this time being condemned and executed. In this case, 1 *Timothy* and *Titus* will have been written in the period of release, and 2 *Timothy* in the second imprisonment, the first trial and the release being referred to in the words 'my first defence' (2 Tim. iv. 16), and 'I was delivered out of the mouth of the lion' (v. 17).

If the three epistles are single wholes from St Paul's pen, this is the only theory that will cover the various allusions. If, for example, 2 Tim. iv. 9–21 was written in the imprisonment of Acts xxviii., the following difficulties are raised:

(*a*) St Paul begs Timothy 'to come shortly' (v. 9), 'to come before winter' (v. 21), although earlier in the same imprisonment Timothy was with him at Rome when he wrote *Colossians* (i. 1), *Philemon* (v. 1), and (perhaps) *Philippians* (i. 1).

(*b*) He says that Titus has gone to Dalmatia (v. 10), and yet he has recently written to him in Crete, where at an earlier date he left him in charge (Tit. i. 5).

(*c*) He explains the fact that only Luke is with him by saying that Demas, Crescens, and Titus have gone elsewhere (v. 10); and yet in the same imprisonment he sends greetings to the Colossians (Col. iv. 10–14) not only from Luke and Demas, but from four other Christians, and to Philemon (vv. 23, 24) from three of these[1], who are here ignored.

[1] Possibly from the four. In *Philemon* the name Jesus Justus is omitted, but it is a possible emendation to read the nominative Ἰησοῦς for Ἰησοῦ, or to add it after the latter.

(*d*) He asks Timothy to bring Mark with him (*v.* 11); and yet earlier in the same imprisonment Mark is with St Paul when he writes to the Colossians (iv. 10) and to Philemon (*v.* 24). He hints, indeed, to the Colossians that Mark may be going to them; but the words to Timothy 'bring him with thee for he is useful to me for service' hardly suggest that he had only just left the apostle, and that he wanted him back at once.

Two further details can be explained if they refer to a period of release:

(*e*) In 1 Tim. i. 3 St Paul refers to an occasion when, on going from Ephesus to Macedonia, he left Timothy at Ephesus. This cannot be the journey mentioned in Acts xx. 1, for St Paul had previously sent him to Macedonia from Ephesus (Acts xix. 22) It is unsafe to assume that he returned to Ephesus before St Paul left that city (see p. 139 f.); but if he did, it is strange that he did not fulfil the charge laid upon him, but for some unknown reason hurried back to Macedonia in time to join in the writing of 2 *Corinthians* (2 Cor. i. 1).

(*f*) Similarly in Tit. i. 5 St Paul refers to an occasion on which he left Titus in Crete, to supply the spiritual needs of the Christians on the island, and to appoint elders in every Church. If this implies that St Paul had just been carrying on successful missionary work in many parts of the island, it can hardly have been during the time that he spent at Crete as a prisoner on his way from Jerusalem to Rome (Acts xxvii. 8, 9), which is the only occasion on which St Luke relates that he visited the island.

The last two points, however, would not be enough alone to require the theory of a second imprisonment. They might easily be explained if we knew more about St Paul's life. St Luke has pressed fourteen years of strenuous activity into as many chapters. From 2 Cor. xi. 23–26 it is clear that St Paul made journeys by land and by sea of which *Acts* contains no record, and which may easily have included a journey from Ephesus to Macedonia, when Timothy was left behind for a time, and a voyage to Crete with Titus.

Further support for the theory of a period of release is found by Lightfoot and others in a supposed journey of St Paul to Spain. Clement of Rome (*Cor.* v., vi.) says: 'Let us set before our eyes the good apostles; Peter who ...having borne witness went to his due place of glory ...Paul...having been a preacher both in the East and in the West, received the noble renown (which was the reward) of his faith, having taught the whole world righteousness, and having come to the boundary of the West[1], and having borne witness before the rulers, so he was released from the world and went to the holy place. To these men of holy life there was gathered a great multitude of elect persons etc.' This passage speaks of the martyrdom of the two apostles as occurring immediately before that of a great multitude of Christians, presumably in the Neronian persecution. Clement's somewhat rhetorical statement need not in itself imply a second imprisonment (see below). 'The boundary of the West' is an expression which might be applied to Spain, in which case a period of release is absolutely required, and the apostle's hope expressed in Rom. xv. 24, 28 was at last fulfilled, after the first imprisonment. But in a letter to eastern readers the expression might be applied not to Spain but to Rome[2], the word 'having

1 $\dot{\epsilon}\pi\grave{\iota}\ \tau\grave{o}\ \tau\acute{\epsilon}\rho\mu\alpha\ \tau\hat{\eta}s\ \delta\acute{v}\sigma\epsilon\omega s$.
2 Thus Ignat *Rom.* 2 uses $\delta\acute{v}\sigma\iota s$ 'West,' and $\dot{\alpha}\nu\alpha\tau o\lambda\acute{\eta}$ 'East,' for Rome and Syria.

borne witness' being joined with 'having come.' And it is to be noticed in any case that Clement does not speak of St Paul as bearing witness more than once. The words in the Muratorian Canon, 'sed et profectionem Pauli ab urbe ad Spaniam proficiscentis,' need not be more than a deduction from Rom. *l.c.* Further, if St Paul was the apostle of Spain, it is surprising that no trace should have survived of Spanish traditions to that effect. The evidence, therefore, for a journey to Spain is far too slender to be of use.

The only evidence of any weight is that derived from 2 Tim. iv. 9–22 a. But if, as will be shewn below, that is very possibly a fragment of an earlier letter, the theory of a release and a second imprisonment falls to pieces. Apart from deductions from the Pastoral Epistles, and St Paul's hope to go to Spain, there is not the slightest reason for thinking that the imprisonment of Acts xxviii. did not end with the apostle's death. St Luke does not mention it, but neither does he mention a release; either would fall outside the plan of his work (see p. 119 f.). His words, however, seem to imply that after the 'two years' some change was made in the prisoner's condition. Clement, as said above, does not speak of St Paul as bearing witness more than once. He naturally estimates his death, and St Peter's, as a martyrdom, in which 'a great multitude of elect persons' was associated with them. But this would not exclude the possibility that St Paul was beheaded before the actual persecution began to rage[1] (in the midst of the persecution he would

[1] It is quite unnecessary to suppose that he died in the later years of Nero's reign, or even under Vespasian (Sanday and Headlam). The tradition that he was beheaded is found in Tert. *De praescr.* 36 and *Scorp* 15, Euseb. *Hist. Eccl.* ii. 25, Lactant. *De morte persec.* 2, Jerome, *De vir. illustr.* 5.

probably have received less humane treatment), and that he was put to death as a Roman citizen, after a formal trial, on the charge, which the Jews had previously brought against him before Felix, of being 'a pestilent fellow, and a mover of insurrections among all the Jews throughout the world' (Acts xxiv. 5). They would have no difficulty in collecting a series of facts (cf. Acts xiii. 50, xiv. 2, 5, 19, xvi 19–24, xvii 5–9, 13, xviii. 5, 6, 12–17, xix. 9, 23–41, xxi. 28, xxiii. 10, 2 Cor. xi. 24, 25), and stating them in such a way as to convince any judge that the prisoner had created disturbance wherever he went. During the good years of Nero's reign such a charge would be sure to meet with condign punishment. For the Emperor to keep a prisoner waiting for two, or even four, years before he took the trouble to give him a trial, was not an uncommon occurrence

One detail may be added. The narrative in Acts xx. 36–38 does not entirely exclude the possibility that St Paul was mistaken in his foreboding[1], and did, after all, return to Ephesus after the first Roman imprisonment; nevertheless it is difficult to think that St Luke would have written his account of this solemn and affecting farewell, and the grief caused by St Paul's words, unless he had known for a fact that the apostle had never revisited Ephesus.

There remain the allusions in 2 Tim. iv. 9–22 a If *2 Timothy* need not be considered as a single whole from St Paul's pen, this passage may be a genuine fragment. And it will be seen that its details, almost without exception, find explanation if it was written to Timothy

---

[1] If the imprisonment of Acts xxviii. ended with his death, his hope of release expressed in Philem. 22 [and ?Phil. ii. 24] was not fulfilled.

when St Paul was a prisoner at Caesarea before being sent by Festus to Rome.

Whatever be the place of writing, *v.* 22 suggests that the passage did not originally stand in its present position. Notice the unusual combination, 'The Lord be with *thy* spirit. Grace be with *you* (plural).' The latter phrase occurs alone as the conclusion of 1 *Timothy*, and [you all] of *Titus*. The former phrase is a natural conclusion to a private letter to an individual.

The contents of the passage can be explained as follows[1]:

St Paul's 'first defence' (*v.* 16), when all the friends who had accompanied him from Europe forsook him, was his trial before the Sanhedrin at Jerusalem (Acts xxiii 1–10). And his words in *v.* 17 'But the Lord stood by me and strengthened me...and I was delivered out of the mouth of the lion'—i.e. from a violent death at the hand of persecutors—are parallel with St Luke's narrative, 'And the night following the Lord stood by him and said, Be of good cheer etc.' (*v.* 11), after which he was delivered from the imminent danger of assassination (*vv.* 12–24).

If Ramsay's suggestion about 'Alexander the coppersmith '(see p 84, n. 1) is right, the 'much evil' which he 'displayed' to St Paul (*v.* 14) may be a reference to the riot at Ephesus.

The cloak (or possibly the cover or case for books), the papyri volumes, and the parchment rolls (of Scripture), which were left at Troas (*v.* 13), were probably left when the apostle was on his way to Jerusalem (Acts

---

[1] In substantial agreement with Bacon, *The Story of St Paul*, p. 198 f., and Erbes who elaborates the theory in *ZNW*. 1909, pp. 195–218.

xx. 13). He decided to walk from Troas to Assos alone, while the others went by boat; and these *impedimenta*, which he could not carry with him on his walk, were either left behind purposely, or by some accident were not put on the boat in charge of the others. St Paul may now have been anxious for the cloak because winter was approaching (*v* 21).

The group of travellers who accompanied the apostle from Europe comprised Sopater, Aristarchus, Secundus, Gaius, also Timothy, Tychicus, Trophimus, and the writer of the narrative, presumably Luke (Acts xx. 4, 5). The first four are not named by St Paul in the present passage, and may have been among those who forsook him at his 'first defence'; or they may have been mentioned in the lost part of the fragment[1]. Of the other four, Luke accompanied him to Jerusalem, was with him (as *v.* 11 here shews) at Caesarea, and travelled with him to Rome, where he sent greetings to the Colossians (iv. 14) and Philemon (*v.* 24). Timothy cannot have travelled as far as Palestine with him, but must have broken his journey somewhere, since St Paul here tells him[2] what happened at Jerusalem, and begs him to come to him. He no doubt obeyed the apostle's summons, and came to Caesarea as quickly as possible, bringing Mark with him[3]. Tychicus and Trophimus also

---

[1] A Macedonian named Aristarchus accompanied him on the voyage from Caesarea (Acts xxvii. 2), and was with him in Rome (Col iv. 10, Philem *v.* 24).

[2] Bacon thinks that the fragment may not have been addressed to Timothy. But in that case the absence of his name would be surprising. The apostle, however, need not necessarily have mentioned every one of his fellow travellers from Europe.

[3] If so, they may have made the voyage with him to Rome, or travelled independently. They were with him in

broke their journey the former because St Paul sent him to Ephesus (*v.* 12), the latter because he fell ill at Miletus (*v.* 20); Trophimus, however, must have recovered in time to be with the apostle in Jerusalem (Acts xxi. 29)[1]. Four other names are mentioned in the fragment, Crescens, Titus, Demas and Erastus. The first two must have joined the apostle at Caesarea, and then, probably commissioned by him, went to Galatia and Dalmatia respectively (*v.* 10). The last two are the only ones which cause difficulty. Demas, after having 'loved this present world and departed to Thessalonica' (*v.* 10), is found with St Paul in Rome as one of his 'fellow-workers' (Philem. 24, Col. iv. 14). But that is a difficulty only if we assume that his repentance was impossible. Erastus, as St Paul tells Timothy, stayed behind at Corinth (*v.* 20). But since Timothy travelled with the group from Corinth (Acts xx. 4), it is not easy to see why he needed this information, if it was he to whom the apostle was writing.

None of the difficulties in the theory is such that it might not be removed if we knew more of the facts between the departure from Corinth and the end of the Caesarean imprisonment. They are certainly not greater than those attaching to any of the rival theories with regard to the composition of the Pastoral Epistles.

Rome, for Timothy joins in the writing of *Colossians*, *Philemon* [and *Philippians*], and Mark sends greeting in the first two of those epistles.

1 Erbes suggests that he did not, and that 'the city' in Acts xxi. 29 means Ephesus, whence 'the Jews from Asia' (*v.* 27) had just come. They 'supposed' that St Paul had brought into the temple his former companion, whereas Trophimus was in reality not in Jerusalem at all. At least they did not arrest Trophimus as they should have done.

4. CONTENTS. The discursiveness of the Pastoral Epistles makes an exact analysis impossible. Sometimes a connexion of thought is barely discernible: but the general outline is as follows.

1 TIMOTHY.

i. 1, 2. Salutation.

i. 3–20. *Introduction.*

i. 3–17. The 'sound teaching' of St Paul's Gospel—of which he was made a minister, having obtained mercy because his former sinful, persecuting life was lived in ignorant unbelief—is contrasted with the teaching of certain Jewish Christians with antinomian leanings, who do not accept the Law as a useful, moral corrective.

i. 18–20. Timothy, his spiritual child, is charged to preserve the true Gospel, which some have repudiated.

ii., iii. *Church Organization and Worship.*

ii. 1, 2. *Prayer* is to be made for all men, because

ii. 3–6. God wills all men to be saved through the one Mediator Jesus Christ.

ii. 7. Of this universal Gospel the apostle was appointed the preacher.

ii. 8. Prayer, therefore, must be made universally.

ii. 9–15. *Women* must wear modest apparel in keeping with their subordination to men, and (*v.* 12) must not speak in public assemblies.

iii. 1–13. *Church Officers:* iii. 1–7. The qualifications of a 'bishop.' iii. 8–13. The qualifications of deacons, including (*v.* 11) their wives.

iii. 14–16. Transition to the next section. The Church must be so ordered because it is the pillar and prop of the Christian truth, of which a formula is quoted.

iv.–vi. 2. *Timothy's attitude to various classes of persons.*

iv. False Teachers. v. 1, 2. Individual Christians. v. 3–16 Widows. v. 17–25. Presbyters. vi. 1, 2. Slaves.

vi. 3–10. Condemnation of false teachers, who make profit out of their religion.

vi. 11–16. Solemn charge to Timothy as to his own manner of life.

vi. 17–21. Postscript:
    vi. 17–19. Charge to rich Christians.
    vi. 20, 21. Warning to Timothy to avoid the false 'knowledge.' Grace.

2 TIMOTHY.

i. 1, 2. Salutation.

i. 3–5 Thanksgiving for Timothy's spiritual state.

1. 6–ii. 13. *The Gospel, and the sufferings which it involves.*

i. 6–11. Timothy is exhorted not to be ashamed of the apostle and of his Gospel.

i. 12–14. He is to follow the apostle's example of endurance.

i. 15–18. The example of Onesiphorus.

ii. 1–3. Timothy is to entrust this Gospel to men who can teach others; and he must shew endurance himself.

ii. 4–13. The certainty of reward for faithful endurance.

ii. 14–iv. 5. *Warnings against errors and contentiousness.*

ii. 14–23 Charge to shun empty and pernicious controversy.

ii. 24–26. The Lord's servant must not be contentious, but tactful in order to win over opponents.

iii. 1–9. A stern rebuke of those who are immoral and unscrupulous.

iii. 10–12. Timothy is exhorted to follow the apostle's example of endurance,

iii. 13–17. And in the face of deceivers to abide by the teaching of Scripture.

iv. 1–8. A solemn charge to him to preach the truth fearlessly, because the apostle himself expects death in the near future.

iv. 9–22. Personal details. Salutations and Grace.

TITUS.

i. 1–4. Salutation.

i. 5–9. The qualifications of a presbyter or 'bishop.'

i 10–16. This is in view of local vices and false teaching, especially of Jewish Christians.

ii. 1–10. Sound teaching to be given to: ii. 1, 2. Older men. ii. 3–5. Women. ii. 6–8. Younger men ii. 9, 10. Slaves.

ii. 11–15. This is because of the divine purposes for which God's saving grace was revealed.

iii. 1–8. And the same divine purposes require Christians to preserve a blameless life in their dealings with all men.

iii. 9–11. Titus is to avoid the folly of the false teachers, and have nothing to do with those who persist in error.

iii. 12–15. Personal details. Salutations and Grace.

PART III
THE CHRISTIAN DOCTRINE OF ST PAUL

INTRODUCTION

Our Lord was the Founder of Christianity; but He founded it less by His teaching than by being Himself the Foundation, other than which no man can lay (1 Cor. iii. 11). He taught the Fatherhood of God, and the brotherhood of men, and, on that basis, the character necessary for those who will inherit the divine Kingdom, which is soon to arrive, and of which He claimed to be the coming Messianic King, an office to which He would pass by death on behalf of His nation, and by resurrection.

This teaching in its main elements must have been known to St Paul, not, of course, through the Gospels, which were not written till after his death, but through intercourse with the first Christians. All its chief truths appear in his epistles. The Fatherhood of God is not stated as a doctrine, but assumed as a fact in every reference which he makes to it. And, as in our Lord's teaching, a sharp distinction is implied between God's relation as Father to us and to His Son Jesus Christ (see 2 Cor. i. 2, 3, Eph. i. 2, 3, Col. i. 2, 3). Though St Paul says more about the spiritual brotherhood of Christians than the natural brotherhood of all human beings, the latter is implied in many of his practical injunctions on conduct. His eschatological teaching will be dealt with below.

But he did much more than echo the truths declared by our Lord. It is a mistake to suppose that St Paul could not have contributed to Christianity anything that is not found in the teaching of Jesus during His earthly life. What he contributed was a system of thought, not constructed out of our Lord's words but, built upon the foundation of His risen and glorified Person. It must be remembered, however, firstly that a system of thought crystallized in the mind of one man, however fertile in imagination and vehement in zeal, within 30 years of our Lord's death, cannot shew a rounded completeness like that of modern systems which have been shaped as the result of previous generations or centuries of thought, and secondly that the apostle's thoughts have been preserved for us only in letters, written for the needs of particular persons or Churches at the moment. It may be taken for granted that we do not know the whole of his Christian teaching. And yet what we do know is marvellous in its range and depth, and on the whole wonderfully harmonious and coherent.

His religious beliefs, like those of every other man, were determined by two main factors, (1) instruction by others, training, tradition, environment, (2) immediate personal spiritual experience. But more clearly than most men he was able to distinguish the latter from the former (cf. Gal. i. 1, 12). The crisis on the road to Damascus did not blot out all that was Jewish and Greek in him, but transfigured it. His early beliefs and tendencies, and his personal spiritual experience, formed the two forces which resulted in the direction taken by his Christian thought, driving him to the conclusions

INTRODUCTION

which, with the help of his great mental powers and intuitive perception, he was enabled in God's providence to reach, and bequeath to the Church.

He does not, like the writer of the Fourth Gospel and 1 *John*, lay the weight of his argument on the Incarnation of the eternal Son He speaks of Him, indeed, frequently, as the Son of God, and in the four passages where he mentions His human birth (Rom. i. 3, viii. 3, Gal. iv. 4, Phil. ii. 5-8) he implies that He was the Son of God—and in the last passage states that He was 'on an equality with God'—before His Incarnation. His pre-existence is recognised also in Eph i. 4, Col i. 15, 16[1]. But the system of doctrine which is characteristically Pauline, while wholly dependent upon His Divinity, lays the chief stress on His Death and Resurrection in their spiritual relation to His Second Coming and the consummation of all things, as the working out of God's eternal plan of salvation for mankind.

It can best be understood by approaching it from the End, and tracing the apostle's thoughts backwards to the Cross. Not that he definitely followed this, or any exact, order in working out his conclusions; in a mind such as his, great truths probably presented themselves as independent certainties, and his reasoning powers were occupied in defining their relative position and bearing upon one another. It is impossible to follow the process of his mind chronologically, the more so

[1] In the Pastoral Epistles His human life is the manifesting or appearing of the pre-existent Christ· 1 Tim iii. 16, 2 Tim. 1. 9, 10; cf 1 Tim 1. 15. And the truth of the Incarnation is expressed in the term 'Mediator' (1 Tim ii. 5), which is elsewhere applied to Christ in Heb viii 6, ix. 15, xii 24 only, as the counterpart of Moses, the mediator of the Old Covenant (contrast Gal. iii. 19, 20).

since the order of the epistles is far from certain. Development of thought there doubtless was; the last stages of it are seen with some clearness in *Colossians* and *Ephesians*; but some writers have greatly exaggerated it. It is chiefly important to see that the several parts of his 'gospel' are links in one chain, in whatever order they may have been forged.

1. ESCHATOLOGY

The prophets of the Old Testament had expected a final age of bliss to be ushered in by the 'day of Yahweh,' the day of Judgment. Their conceptions of this age, and day, were taken over by the apocalyptic writers, but to a large extent developed and altered, especially by those who attained to a belief in a new heaven and a new earth, a spiritual transformation, a 'regeneration' of all things. And prophets and apocalyptists alike expected that the great consummation for which they severally hoped was to occur in the near future. Jewish thought had reached also the conception that the introduction of the new age would be the work of a God-sent Agent, either of earthly or of heavenly origin. Writers differed widely in their descriptions of his nature and functions, but the hopes of an Individual, whom some called 'Messiah,' i.e. Χριστός, 'Anointed,' and some 'the Son of Man,' 'the Beloved,' 'the Elect' and other titles, tended gradually to become more distinct.

Then our Lord claimed to be the fulfilment of these hopes. And Saul of Tarsus, who inherited them with his Jewish blood, learnt from the Christians whom he persecuted that they were convinced that the claims of Jesus had been proved true by His Resurrection from

ESCHATOLOGY

the dead. The Galilean who had lived and moved with them had become the heavenly Man who would soon arrive in glory at the Last Day to inaugurate the Kingdom of God on earth.

And then came the crisis. Jesus the heavenly Man, crucified and risen, revealed Himself to Saul, and at one stroke the eschatology of the despised Christians became the eschatology of St Paul the apostle. The parousia of the Messiah would be the parousia of the risen Jesus. Inherited Jewish hopes were transfigured in the dazzling light of personal experience. In his epistles, however, he nowhere spends a sentence on proving that Jesus is the Messiah of Jewish expectations[1]. The identity of Jesus and the Christ had been the subject of early apostolic teaching (Acts ii. 36, iii. 18, 20, 26, iv. 11, 27, v. 30, 31, 42, vii. 52, 56, viii. 5, 35, x. 38, 42, 43, xviii. 28), and St Paul taught the same (ix. 20, 22, xiii. 23–33, xvii. 3 (cf. *v.* 7), xviii. 5, xxvi. 23, xxviii. 23). But in writing his epistles to meet the immediate needs of those who were already Christians, he assumes their acceptance of this fundamental truth which he had taught them by word of mouth when he converted them.

We enter, then, upon the study of his teaching in the epistles by noting his expectations of the events to take place at what is popularly called 'the end of the world.'

1. The time of the End is expressed in an Old Testament phrase, or varieties of it: 'the Day of the Lord (Jesus)' (1 Cor. v. 5, 1 Thes. v. 2, 2 Thes. ii. 2), of our Lord Jesus (Christ) (1 Cor. i. 8, 2 Cor. i. 14), of Jesus Christ (Phil. i. 6), of Christ (ii. 16); 'that Day' (2 Thes.

---

[1] Rom. ix 5 contains a passing allusion to the Israelite descent of the Messiah, and i 3 to His Davidic descent; cf. 2 Tim. ii 8.

i. 10; cf. 2 Tim. 1. 12, 18, iv. 8); 'the Day' (Rom. xiii. 12, 1 Cor. iii. 13, 1 Thes. v. 4; cf. Rom. ii. 5, 16).

2. It will be a time when all will be judged by God (Rom. ii. 3, 5, 12, 16, xiv. 10, 2 Thes. ii. 12), or by Jesus Christ[1] (Rom. ii. 16, 1 Cor. iv. 5, 2 Cor. v. 10; cf. 2 Tim. iv. 1, 8). And good and bad will receive the due reward of their deeds (Rom ii. 6, 2 Cor. v. 10). The good will obtain salvation (Rom v. 9, 10, 1 Cor. iii. 15, v. 5, 1 Thes. v. 9), life with Christ (Phil. i. 23, 1 Thes. iv. 17), praise from God (1 Cor. iv. 5), rest (2 Thes i. 7), eternal life (Rom. ii. 7). The wicked will suffer wrath (Rom. v. 9, xii. 19, xiii. 5, 1 Thes. i. 10, ii. 16, v. 9[2]; Rom. i. 18, ii 5, 8, iii 5, Col. iii 6, Eph. v. 6), destruction (1 Thes. v 3, 2 Thes i. 9), affliction (2 Thes. i. 6), wrath and indignation, affliction and distress (Rom. ii. 8), vengeance (2 Thes i. 8).

3. The Advent of Jesus Christ is variously spoken of: 'The Parousia of our Lord Jesus Christ' (with all His holy ones[3]) (1 Thes. iii. 13, v 23; cf. ii. 19). 'The manifestation of His Parousia' (2 Thes ii. 9). 'They that are Christ's [will rise] at His Parousia' (1 Cor. xv. 23). 'To await His Son from heaven' (1 Thes. 1 10). 'The Lord Himself with a shout of command, with the voice of an archangel, and with the trump of God[4], shall descend from heaven' (1 Thes iv. 16) 'The revealing of our Lord Jesus Christ from heaven with the angels of His power in a flame of fire' (2 Thes. i 7). '...heaven, whence we

---

1 In the Jewish Apocalypses and in the Synoptic Gospels a similar variety of expectation is seen, God judges either in His own Person or through the agency of the Messiah.
2 In these first six passages the eschatological term '*the* wrath' is used.
3 Saints, or angels, or possibly both.
4 Cf. 'the last trump' (1 Cor. xv. 52).

ESCHATOLOGY

eagerly expect as a Saviour the Lord Jesus Christ' (Phil. iii. 20). 'Until the Lord come' (1 Cor. iv. 5). 'When He comes in order to be glorified in His holy ones and to be marvelled at in all them that have become believers' (2 Thes. i. 10). 'When Christ is manifested' (Col. iii. 4). See also 1 Tim. vi. 14, 15, 2 Tim. iv. 1, Tit ii. 13.

These passages for the most part picture the Advent of Christ as a visible event, much as it was pictured in Jewish Apocalypses. And two further features of Jewish expectation are preserved:

4. It will be in the near future[1]. St Paul expects that he and some, at least, of his readers will still be alive when it occurs (1 Cor. xv. 51, 1 Thes. iv. 15, 17). He and his contemporaries are they 'upon whom the ends of the ages are come' (1 Cor. x. 11). He advises the Corinthians not to marry, because the time is short, the world is passing away, and the tribulation of the End is imminent (1 Cor. vii. 28–31). 'The night is far spent, the day is at hand' (Rom. xiii 12). 'The God of peace shall bruise Satan under your feet shortly' (Rom. xvi. 20). 'Behold now is the acceptable time, behold now is the day of salvation' (2 Cor. vi 2).

5. It will be sudden. 'The day of the Lord as a thief in the night so it cometh.... Sudden destruction cometh upon them as pangs upon a woman with child' (1 Thes. v. 2, 3).

Two passages may here be studied which are unique in St Paul's writings, dealing respectively with events before and at the Advent.

[1] At the end of his ministry this thought may perhaps have faded away. It finds no expression in *Colossians* and *Ephesians* It is not, however, denied in Eph. ii. 7, iii. 21, where the ages and generations of the future perfected life are spoken of.

6. 2 Thes. ii. 3–12. The apostle warns his readers not to think that 'the day of the Lord has (actually) set in,' or 'is present.' 'Because (it will not occur) except the apostasy come first, and the man of lawlessness be revealed, the son of perdition, who opposeth and exalteth himself against everyone called God or an object of reverence, so that he sitteth in the temple of God, giving himself out to be God.... And now ye know the restraining force, that he [i.e. the man of lawlessness] may be revealed (only) in his proper time. Only the restrainer is now (present) until he be taken out of the way. And then shall the lawless one be revealed, whom the Lord Jesus will destroy with the breath of His mouth, and bring to nought by the splendour of His Parousia, him whose parousia is according to the working of Satan in all power[1], and signs, and false portents, and in all deception of unrighteousness to those who are being lost etc.'

This appears to be based partly on the language of Dan. xi. 36, and to refer to the mysterious conception held by many Jews of a supremely malignant power, who may be described almost as the devil in human shape. Immediately before the Last Day he would exercise his terrible power, but would then be destroyed by God. Such a Figure is probably referred to in Mk xiii. 14, 'the abomination of desolation standing where he[2] ought not.' St Paul declares that the Lord Jesus will destroy him. The man of lawlessness sets himself up as a counterpart of Christ[3]; his arrival is a parousia,

[1] I e. 'displayed in sheer force.'
[2] Notice the masculine pronoun.
[3] In 1 John ii. 18, iv. 3 the word Antichrist is used; the spirit of error is the spirit of Antichrist, 'and even now there are many Antichrists.'

accompanied by signs and portents. But, says the apostle, the great moral apostasy from God which comes with the man of lawlessness will not occur quite immediately. The restraining power of the Roman empire with its genius for law and order, represented by the Emperor, 'the restrainer,' for the moment keeps the awful catastrophe in check. This is the most generally accepted explanation of the passage, the details of which must be studied in commentaries[1].

7. 1 Cor. xv. 24–28. St Paul here deals with the relation of Christ to God the Father at the end of time. After speaking of the Resurrection of Christ the Firstfruits and afterwards of those who are Christ's at His Parousia, he proceeds: 'then (cometh) the end, when He delivereth up the Kingdom to God even the Father, when He hath annulled every rulership and every authority and power. For He must reign until He hath placed all His enemies under His feet. The final enemy that shall be annulled is death, for He hath subjected all things under His feet. But when it says "all things have been subjected" it is clearly exclusive of Him who subjected all things to Him. But when He hath subjected all things to Him, then shall the Son also Himself be subjected to Him who subjected all things to Him, that God may be all in all.'

This might at first sight seem to teach that Christ's Messianic reign, beginning at the Parousia, would continue until He had subdued all opposing powers, including the last of them, death. This Messianic reign would thus be analogous to the millennium of Rev. xx.

---

[1] See also Bousset, *The Antichrist Legend*, and H A. A. Kennedy, *St Paul's Conceptions of the Last Things*, pp. 207–221.

274 THE CHRISTIAN DOCTRINE OF ST PAUL

But this expectation is not found in the Gospels, and cannot with probability be seen here[1]. We must suppose that St Paul thought of death as destroyed when Christians rise at the Parousia. His conceptions need not involve the lapse of time. At the Parousia Christ is King, He puts down all opposing powers by His coming, and in the same timeless act delivers up the Kingdom to God the Father. His final and eternal 'subordination' to the Father does not imply an essential inequality of nature[2], for the apostle shews on every page that he believes Christ to be fully and utterly Divine. But the thought of subordination is bound up with the closing words of the passage, 'that God may be all in all,' and finds an echo in 1 Cor. xi. 3, 'the Head of every man is Christ, and the Head of Christ is God.' In the sphere of time, Christ is the supreme divine Head in relation to created things and beings; in eternity, God the Father is the supreme Head of all.

2. THE HOLY SPIRIT

But if St Paul's thought had not advanced beyond the expectation that Jesus was soon to return as the Messiah of the best Jewish hopes, he would have done no great work for Christianity. As far as he was concerned Christians would have continued to be what he in his persecuting days had thought them—a mere Jewish sect, holding notions about the Messiah that were condemned as pernicious and blasphemous.

[1] See Charles, *Eschatology*, pp. 349 f., 389 f.
[2] It was owing to the undue stress laid on this passage by Marcellus of Ancyra that the clause 'whose kingdom shall have no end' was inserted in the orthodox creed of the Church.

A fresh thought regarding the Last Day comes before us, not in the apocalypses but in the later prophets of the Old Testament, i.e. that the perfecting of God's people, to fit them for the ideal conditions of the divine sovereignty, would be wrought by the outpouring of God's Spirit; see Is. xliv. 3, Ezek. xxxvi. 27, xxxvii. 1–14, xxxix. 29, Joel ii. 28 f. This thought entered into the prediction uttered by John the Baptist, 'He that is mightier than I cometh after me.... He shall baptize you with the Holy Spirit' (Mk i. 7, 8). St Paul nowhere speaks explicitly of the outpouring of the Spirit as an event which will accompany the Messiah's Advent; and yet it was more effectual in the building up of his system of doctrine than any other eschatological idea. As in the case of the Messiahship of Jesus, the Jewish hope of the gift of the Spirit was transfigured by personal experience. Simon Peter and the rest of the earliest disciples underwent their experience on the day of Pentecost, the repentant Saul a little later. That they were in very truth endued with the Holy Spirit of God they all knew with the unshakeable conviction that the deepest experience can bring. In Acts ii. 17–21 the prophecy of Joel is recognised as finding fulfilment at Pentecost. But St Paul went much further, and worked out all the far-reaching consequences involved.

He thought of it in this way: the greatest of all the conditions accompanying the Messiah's Advent, the full and complete outpouring of the Spirit, *had already begun to make itself felt*. Christians had already received 'the firstfruits of the Spirit' (Rom. viii. 23), 'the pledge, or first instalment, of the Spirit' (2 Cor. i. 22, v. 5), which like a seal ensured to them the promise of the coming inheritance (Eph. i. 13. 14, iv. 30).

3. THE CHRISTIAN'S TRANSFERENCE INTO THE MESSIANIC KINGDOM

This thought is immeasurably important in St Paul's Christianity, and the student cannot be too careful to grasp it clearly. The gift of the Spirit, and therefore every blessing which is in store for God's elect in the ideal future, is theirs partially, potentially, proleptically, *now*. 'We know in part, and we prophesy in part; but when that which is perfect is come, then that which is in part shall be done away' (1 Cor. xiii. 9, 10). The present condition is to the future perfected condition as childhood to manhood (*v.* 11), or as a blurred vision in a mirror to a vision face to face (*v.* 12). Mostly, however, St Paul does not express in words the partialness or potentiality of what has been granted; he assumes that his readers will understand him, and uses exactly similar language for the present condition of Christians and their destined perfected condition. The latter was to be the final end of a process already begun.

The perfected condition is expressed, for example, in the words 'the kingdom of God' (1 Cor. xv. 50, 2 Thes. i. 5; cf. 2 Tim. iv. 1, 18); 'salvation,' or 'be saved' (Rom. v. 9, xiii. 11, 1 Cor. iii. 15, v. 5, 1 Thes. v. 8, 9; cf. 2 Tim. ii. 10); 'redemption' (Rom. viii. 23, Eph. i. 14, iv. 30); 'life,' or 'eternal life' (Rom. ii. 7, vi. 22, 2 Cor. v. 4); 'sonship[1]' (Rom viii. 23);

[1] υἱοθεσία, 'a making or constituting sons.' If it is translated 'adoption' it must be remembered that the word meant in Roman law a much more complete and irrevocable membership of the family than it means with us. But even so, it can in human life be only a legal fiction, whereas St Paul is thinking of a spiritual sonship which is *real*, produced by a real, living union with the Father. In the ideal future this union will be revealed in its perfection.

THE CHRISTIAN AND THE MESSIANIC KINGDOM 277

'inheritance[1]' (Eph 1. 14, Col. iii. 24); 'glory' (Rom. v. 2, viii. 18, 21, 1 Cor. xv. 43, 2 Cor. iv. 17, Phil. iii. 21, Col. i. 27, iii. 4; cf. 2 Tim. ii. 10); 'that which is perfect' (1 Cor. xiii. 10).

But the present condition is expressed in precisely parallel terms. In some passages the fact that that condition is a process tending towards the perfected condition makes it impossible to distinguish between present and future. Compare the future tense in the statement that the wicked 'shall not inherit the kingdom of God[2]' (1 Cor. vi. 9, 10, Gal. v. 21) with the present tense in the parallel statement that 'no fornicator...hath any inheritance in the kingdom of Christ and of God' (Eph. v. 5). 'The kingdom of God is not eating and drinking, but righteousness, and peace, and joy, in the Holy Spirit' (Rom. xiv. 17); it is not 'in word but in power' (1 Cor. iv. 20); God has 'translated us into the kingdom of the Son of His love' (Col. i. 13); He 'calleth [*v.l.* called] you into (or unto) His kingdom and glory' (1 Thes. ii. 12; cf. 1 Tim vi 12, 2 Tim. i. 9). Salvation is a process to be worked out fully (Phil. ii 12; cf. 1 Tim. ii. 4, 2 Tim. iii. 15); Christians are 'being saved' (1 Cor. i. 18, xv. 2, 2 Cor. ii. 15), and they 'were, *or* have been, saved' (Rom. viii. 24, Eph. ii. 5, 8; cf. 2 Tim i. 9), and 'bought'

---

1 In English law a person is not legally 'heir' till the death of the testator who has made him so. In Roman law his legal position during the testator's life was much more secure. This made it possible for St Paul to use the word to describe the relationship of Christians to God who does not die. He was also accustomed to it from its use in the Old Testament for the possession of the promised land by Israel; see Westcott, *Hebrews*, pp. 167-9

2 This, and the passages which follow, shew that it is inaccurate to say that the kingdom of God is the Church. The members of the Church possess all the privileges involved in being under God's sovereignty.

(1 Cor. vi. 20, vii. 23, Gal. iii. 13). 'Life,' 'eternal life' is God's present gift to those who are in Christ (Rom. vi. 4, 23, viii. 2, 10, 2 Cor. iv. 10, 11, Col. iii. 3; cf. 1 Tim. i. 16, vi. 12, 2 Tim. i. 1). 'Perfect' is applied to Christians now (1 Cor. ii. 6, xiv. 20, Phil. iii. 15, Col. iv. 12), although St Paul elsewhere denies that he is already 'perfected' (Phil. iii. 12; cf. 1 Cor. xiii. 10). Christians are 'saints' now (Rom. i. 7, viii. 27 and frequently), though sanctification is a life-long action of the Holy Spirit and of the indwelling Christ (Rom. vi. 19, 22, Eph. v. 26, 1 Thes. iv. 3, v. 23, 2 Thes. ii. 13). To attain to 'glory' is likewise a process (2 Cor. iii. 18). And see the use of the terms 'redemption' (Rom. iii. 24, 1 Cor. i. 30, Eph. i. 7, Col. i. 14; cf. 1 Tim. ii 6, Tit. ii. 14), 'sonship' (Rom. viii. 15, Gal. iv. 5, Eph. i. 5) and 'sons' (Rom. viii. 14, Gal. iii. 26, iv. 7); 'heirs,' 'inheritance' (Rom. viii. 17, Gal. iii. 29, iv. 7, Eph. 1. 18, v 5; cf. Tit. iii. 7).

A study of these passages will shew what St Paul meant by the 'pledge, or firstfruits, of the Spirit,' and the 'translation into the kingdom of the Son of God's love.' Christians are already transferred from the old into the new, and are already (potentially) in possession of the blessings of the Messianic age.

The condition out of which they are transferred St Paul calls, in echoes of Jewish language, 'this age' (R.V. 'world') (Rom. xii. 2, 1 Cor. i. 20, ii. 6–8, iii. 18, 2 Cor. iv. 4), 'the age of this world' (Eph. ii. 2), 'the age of the present evil' (Gal. i. 4), which is under the domination of 'the god of this age' (2 Cor. iv. 4), 'the prince of the authority of the air' (Eph. ii. 2), 'the world-rulers of this darkness' (Eph. vi. 12), 'the authority of darkness' (Col. i. 13); and the terms 'rulerships' (ἀρχαί), 'authorities' (ἐξουσίαι), 'powers' (δυνάμεις), 'lordship' (κυριότης) (Rom. viii. 38, 1 Cor. xv. 24, Eph. i. 21, ii. 2, iii. 10, vi. 12, Col. i. 13, ii. 10, 15) and 'elements' (στοιχεῖα) (Gal iv. 3, 9, Col. ii. 8, 20) contain, more or less explicitly, the same thought of quasi-personal forces opposed to the sovereignty of God.

4. THE NATURE OF MAN

This conviction of the transference of Christians from the old condition to the new profoundly influenced St Paul's ideas as to the nature of man. Every man born into the world consists of ψυχή (*psyche*, 'soul'), and σῶμα ('body'). The former is the natural life, the non-corporeal element in human nature. 'The first man Adam became a living *psyche*' (1 Cor. xv. 45). This included νοῦς, 'mind,' 'intellectual faculty' (Rom. vii. 25, 1 Cor. xiv. 14, 15), and καρδία, 'heart,' a wider term covering the ideas of mind, emotion, and will *Psyche* is in itself a word implying neither blame nor praise; it is neutral and colourless. And the same is true of 'body.' St Paul was quite untouched by the tendency to think of the body as something evil because it is material.

But when the ordinary, natural man becomes a Christian, translated (potentially) into the Messianic kingdom, he is at once (potentially) immersed in, filled, permeated, with the divine Spirit. He is not a being composed of body, soul, and spirit[1], but of body and soul plunged into a new world of being, a spiritual atmosphere, a spiritual ocean; he is in possession of an

[1] In a single passage, 1 Thes. v. 23, they are mentioned in a way that might suggest that. And this has led some writers to use the word 'trichotomy' in dealing with St Paul's ideas on psychology.

all-pervading divine force. See Rom. viii., 1 Cor. ii., xii. The Christian is thus a different being from the ordinary, natural man. And this contrast is expressed by the adjectives πνευματικός, 'spiritual,' and ψυχικός, 'psychic,' 'natural.' See 1 Cor. ii. 14, 15 and xv. 44, 46, in the former of which the adjectives are applied to the mind, in the latter to the body. Occasionally St Paul uses *pneuma*, 'spirit,' loosely of the mind and feelings, much in the sense of 'heart' (e g. 1 Cor. ii. 11, v. 3, xvi. 18, 2 Cor. ii. 13, vii. 13, Col. ii. 5); but in the great mass of passages the Christian's 'spirit' is that which he possesses, or in which he lives, in virtue of his having been transferred into the new condition of existence in the Spirit of God. Thus there are passages in which the Christian's spirit and God's Spirit are not strictly distinguishable (see next section).

That which at present prevents man from living in the full and actual condition of 'spirit' is *Sin*. And the element in him which affords sin its handle and instrument is not the *psyche* but the *body*. When considered from the spiritual point of view the body holds a noble place in man's life. The sinful heathen 'dishonour their bodies' (Rom. i. 24); a fornicator sins against his body (1 Cor. vi. 18) The body supplies St Paul with one of his greatest metaphors for the unity of Christians in Christ (1 Cor. xii.). The bodies of Christians can be 'presented as a living sacrifice, holy, acceptable to God' (Rom. xii. 1); they are 'limbs of Christ' (1 Cor. vi. 15), and 'the temple of the Holy Spirit' (*v.* 19). Christians can 'glorify God in their body' (*v.* 20), and 'be holy in body and in spirit' (vii 34) The life of Jesus can be manifested in their body (2 Cor. iv. 10), and Christ be magnified in it (Phil. i 20) All this is in the present.

But finally, when that which is perfect is come, their bodies when raised will be perfectly 'spiritual' (1 Cor. xv. 44). The Holy Spirit that dwells in Christians will 'quicken their mortal bodies' (Rom. viii. 11), and those bodies will be 'redeemed' (v. 23), and 'conformed to the body of Christ's glory' (Phil. iii. 21). St Paul expects to be, not divested of the material body—'unclothed,' 'naked'—but 'clothed upon' with the 'habitation which is from heaven,' i.e. the heavenly body, 'that what is mortal may be swallowed up by life.' That was God's purpose, and He pledged it by the 'first instalment of the Spirit' (2 Cor v. 1–5). 'This corruptible thing must put on incorruption, and this mortal thing must put on immortality. And when this mortal thing shall have put on immortality, then shall come to pass the saying that is written, Death is swallowed up into victory[1]' (1 Cor. xv. 53, 54).

On the other hand, when considered as the handle and instrument of sin it is described as 'the body of sin' (Rom. vi. 6), 'the body of this death' (vii. 24), 'dead because of sin' (viii. 10); it is 'the body of our humiliation' (Phil. iii 21), and must be kept in control by the sternest discipline (1 Cor. ix. 27).

But more often St Paul expresses this by employing the word *flesh*. In Old Testament language 'flesh' stood for the material in man, as distinct from the non-material, the 'spirit' (cf. Rom i. 3, ii. 28, iv. 1, ix. 3, 5, 8 and elsewhere). But when the meaning of 'spirit' is raised by St Paul to a higher plane, that of 'flesh' is thrust to a lower one. His own bitter experience of the internal war involved in living the spiritual life, owing to the

[1] εἰς νῖκος, the LXX equivalent in Is. xxv. 8 for a Hebrew word meaning 'for ever.'

fact that the hostile force of sin employed as its handle and instrument the body which is made of flesh, led him for the most part to prefer 'flesh' to 'body' as the right word with which to express a moral contrast with 'spirit' (Rom. vii. 5, 18, 25, viii. 3–13, xiii. 14, 1 Cor. v. 5, Gal. v. 16, 17, 19, 24, vi. 8). And as he used ψυχικός, 'psychic,' so he could use σαρκικός, 'fleshly,' and σαρκινός, 'made of flesh,' in the sense of non-spiritual (Rom. vii. 14, xv. 27, 1 Cor. iii. 1, 3, ix. 11, 2 Cor. i. 12, x. 4), which sometimes, from the nature of the case, verges on 'unspiritual' or 'sinful.'

5. THE WORK OF THE SPIRIT IN THE CHRISTIAN

1. The ultimate aim of the Spirit's work is to bring to completion 'the age-long purpose' of God (Eph. iii. 11; cf. 2 Tim. i. 9, Tit. i. 2). This purpose was shewn in the 'calling' of Christians (Rom. viii. 28), their 'election' (ix. 11), and their 'foreordaining' (Eph. i. 11), in accordance with God's good pleasure which was purposed in Christ for a working out of His plan in the fulness of the times, i.e. to sum up all things in Christ (v. 10). This includes the blessings enumerated above, which comprise the perfected condition of Christians, all of which are potentially won already.

2. The present nature of the Spirit's work.

(a) It is an atmosphere in which Christians 'walk about' (Gal. v. 16), 'live, and walk straight' (v. 25), and with which they are filled (Eph. v. 18). He dwells in them (Rom. viii. 11, 1 Cor. iii. 16, vi. 19; cf. 2 Tim. i. 14), and if He dwells in them, they are 'in [the condition or atmosphere of] spirit' (Rom. viii. 9); in [the] Spirit they are fervent (xii 11), and have joy (xiv. 17, 1 Thes. i. 6), and freedom (2 Cor. iii. 17), they have a 'common share in the Holy Spirit' (xiii. 13), and hence a 'unity of the Spirit' (Eph. iv. 3).

(*b*) It is a power working in their moral life. In it they abound in hope (Rom. xv. 13; cf. Gal. v. 5); their character is an epistle of Christ written by the Spirit of the Lord (2 Cor. iii. 3), and it exhibits 'the fruit of the Spirit' (Gal. v. 22; cf. vi. 8).

(*c*) It is the Source of spiritual blessings: the love of God (Rom. v. 5); life and peace (viii. 6), leading (viii. 14; cf. Gal. v. 18); assurance of recognition as God's sons (viii. 15, 16; cf. Gal. iv. 6); help and intercession (viii. 26); manifold *charismata* (1 Cor xii.); revelation of the inconceivable blessings prepared for the spiritual man, i.e the Christian (ii. 10–16).

6. THE SPIRIT OF CHRIST

A further truth essential to St Paul's teaching emerged from his personal experience, and from that of the first Christians. When he was endued with the Holy Spirit of God, he knew it to be the Spirit of the crucified and risen Christ. Whether any reasoning helped him to form this conclusion we cannot tell. It is not impossible that such passages as Is. xi. 2, xlii. 1, which speak of the divine inspiration of the Messianic prophet[1], may have done something to define and strengthen his intuitive certainty. We can see only the results in his teaching. He is so unutterably sure that he is filled with the Spirit of the risen Lord that the language which he uses about

[1] Cf. Acts x. 38.

Christ and about the Holy Spirit is sometimes hardly distinguishable. The Spirit of God and the Spirit of Christ are one and the same (Rom. viii. 9). Christ and the Holy Spirit are spoken of in parallelism (ix. 1). 'He that is joined to the Lord [i e. Christ] is one spirit' (1 Cor. vi. 17). 'The Spirit of His Son[1]' (Gal. iv. 6) His Spirit in the inner man is equated with Christ dwelling in your hearts by faith (Eph iii. 16, 17). 'The supply of the Spirit of Christ Jesus' (Phil. i. 19). And most explicitly 'The Lord is the Spirit' (2 Cor. iii. 17), 'the Lord Spirit[2]' (v. 18). 'The last Adam became a life-giving Spirit' (1 Cor. xv. 45).

7. 'IN CHRIST'

Thus if the Holy Spirit of God is the Spirit of Christ, it is equally true to say either that the Holy Spirit or Christ is in Christians, and they in Him. No thought is more characteristic of St Paul than that which he expresses by 'in Christ,' 'in the Lord,' and the like.

1. The heavenly calling of Christians is 'in Christ Jesus' (Phil iii. 14; cf. 2 Tim. i. 9), and their election (Eph. i. 4). 'In Christ' is performed the saving act which places them (potentially) in the perfect condition which they are finally to reach: Forgiveness (Eph. i. 7, iv. 32, Col. i. 14), Redemption (Rom. iii. 24, Eph. i. 7, Col. i 14), Freedom from condemnation (Rom. viii. 1), and from law (Gal. ii. 4), Justification (v. 17), Life (Rom. vi. 11, 23, viii. 2). In Christ Jesus they derive their spiritual being from God (1 Cor i. 30), they become a new creation (2 Cor v 17; cf. Eph ii. 10,

---

[1] Cf. St Luke's language, 'He hath poured forth this' (Acts ii. 33), 'the Spirit of Jesus allowed them not' (xvi. 7).
[2] ἀπὸ κυρίου πνεύματος See *J. Th. S.* Oct. 1915, pp. 60–65.

Col. ii. 11, 12), and are 'filled' by union with the whole 'Fulness' of the Godhead which dwelleth in Him bodily (Col. ii. 10); and thus they have 'a share, *or* fellowship, in Christ' as they have in the Spirit (1 Cor. i 9); God gave them grace and kindness 'in the Beloved,' 'in Christ Jesus' (Eph. i. 6, ii. 7); 'in Him' they were 'made His lot' (i. 11); 'in Christ' He blessed them with every spiritual blessing in the sphere of heavenly things (i. 3), and raised them together and made them sit together in the sphere of heavenly things (ii. 6).

The process, also, by which this potential perfection is made real and actual is 'in Christ'. they are sanctified (1 Cor. 1. 2), rooted and built up (Col. ii. 7), and taught (Eph iv. 21); their hearts and thoughts are guarded (Phil. iv. 7); God always leads them in triumph (2 Cor. ii. 14). 'In Christ' they are one body (Rom. xii. 5; cf Gal. iii. 28, v. 6); in particular Jews and Gentiles are made one (Eph. ii 13, 15, 22, iii 6), the whole building 'grows into a holy temple in the Lord' (ii 21), and in Him they have boldness, and access to God (iii. 12).

And the ultimate end of this process is also 'in Christ': salvation (Rom v. 10, 'in His life'), and life (1 Cor. xv. 22).

2. St Paul is also led to employ the expression in a large number of passages with less doctrinal precision, but in a free and incidental manner which implies the doctrine quite as forcibly as it is taught in definite statements 'In Christ' he speaks (Rom. ix. 1, 2 Cor. ii. 17, xii. 19), testifies (Eph. iv. 17), is persuaded (Rom. xiv. 14), boasts (xv. 17, 1 Cor. xv 31, Phil. i 26), is confident (Gal. v. 10, Phil ii. 24, 2 Thes. iii. 4), hopes (Phil. ii. 19); he salutes his readers (Rom. xvi 22, 1 Cor. xvi. 24, cf. *v.* 19, Phil iv. 21), and exhorts them (1 Thes. iv. 1);

he asks for a reception of Phoebe (Rom. xvi. 2) and Epaphroditus (Phil. ii. 29); he has an 'open door' (2 Cor. ii. 12); he is a prisoner (Eph. iv. 1), and his bonds are manifest (Phil. i. 13). 'In Christ' Christians can have encouragement (ii. 1), and power (Eph. vi. 10); they can rejoice (Phil. iii. 1, iv. 4, 10), stand fast (iv. 1, 1 Thes. iii. 8), and be of one mind (Phil. iv. 2); their labour is not in vain (1 Cor. xv. 58), children are to obey their parents (Eph. vi. 1), in the Lord.

In several other passages 'in Christ,' 'in the Lord,' and the like, are simply equivalent to 'Christian,' a word which St Paul never uses[1] because in his day it was still a nickname employed by opponents. See Rom. xvi. 3, 7–13, 1 Cor. iii 1, iv. 10, 15, 17, vii. 22, 39, ix. 1, 2, xv. 18, 2 Cor. xii. 2, Gal. i. 22, Eph. i. 1, Phil. i. 1, 14, Col. i. 2, 1 Thes. 1. 1, ii. 14, iv. 16, v. 12, 2 Thes. i. 1.

3. The same great truth is stated also, though less frequently in explicit language, from the converse point of view. Christ is in Christians; see 2 Cor. xiii. 5, Col. i. 27. Ideally, potentially, He takes the place of man's Self, so that as a Christian it is not he that lives his life but Christ (Gal. ii. 20); and St Paul describes God's purpose in converting him in the words 'it pleased God...to reveal His Son in me' (i. 15, 16). But this is, in fact, a gradual process, so that he prays for his readers that 'Christ may be formed in you' (iv. 19), and that 'Christ may dwell in your hearts by faith' (Eph. iii. 17).

8. CHRISTIANS

1. Those who are in Christ, and Christ in them, live one Life, like the limbs of a body, or the parts of a

[1] It occurs only in Acts xi 26, xxvi. 28, 1 Pet. iv. 16.

building. For the latter see 1 Cor. iii. 9, 16, 17, 2 Cor. vi. 16, Eph. ii. 21. The former is St Paul's favourite simile; see Rom. xii. 4, 5, 1 Cor. vi. 15, x. 17, xii. 12–27, Eph. i. 23, ii. 16, iv. 4, 12, 13, 15, 16, v. 30, Col. i. 18, 24, ii. 19, iii. 15. In some of these passages it is not a mere simile, but a vivid and significant metaphor for the real oneness of Christians in Christ. (1) He is the Whole Body of which they are the members[1] (1 Cor. xii. 12, 27, Eph. iv. 12, 13, v 30, Col. i. 24), so that St Paul can say that 'in Him dwelleth all the Pleroma of the Godhead *bodily-wise*, $\sigma\omega\mu\alpha\tau\iota\kappa\hat{\omega}\varsigma$ (Col. ii. 9). (2) He is the chiefest member, the Head, by which the whole body derives its nourishment and cohesion[2] (Eph. iv. 15, 16, Col. i. 18, ii. 19).

2. And the body is the Church, the *Ecclesia*, a word derived from the LXX (where it represents the Hebrew *ḳāhāl*, the assembly of Israel). It occurs frequently in St Paul's epistles, sometimes for the whole body of Christ, sometimes for the Christian community in a particular town, so that it can be used in the plural, in three passages (Rom. xvi. 5, 1 Cor. xvi. 19, Philem. 2) it is even a group of Christians meeting in a particular house.

3. A further line of thought, which St Paul inherited from his Jewish faith, and applied to Christians, is that God made them the objects of His knowledge and determination from the beginning. (1) He 'called' them, 'according to purpose' (Rom. viii. 28), to receive the blessings won for them by Christ. This thought occurs *passim*. (2) Before calling them, He had 'set them

[1] Cf. John xv. 1.
[2] That a modern physiologist would demur to this does not lessen the value of the metaphor as St Paul employed it.

apart' (Rom. i. 1, Gal. i. 15, Eph. i. 5, 11). (3) And had 'foreknown' them, as He had foreknown Israel (Rom. xi. 2). These three stages (with the subsequent stages 'justified' and 'glorified') are enumerated in Rom. viii. 29, 30.

And Christians are divinely 'elected' or 'selected' from the mass of mankind (Rom. viii. 33, xi. 5, 7, 28, xvi. 13, Eph. i. 4, Col. iii. 12, 1 Thes i. 4; cf. 2 Tim. ii. 10, Tit. i. 1); God's 'purpose was according to the principle of selection' (Rom. ix. 11). The incidental way in which St Paul speaks of it as a recognised truth as early as 1 *Thessalonians* shews that it must have formed part of his preaching from the first[1].

4. Thus non-Christians, i.e. 'psychic,' non-spiritual men, and Christians, i.e. spiritual men, stand over against each other as two distinct creations, or families. The former are sons, children, of the flesh (Rom. ix. 8), of wrath (Eph. ii. 3), of disobedience (ii. 2, v. 6), the latter of God (Rom viii. 14, 16, 17, 19, 21, ix. 8, Gal. iii. 26, iv. 6, 7, Phil. ii. 15). And these families are descended from, and represented by, two distinct founders or heads, the former being 'the first Adam,' the latter 'the last Adam' (Rom. v. 12-19, 1 Cor. xv. 21, 22, 45, 47). The change, the 'translation,' from the former to the latter condition is described metaphorically as the 'putting off the old man,' i.e. the old self derived from the first Adam, and the 'putting on the new man'

[1] Foreknowledge, determination, selection, and calling, considered in the abstract would logically exclude man's responsibility, and power of choice and voluntary action. But St Paul shews in many passages a clear recognition that in practice the latter are not excluded. He does not attempt any formal synthesis, he simply asserts both sides of the paradox Hence Pelagians and Arminians, and their opponents, could alike claim the support of his words.

derived from, and existing in, Christ (Eph. iv. 22, 24, Col. iii. 9, 10, cf. Rom. xiii. 14), or the crucifying of the old self (Rom. vi. 6).

5. And from this point St Paul was able to look forward to the final consummation, when all mankind, with the redemption of their bodies, would be fully revealed as sons of the new spiritual family, or sons of God; and with them, and dependent upon them, the whole creation which at present groans and travails in the pain of bringing to birth a perfected world (Rom. viii. 22, 23). Then all will come, i.e. all as one body, 'unto a perfect man, unto the measure of the stature of the fulness of Christ' (Eph. iv. 13), and God's age-long purpose will be accomplished of 'summing up all things in Christ, the things in heaven and the things on earth' (1 10). In a word, that which is now potential will then be actual.

9. DELIVERANCE FROM SIN AND LAW

We have now traced St Paul's two-fold thought: (1) of the Last Day, when Christ shall appear in person, and Christians will reach the consummation of the spiritual life in accordance with God's age-long plan; (2) of the present life of Christians, which is ideally and potentially the perfected life, into which they have been 'translated' from the old non-spiritual condition, but which is in fact a process of sanctification which is being worked by the power of the Holy Spirit and of the indwelling Christ.

We have next to consider what this translation, or transference, from the old to the new involved. St Paul's thought at this point was influenced neither by Jewish nor Greek thought, but solely by his own spiritual experience. He was profoundly conscious that the change which had been wrought in himself was a deliverance from the power of sin. The principal passage is Rom. vii. 14–25, where he describes the internal warfare that raged in him between his flesh with its inclination to sin, and his mind which wanted to serve God. Deliverance comes from God alone through Jesus Christ our Lord.

But if Christians are thus delivered through Jesus Christ, what is the condition of non-Christians? Non-Christians were either Jews or Gentiles. *Jews* had been given a divinely appointed law which was intended to deliver from sin, and lead to life (Rom. vii. 10 a). In its true nature it was 'holy and righteous and good[1]' (*v.* 12), and spiritual (*v.* 14). In his true inner self St Paul consents to the law that it is good (*v.* 16), and delights in it (*v.* 22). And *Gentiles*, though they did not possess a law of the same explicit kind as that of the Jews, nevertheless possessed the divine law of conscience written in their hearts (Rom. ii. 14, 15), given them with the same purpose.

But the law failed in its object; it failed in the case of Jew and Gentile alike (Rom. i., ii.). It could make a man 'righteous' before God only if he kept all its requirements perfectly (Gal. v. 3); 'not the hearers of law are righteous before God, but the doers of law shall be constituted righteous' (Rom. ii. 13); 'Moses writes that the man that doeth the righteousness which comes from law shall live by it' (x. 5). But there is something in the nature of man which prevents him from keeping

[1] In 1 Tim. i. 8–10 the statement that 'the law is good' is made from a different point of view

DELIVERANCE FROM SIN AND LAW

the law perfectly, i.e. the tendency of his fleshly nature to sin To make righteous was something which the law was unable to do; it was weak through man's flesh (viii. 3).

This tendency to sin is found in every human being born of Adam. It is as inevitable and 'natural' as the downward drag of gravitation; and the responsibility of man's will in the effort to climb upwards is as little annulled in the one case as in the other[1]. Augustine's expression *peccatum originis*, 'original sin,' is not found in the Bible, but is capable of conveying a real truth if St Paul is rightly understood. If the consequence of the transference of the Christian into the new family in Christ is potential righteousness, the consequence of the birth of the human race in Adam is *potential sin*. It is a mistake to draw a distinction between original sin and original guilt; if they are potential, they are identical. It is in this potential sense of original sin that St Paul says 'As through one man's disobedience the many were constituted sinners, even so through the obedience of the one shall the many be constituted righteous' (Rom. v. 19); and it is potential guilt that is implied in the words 'we were by nature children of wrath even as the rest [of mankind]' (Eph. ii. 3)[2]. But it is a mournful fact that this potentiality of sin has in every human being, except Jesus, become actual, and therefore 'death passed unto all men, because all sinned' (Rom. v. 12).

This tendency to sin is the burden of St Paul's cry

[1] See Sanday and Headlam, *Romans*, pp. 136–8.
[2] In this sense Article IX in the English Prayer Book must be understood. It should be noted that its expression 'original righteousness' is without warrant in the Bible; 'original innocence' would be a much better term.

in Rom. vii. 14–25. It is such that a law commanding him not to sin has precisely the opposite effect to that which was intended. It makes him sin. He says he would not, for example, have known covetous desire had it not been for the tenth commandment (vii. 7); 'through law comes knowledge of sin' (iii. 20); 'the power of sin is the law' (1 Cor. xv. 56). Sin simply made use of the law as an occasion or handle (Rom. vii. 8); innocence was life, but when the law came, sin sprang into life and brought with it spiritual death (v. 9)[1]. This spiritual death, of which physical death is the outward expression, is 'the curse of the law' (Gal. iii. 13), i.e. the curse attached to the non-observance of any single one of all its commands (v. 10). Man's tendency to sin, then, produced the terrible anomaly that the commandment which was intended to lead to life, did in fact lead to death (Rom. vii. 10) and became a curse; and no law was, in fact, given which could make alive (Gal. iii. 21). Therefore, man being what he is, righteousness cannot be gained by obedience to law (Rom. iii. 20, Gal. ii. 16, iii. 11).

St Paul, however, does not let go the thought that the law had a real, though temporary, place in God's plan. By exciting to action man's sinful tendency, it shewed up the true sinfulness of sin (Rom. v. 20[2], vii. 13, Gal. iii 19), and thus, by its very inability to justify and save, pointed on to something better. 'Through law I died to law' (Gal. ii. 19); it was 'our παιδαγωγός unto Christ' (iii. 24), i.e. the guardian and attendant of

[1] For the connexion between sin and death see also Rom. v. 12, 14, 17, 21, vi. 16, 21, 23, vii 5, 13, 24, viii 2, 6, 1 Cor. xv. 21, 56.
[2] In this passage ἵνα virtually expresses a result, not strictly a purpose; cf. 1. 20 εἰς τὸ εἶναι κτλ.

our childhood to make us fit for the privilege of adult life as sons. Thus 'Christ is the end of law unto [i.e. leading to and resulting in] righteousness to everyone that believeth' (Rom. x. 4).

10. RIGHTEOUSNESS, GRACE, AND FAITH

1. But what did St Paul mean by 'righteousness'? Jewish ethical ideas were largely dominated by forensic, legal notions. Social duties were 'owed' by man to man. If this debt was not paid, it was as though there were a lawsuit between them, in which the debtor were proved to be in the wrong, i.e. guilty, and the injured person in the right, i.e. 'righteous' Similarly in the case of moral duties towards God, all sins were 'debts' (cf. Mat. vi. 12), and God could always shew Himself to be in the right or 'righteous' (Rom. iii. 26), and the sinner in the wrong (cf. Exod. ix. 27, Ps. li. 4). Since, then, no man could keep all the requirements of the law, no man could be 'righteous' before God.

But St Paul teaches that in the Gospel of Christianity a new method of obtaining righteousness is revealed (Rom. iii. 21). God does not merely acquit, or impute righteousness to, a man though he is guilty; that is not even human justice, much less divine. The Christian, as we have seen, is 'translated' from the old condition in which righteousness was impossible into the new condition of oneness with Christ. Christ is perfectly righteous, and *in Him* the Christian is potentially, proleptically, righteous; ideally sin is now for him impossible (Rom. vi. 1–11, 15–23, vii. 1–6). God treats us, as Augustine says, 'non quales sumus sed quales futuri sumus'—'not as we are, but as we are going to be.' It is, in fact, one of the many aspects of the final consummation in the divine Kingdom, which is (potentially) ours *now*; 'having been justified now in His blood' (Rom. v. 9); 'that we might become the righteousness of God in Him' (2 Cor. v. 21).

2. Obviously this is not what we deserve; it is sheer kindness on God's part, 'which He freely bestowed upon us in the Beloved' (Eph. i. 6). This St Paul calls χάρις, *Grace*, and his pages are full of the thought.

3. But on the other hand grace is not bestowed 'automatically,' indiscriminately on everyone. We are not translated from the old condition into the new against our will. Our whole being must co-operate by desiring and accepting the transference, thus being united with Christ and obtaining all the blessings which that involves. This desire and acceptance with the whole being St Paul calls πίστις, *Faith*. It is far from being a mere intellectual acceptance of facts about Christ. It is that condition or attitude of our being which performs our necessary part in making real the transference already ideally enacted. It includes a trust in God, a self-delivery, a self-abandonment to God for Him to do what we cannot do for ourselves. It is a living, experimental acceptance of oneness with Christ, which, from the nature of the case, springs from repentance (Rom. ii. 4[1]), and issues in a life of sanctification

[1] Only here, and in 2 Cor. vii 9, 10, does St Paul use the word 'repentance.' But that does not imply that he thinks little of its necessity. The longing desire for righteousness, and the intense conviction that nothing but the transference in Christ from the old to the new can give it, so obviously involve sorrow for sin, and 'change of mind' (which is the meaning of μετάνοια) that he does not dwell upon it in writing to Christians, all of whom he regards as having experienced it. In Rom. ii. 4 he addresses non-Christians, who need it, and

by which the potential becomes actual. A man who does not live the life of sanctification allows his transference into the new order to remain nominal, and therefore null and void. He must 'work out his own salvation with fear and trembling, for it is God that worketh in him both to will and to work for His good pleasure' (Phil. ii. 12, 13). St Paul in no sense teaches that faith is *opposed to* works, but only that faith must, in the order of effectiveness for obtaining righteousness, *precede* works[1]. For a Christian to move the works of the law, for example circumcision, into the primary place is to be 'nullified from Christ,' and to 'fall from grace' (Gal. v. 4).

This teaching on faith, like that of grace, is paramount in St Paul's system. 'By grace ye have been saved through faith' (Eph. ii. 8); both are the gift of God (*ib.*), and the two are mutually necessary and complementary, not only for the act of transference into the new condition but also for the process of sanctification which must follow.

11. JEW AND GENTILE

The deduction from this is inevitable. If Christians are delivered from the law, and from the sin which it excited, if they are translated into the kingdom of Christ by God's sheer kindness, appropriated by them through faith, all distinction of Jew and Gentile in God's sight necessarily vanishes. Jews as such, and

in 2 Cor. vii. 9, 10 he is not writing doctrinally, but very practically to Christians guilty of a particular sin.

[1] In Jam ii. 14–26 is taught the complementary truth, which St Paul would have been the last to deny, that 'faith apart from works is dead.'

Gentiles as such, belong to the old condition. Once translated into the new they become united as one body in Christ, one Spirit. This was not a truth which St Paul could have learnt from any earlier Jewish writings. The universalism to be found in several of them after the exile was a readiness to receive Gentiles into the Jewish Church with all its privileges. Some Jews went further, and were willing to admit Gentiles to a partial share of Jewish privileges on condition of a partial acceptance of Jewish rules of life. But St Paul was the apostle of the Gentiles because he taught—not a universalistic Judaism, but—a universal Christ in whom all distinctions are transcended. See the following passages: Rom i. 16, ii. 9–11, iii. 22, 29, 30, ix. 24–26, x. 4, 11, 12, xi. 32, 1 Cor. i 24, xii. 13, Gal. iii. 7–9, 14, 28, v. 6, vi. 15, Eph. ii. 11–18, iii. 6, Col iii. 11. His universal Gospel was thus the only possible conclusion from the whole course of his argument that we have hitherto traced. It was in no sense derived from his Hellenism, though the line along which his thoughts moved may perhaps have been rendered easier by his upbringing as a Jew of the Dispersion, which would give him a natural sympathy towards the better class of Gentiles, such as were attracted by Jewish monotheism.

On the other hand the rejection of the Jews as Jews from their privileged position before God caused him acute grief. But he thought the matter out, and wrote his conclusions in Rom. ix.–xi. (see pp. 199 ff.).

The apostle illustrates his teaching in this and the two foregoing sections by means of Old Testament exegesis of a kind which would appeal to his Jewish contemporaries, Rom. iv , ix. 7–9, Gal. iii., iv. 21–v. 1. At Sinai God made a 'covenant' with Israel, i e. a promise of blessing on

JEW AND GENTILE

condition that they observed the Mosaic Law. But centuries earlier than this (Gal. iii. 17), God made a covenant with Abraham in which no conditions of obedience to law were laid down, and no human mediator, or angelic agents, were needed (*v.* 19). He did this because Abraham had obtained the righteousness which comes from faith (Rom. iv. 13-25). It was also earlier than his circumcision, which was only a seal of the righteousness which he had previously won through faith (Rom. iv. 1-12), but which became, in Israelite thought, one of the principal 'works of the law.' This covenant was therefore a 'promise,' independent of works, and arising out of God's sheer kindness

But this covenant or promise had reference to a 'seed' (Rom. iv. 13, 16, Gal. iii. 16), which has proved to consist not of Abraham's physical, but his spiritual descendants in Christ, 1 e those who share his faith and obtain his righteousness promised to them, and won for them by Christ (Rom. iv. 11, 12, 16, 17, 23-25, Gal. iii. 6-9, 14). Thus Jews on the one hand, and all who have faith on the other, are represented allegorically in Abraham's son by Hagar a slave-woman, and in his son by Sarah a free woman. The slavery of the Law and the freedom of the Gospel thus stand in two categories (Gal. iv. 21-v. 1):

Hagar	Sarah
Ishmael born after the flesh	Isaac born after the Spirit
The Old Covenant at Sinai	The New Covenant[1]
The Law	The Promise
The earthly Jerusalem	Jerusalem that is above
Slavery	Freedom

Those who belong to the former are 'children of the flesh,' to the latter 'children of the promise' (Rom. ix. 8,

[1] Cf 1 Cor. xi. 25, 2 Cor. iii. 6, 14.

Gal. iv. 28, 29). And it is a 'promise of the Spirit' (Gal. iii. 14, Eph. i. 13; cf. iii. 6). Elsewhere St Paul regards all the pre-Mosaic covenants in the same light, as promises (cf. Rom. ix. 4) of which Christians are the true heirs (Rom. xv. 8, Eph. ii. 12).

12. THE CROSS

1. It will be clear from all that has been said up to this point how vital to St Paul's Christianity is the truth of the transference of Christians from the old condition into the new, i.e. into the kingdom of Christ, the life of the Spirit. But one further step backward must be taken. How was this transference made possible? St Paul's answer is that Christ who died and rose, Christ in whom we live and who lives in us, Himself passed from the old condition to the new. He became the Founder, Head, Representative, of the new spiritual family by doing so (Col. i. 18; cf. Rom. viii. 29). The old condition meant sin, and therefore involved death. Christ's death was due to sin; not His own sin; but God in His love for men made His sinless Son 'to be sin on our behalf' (2 Cor. v. 21). Nowhere in the Pauline epistles is death actually described as the 'punishment' for sin, nor is God ever said to have punished His Son. But spiritual death is, in fact, the inevitable result of sin (Rom. vi. 23), and physical death its necessary outward expression. St Paul calls them both 'death' without distinction. In the case of Christ the outward expression took the form of the most shameful death that could be inflicted (Phil. ii 8), corresponding with the curse laid by the law upon the world's sin which He took upon Himself (Gal. iii. 10, 13). If He had died

and remained dead—in other words, if His continued existence after death had not differed in kind from that of all human beings who had died before Him—death would have been the result of sin ('punishment' as we say) pure and simple. But this was not the purpose that the love of God had in view. His design was that death should lead to life, so that death should not merely be the result of the sin with which Christ identified Himself, but should also be a death *unto* sin, the climax and consummation of that spiritual death unto sin which He exhibited throughout His earthly life by perfect humility and obedience (Phil. ii. 8). His death—continually during His life, and finally upon the Cross— freed Him from the world's sin, and He was carried over, 'translated,' into the new condition of the Resurrection life.

His life out of death was then available for all men; and Christians are those in whom He lives. Hence not only is His life theirs, but His method of gaining life is also theirs; 'One died on behalf of all; then all died; and He died on behalf of all that they who live might no longer live unto themselves, but unto Him who on their behalf died and was raised' (2 Cor v. 14, 15; Rom. v. 8, vi. 2, 8, 11, vii. 4, x 9, Gal. ii. 20, vi 14, Col. ii. 20, iii. 3; cf. 2 Tim. ii. 11).

It is inaccurate and misleading to say simply that the Cross is the centre of St Paul's religion. Its centre is the *transference* from death to life, from the old to the new. 'It is Christ that died, yea rather that is risen again' (Rom. viii. 34). Sometimes he refers to the former (Rom. iii. 25, v. 6–8, viii. 3, 32, xiv 15, 1 Cor. i. 13, 17, 18, 23, 24, ii 2, 8, v. 7, vi 20, vii 23, viii. 11, xi. 26, Gal. 1. 4, ii. 21, iii. 1, 13, v. 11, vi. 12, 14, Eph. i. 7

ii 13–16, v. 2, 25, Phil. iii. 18, Col. i. 20, 22, ii. 14, 1 Thes. ii. 15), or to the latter (Rom. i. 4, viii. 11, x. 9, 1 Cor. vi. 14, xv. 12–21, Gal. i. 1, Eph. i. 20, ii. 5, 6, Col. 1. 18, 1 Thes. i. 10, cf. 2 Tim. i. 10, ii. 8); but he also coordinates them (Rom. iv. 24, 25, vi. 3–11, vii. 4, viii. 34, xiv. 9, 1 Cor. xv. 3, 4, 2 Cor. iv. 10–14, v. 14, 15, xiii. 4, Gal. ii. 20, Phil. ii. 8, 9, iii. 10, Col. ii. 12, 20 with iii. 1, 1 Thes. iv. 14, v. 10), and each without the other is to him unthinkable[1].

And the recognition that his doctrine rests not upon something static but upon a *movement*, a transference, meets the criticism of some writers that his system is not coherent, and therefore not a system. On the one hand is the immanent Christ, the motive power—by His Spirit—of man's ethical life. On the other is the human Christ who died as an offering for sin for man's salvation, which is a 'legal' transaction. And it is thought that the two conceptions, mystical and legal, are taught by St Paul separate and unrelated. But this would be surprising in a teacher of his mental ability, and the more so when it is remembered that both are clearly represented within the limits of one and the same epistle, that to the Romans. The mystical conception—rendered easier to him by his upbringing among Greeks—was an expression of his daily spiritual experience; and the legal conception—rendered easier to him by his upbringing in the Jewish sacrificial system—was the satisfaction of his dire spiritual need. And so far from these being in his mind unrelated, his doctrinal

---

[1] 'There can be no salvation from sin unless there is a living Saviour. this explains the emphasis laid by the apostle on the resurrection. But the Living One can only be a Saviour because He has died. this explains the emphasis laid on the Cross.' Denney, *The Death of Christ*, p. 88 f.

centre of gravity consisted precisely in the relation between them.

2. But beside shewing what the Cross meant to man, St Paul also made it clear what it meant to God. First and foremost it was the action of God's love, and—which is one and the same—of Christ's love (Rom. v. 8, viii. 37, 2 Cor. v. 14, Gal. ii. 20, Eph. ii. 4, v. 2, 25, 1 Thes. ii. 16; cf. Tit. iii. 4). What was true of the Gentiles was true of all men: they were 'dead in trespasses and sins' (Eph. ii. 1, 5), 'alienated from the life of God' (iv. 18), 'alienated and enemies' (Col. i. 21). Their state of mind in the old condition of 'flesh' was 'enmity against God' (Rom. viii. 7) And God reconciled them to Himself (Rom. v. 10, 2 Cor. v. 18, 19, Eph. ii. 16, Col. i 20, 22). No New Testament writer says that God was reconciled to man; God is always Love, and it is man that needs to be brought back to Him, that His love may be satisfied. God's attitude to sin, which is the very negation of His Life, is described by St Paul and other Biblical writers as 'wrath' (see p. 270). This is a word derived from human nature; but it can be employed as expressing a real truth provided it is kept free from the thought of vindictiveness and all the other wrong motives by which, in man's frailty, the purity and righteousness of human anger are sullied. God's necessary, inevitable, attitude to sin is entirely compatible with His love for sinners. Sin is so hateful that His love wants to save us from it. And when St Paul, using the language of Old Testament sacrifice, speaks of Christ as 'propitiatory' (Rom. iii. 25), he does not say that God is propitiated; the sin is done away, and the sinner forgiven, i.e. brought back into the union with Him that sin had broken. Though it is true that the

thought of sacrifice may, in St Paul's mind, underlie all his references to Christ's death, yet it is not often that he actually speaks of it as sacrificial: 'Christ our Paschal Victim has been sacrificed for us' (1 Cor. v. 7). 'This cup is the new covenant in My blood' (xi. 25), a variant form of our Lord's words as given in Mk xiv. 24, referring to the covenant ceremony in Exod. xxiv. 3–8. 'Christ ...gave Himself up on your behalf an offering and a sacrifice to God for an odour of sweet scent' (Eph. v. 2). And the thought is probably to be found in the expression περὶ ἁμαρτίας, 'for sin' (Rom. viii. 3; cf. the *var. lect.* in Gal. i. 4, περὶ τῶν ἁμαρτιῶν ἡμῶν), which is used in the LXX as equivalent to a substantive, 'sin-offering'; see the quotation in Heb. x. 5. The large place which the thought holds in our mind—and rightly holds if rightly understood—is probably due more to the Epistle to the Hebrews than to St Paul. But he shews the way in which it can be rightly understood. He is far more ready to regard Christ's death, the means of our salvation from sin, as part of a plan conceived and carried out by the will of God (cf. Gal. i. 4) for the satisfaction of His love than an appeasement offered by His Son and evermore put forward by us, as a satisfaction of His justice[1]. Man's salvation was (potentially) secured 'at a price' (1 Cor. vi. 20, vii 23), i e. at great cost; but the apostle says nothing to exclude the idea that the cost was paid, or felt, by God the Father as really as by His Son.

[1] The corresponding sacrifice, well pleasing to God, which is to be offered by Christians is the presentation of their bodies to do His will (Rom. xii. 1) 'The moment God is forgotten as the ground of sacrifice, the moment sacrifice is regarded, not as an act of obedience to the divine will, but as a means of changing the divine will, there is the germ of every dark superstition.' F. D. Maurice, Letter to R. H. Hutton on *Tracts for Priests and People*, no. xiv.

13. THE SACRAMENTS

St Paul's Gospel, then, is life gained through death, granted in Christ by God's grace, or free kindness, and appropriated by man's faith. And because man is possessed of a body, spiritual death unto sin finds its necessary outward expression in physical death. But for the same reason sacraments find a place in the divine plan, which in its various aspects is described as a 'mystery[1]'; see [Rom. xvi. 25], 1 Cor ii. 1, 7, iv. 1 (plur.), xv. 51, Eph. i. 9, iii 3, 4, v. 32, vi. 19, Col i. 26, 27, ii 2, iv. 3.

1. *Baptism.* Grace on God's part and faith on man's are the spiritual means, and Baptism the sacramental means, whereby the blessings are obtained which result from union with Christ (Gal. iii. 27). The whole Church has 'one faith, one baptism' (Eph. iv. 5). In Baptism God gives outward expression to His grace, and man to his faith. Hereby a man (potentially) dies to sin in union with Christ's death to sin, and rises to new life in union with Christ's Resurrection life; and the act of plunging beneath the water suggests to St Paul burial with Christ, an ocular demonstration of death (Rom. vi. 3, 4, Col. ii 12, 20, iii. 1–3; cf. Tit. iii 5) This (potential) transference of the baptized person, in union with Christ, from the old condition to the new, constitutes him a member of the one Body filled with the one Spirit (1 Cor. xii. 13). It is analogous with the passage of Israel from Egyptian slavery to freedom and life effected by their baptism 'unto Moses in the cloud and in the sea' (x. 1, 2).

[1] Patristic writers, e g Chrysostom and Gregory of Nazianzus applied the term to the Holy Communion; and later it was used more generally, as equivalent to 'sacrament'

2. *Holy Communion.* Κοινωνία, 'communion,' is a common share or participation in something, and the consequent unity or fellowship. As in the case of baptism the spiritual finds its outward expression in the sacramental. Christians were 'called into the communion of His Son' (1 Cor. i. 9); and the apostle speaks of 'the communion of the Holy Spirit' (2 Cor. xiii. 13), and of 'communion of Spirit' (Phil. ii. 1). This is a continual share in the life of the risen Christ, granted by God's grace, and appropriated by man's faith. Sacramentally this is expressed in 'communion of the blood of Christ' and 'communion of the body of Christ' (1 Cor. x. 16), by continually partaking of which 'ye proclaim the Lord's death till He come' (xi. 26). When the Israelites passed from the death of slavery to the life of freedom they needed continual divine nourishment by manna and water; and for that purpose 'they did all eat the same spiritual food [as we], and did all drink the same spiritual drink; for they drank from the spiritual rock that followed them, and the rock was Christ' (x. 3, 4). And this share in the 'cup of the Lord' and 'the table of the Lord' (*v.* 21) perpetuates the membership of Christians in the one Body of Christ· 'we, the many, are one bread [*or* loaf], one body, for we all share in the one bread' (*v.* 17). St Paul could have said that it is the sacramental means whereby 'Christ is formed in' us (cf. Gal. iv. 19).

3. Similarities can be pointed out between the phraseology and ideas in St Paul's teaching and those connected with the mystery religions of his day[1].

---

[1] This is done, perhaps with some exaggeration, by Reitzenstein, *Die Hellenistischen Mysterienreligionen*, pp. 160–204.

THE SACRAMENTS

(a) Phraseology. Some examples are μυστήριον 'mystery,' μυεῖσθαι 'be initiated' (Phil. iv. 12), μεταμορφοῦσθαι 'be transformed' (Rom. xii. 2, 2 Cor. iii. 18), μετασχηματίζειν 'change the appearance of' (Phil. iii. 21), λογικὴ λατρεία 'service offered by the reason' (Rom. xii. 1), φωτίζεσθαι 'be illuminated' (Eph. i. 18), τέλειος 'perfect' (1 Cor. ii. 6, xiv. 20 [R.V. 'mer.'], Phil. iii. 15, Col. iv. 12), τελειοῦσθαι 'be perfected' (Phil. iii. 12).

(b) Ideas. Words might be adopted for literary effect, but with quite altered significance. Ideas are more important. St Paul's religion and that of the mysteries can alike be described as 'mystical.' Far removed from mere individual ethics, they are intended to satisfy the desire of the human soul to be delivered from evil by union with the Divine. The mystery religions were very various. Some lifted their devotees to a considerable degree of spirituality, others were crude and barbarous in the extreme. But the underlying desire was the same. Their mystical enthusiasts, like St Paul, would contrast 'spirit' with *psyche*, and with the body or the flesh, the heavenly with the earthly body; and they would long to put on the heavenly. They were initiated by a cleansing bath, which resulted in a spiritual illumination; they emerged new men, re-made, reborn. And having been initiated, they were united sacramentally, by the partaking of blood, or by a sacred feast, with the death and new life of a god, and became thereby perfected. It is true that ceremonial washings and sacrificial feasts were to be found in Judaism, but there is no evidence that Jews untouched with foreign thought regarded them as producing the mystical results claimed both in the mysteries and in Christianity.

If, then, the mystery religions supplied St Paul with some of his vocabulary, and moulded the shape of some of his ideas, it is not more than we should expect in one who was a Jew of the Dispersion, however zealously he followed Hebrew law and Pharisaic traditions, and who, after his conversion, dedicated every power of mind and sensitive understanding to his apostleship of the Gentiles. He might well feel that if Christ was 'the end of the law,' He was also the end of the mysteries, being Himself the Mystery.

His probable attitude is well described by a modern Jewish writer[1], whose words are worth quoting at some length. 'May he not have cast a wistful eye over the border [from his own religion to that of the Hellenists among whom he lived], where the votaries of the Hellenistic mystery religions were claiming that they could conquer sinfulness at a bound? Those who with humble faith passed through the rites of initiation were mysteriously re-born; they died to live again; they were endowed with a fresh and supernatural strength; they were invested with a new personality, which enabled them to conquer, and rise superior to, the solicitations of sin. The god had entered into them, and under the appearance of the old body there now dwelt a divine spirit, the source of a new and a higher life. It is admitted on all hands, though by some reluctantly, that the terminology of Paul shews the influence of the theology of the "mysteries." But did he use the terminology without knowing something of the ideas which underlay them[2]? Doubtless he thought the whole

[1] C. G. Montefiore, *Judaism and St Paul*, pp. 116–119.
[2] In a footnote Reitzenstein's view is referred to with approval, that 'it is not a question of borrowing. It is a question of the subtlest form of unconscious influence.'

business false and blasphemous and unclean, but for all that he may have felt some secret allurement, some half-conscious interest, some hidden feeling, "how grand it would be if there were a means of becoming *really and truly* a new creature, of triumphing over sin and the Yetzer ha-Ra[1] and the evil heart once and for all!" Then one would have received that new heart and that new spirit which the Prophets had declared was to be the gift of God to Israel in the Messianic age....Then to this mobile, eager, yearning soul, with his gloomy and pessimistic religion[2], comes the great illumination. Jesus of Nazareth was the Messiah, the Son of God.... The votaries of the mysteries are trying to get from idols and false gods what can only be got from the One True God, the God of Israel, who is also the God of the spirits of all flesh. In the death and in the resurrection of His divine Son...lies the only efficacious mystery. With him all men must die, in order that with him all may live Here is the true dying to live. Here are the true I in Thee and Thou in Me.'

[1] A Jewish expression for man's tendency to sin.
[2] Such is Mr Montefiore's idea of St Paul's religion before his conversion, in contrast with the orthodox Rabbinic religion, which he assumes to have been similar to that which appears four centuries later.

LITERATURE

The literature on St Paul is very large. The following list contains only a selection of works in English exhibiting widely different ideas and points of view.

Commentaries on the Epistles

Cambridge Greek Testament: *Romans*, R. St J. Parry, 1912. 2 *Corinthians*, A. Plummer, 1903. *Ephesians*, J. O. F. Murray, 1914. *Colossians* and *Philemon*, A. Lukyn Williams, 1907. 1, 2 *Thessalonians*, G. G. Findlay, 1904. 1, 2 *Timothy, Titus*, J. H. Bernard, 1899.

Macmillan's Commentaries: *Galatians, Philippians, Colossians* and *Philemon*, J. B. Lightfoot. *Ephesians*, J. Armitage Robinson. 1, 2 *Thessalonians*, G. Milligan.

International Critical Commentary: *Romans*, W. Sanday and W. Headlam, 5th ed. 1902. 1 *Corinthians*, Bp. Robertson and A. Plummer, 1911. 2 *Corinthians*, A. Plummer, 1915 *Ephesians* and *Colossians*, T. K. Abbott, 1897. *Philippians* and *Philemon*, M. R. Vincent, 1897.

Century Bible: *Romans*, A. G. Garvie. 1, 2 *Corinthians*, J Massie. 1, 2 *Thessalonians* and *Galatians*, W. F. Adeney. *Ephesians, Colossians, Philemon* and *Philippians*, G. Currie Martin. 1, 2 *Timothy, Titus*, R. F. Horton.

Separate commentaries *Romans*, Bp. Gore, London, 1899. 2 *Corinthians*, A. Menzies, London, 1912. *Galatians* ('Historical Commentary on'), W. M. Ramsay, London, 1899. C. W. Emmet, London, 1912. *Ephesians*, Bp. Gore, London, 1900. *Colossians*, Bp. H. J. C. Knight. 1 *Thessalonians*, A. Plummer, London, 1918.

Other works on the Epistles

F. J. A. Hort. Prolegomena to the Epp. to the Romans and Ephesians. London. 1895.

E. H. Askwith. The Destination of the Ep. to the Galatians. London. 1899.

E. H. Askwith. An Introduction to the Thessalonian Epistles. London. 1902.

J. H. Kennedy. The Second and Third Epistles to the Corinthians. London. 1900.

H. St J. Thackeray. The Relation of St Paul to contemporary Jewish Thought. London. 1900.

Kirsopp Lake. The Earlier Epistles of St Paul. London. 1911.

J. Moffatt. An Introduction to the Literature of the New Testament (2nd ed) Edinburgh. 1912.

G. A. Deissmann St Paul (transl. L. R. M. Strachan). London. 1912.

W. S. Muntz. Rome, St Paul, and the early Church. London. 1913.

A Companion to Biblical Studies. Ed. W. E. Barnes. Cambridge. 1916.

St Paul's Life and Times

Jas Smith. The Voyage and Shipwreck of St Paul London. 1848. 4th ed. 1880.

W. J. Conybeare and J. S. Howson. The Life and Epistles of St Paul. 2nd ed. London. 1856. People's edition. London. 1862

F. W. Farrar. The Life and Work of St Paul. London. 1879. Illustr. ed. 1904.

J S. Howson. The Companions of St Paul. London. 1883.

J. Iverach. St Paul · his Life and Times. London. 1890.

F. J. A. Hort. Judaistic Christianity. London. 1894.

A. C. McGiffert. History of Christianity in the Apostolic Age. Edinburgh. 1897.

W. M. Ramsay The Church in the Roman Empire. London. 1893.

—— St Paul the Traveller and the Roman Citizen. 3rd ed. London. 1897.

—— Pauline and other Studies. London. 1906.

—— The Cities of St Paul. London. 1907.

G. H. Gilbert. The Student's Life of St Paul. New York. 1899.
J. V. Bartlet. The Apostolic Age. Edinburgh. 1900.
B. W. Bacon The Story of St Paul. London. 1905.
H. Weinel. St Paul, the Man, and his Work (transl. Bienemann). London. 1906.
E. von Dobschutz. The Apostolic Age (transl. Pogson). London. 1909
P. Gardner. St Paul's Speeches in the Acts (in *Camb. Biblical Essays*). London. 1909.
R. W. Pounder. St Paul and his Cities. London. 1913.
E. B. Redlich. St Paul and his Companions London. 1913.
C. H. Watkins St Paul's Fight for Galatia London. 1914.
J Paterson Smyth. The Story of St Paul's Life and Letters. London. 1917.

St Paul's Teaching

O. Pfleiderer. Paulinism (transl. Peters). London. 1877.
────── The Influence of the Apostle Paul on the Development of Christianity. London 1885.
G. Matheson. The Spiritual Development of St Paul. Edinburgh. 1890.
A. Sabatier. The Apostle Paul (transl Findlay). London. 1891.
A. B. Bruce. St Paul's Conception of Christianity. Edinburgh. 1894.
S. Baring Gould. A Study of St Paul. London. 1897.
D. Somerville. St Paul's Conception of Christianity. Edinburgh. 1897.
O. Cone. Paul, the Man, the Missionary, and the Teacher. London. 1898.
W. Lock Paul the Master Builder. London. 1899.
R. J. Knowling. The Testimony of St Paul to Christianity. London. 1903.
H. A A. Kennedy. St Paul's Conception of the Last Things. London. 1904.

LITERATURE

H. A. A. Kennedy. St Paul and the Mystery Religions. London. 1913.
J. M. Campbell. Paul the Mystic. London. 1907.
W. P. Du Bose. The Gospel according to St Paul. London. 1907.
J. Weiss. Paul and Jesus (transl. Chaytor). London. 1909.
R. J. Fletcher. A Study of the Conversion of St Paul. London. 1910.
J. R Cohu. St Paul and Modern Research London 1911.
J. Denney. The Death of Christ 2nd ed. London. 1911.
P. Gardner. The Religious Experience of St Paul. London. 1911.
E. H. Gifford The Incarnation: A Study of Phil. ii. 5–11. 2nd ed. London. 1911.
H. L. Goudge. The Mind of St Paul, as illustrated by his Second Epistle to the Corinthians. London. 1911.
S. N. Rostron. The Christology of St Paul. London. 1912.
A Schweitzer. Paul and his Interpreters (transl. Montgomery). London. 1912.
C. G Montefiore Judaism and St Paul London. 1914.
R. H. Strachan The Individuality of St Paul. London. 1916.

INDEX

Abraham, 4, 35, 177 f, 191, 194 f, 199, 297
Achaia, xv, 30, 67 n, 72, 79, 82, 162, 169, 181, 215
Achaicus, 149
Adam, 161, 191, 196, 288, 291, the Second, Last, 162, 284, 288
Adramyttium, 109
Adria, 112
Advent, the, 78, 124, 127 f, 132–5, 155, 159, 190, 240, 267, 268–75, *and see* 'eschatology'
Agabus, 23, 25, 94
ager Romanus, 116 n
Agrippa I, 27, 97 n, 105, 106 n
Agrippa II, 5, 16, 106–8, 119
Alexander, 84, 98, 259
Alexandria, -drian, 6, 7, 9, 78
amanuensis, 2, 122
Amphipolis, 57 n, 62
Ananias, 15 f, the high priest, 100, 104
Anastasis, 65, 67
Ancyra, 52
angels, 126 n, 206 n, 209, 224, 270 n, 297, worship of, 7, 206
Antichrist, 132, 134, 272 n
Antioch, Pisidian, 33–6, 38, 39, 51, 52, 54, 66, 72, 76 n, 77 n, 78, 79, 95
Antioch in Syria, xv n, 21, 22 f, 25, 28 f, 30, 39, 41, 42, 44 f., 74, 76 f., 169, 171
Antipatris, 103
antitheses, 250
Antonia, castle of, 99
Apameia, 54, 79
Aphrodite, 70, 83
Apollonia, 62, 86
Apollos, 78 ff, 137 n, 150–2, 162, 183
Apphia, 212
Appius, Forum of, 117

Aquila, xviii, 70 f, 72 n, 74 f, 78, 135, 182, 183, 187–9
Arabia, 17 f, 27, 169, 176, 179 n.
Aratus, 68
Archippus, 204, 211, 212
Areopagus, 65
Aretas, xiii f, 18
Aristarchus, 83, 85, 87, 109, 113 n., 204, 210, 260
Aristobulus, the household of, 227
Artemis, 82–5
asceticism, 7, 206, 250
Asia, 51, 54, 55, 76 n, 79 n, 83 n, 87 n, 89, 92 n, 98, 135, 136, 169, 183, 204
Asiarchs, 83
Assos, 90, 260
Athens, 6, 64–9
Atonement, Day of, 110
Attalia, 33, 39. 54
Augustan cohort, 109

Baptism, 40, 78, 79, 151, 157, 161, 197, 303
Barjesus, 31 f
Barnabas, 11, 19, 22, 23–5, 27, 28 f, 30–4, 36–9, 41–5, 50, 52, 169, 171 n, 177
Bernice, Berenice, 16, 106, 107 n
Beroea, 63 f, 86, 95
bishop, 237, 243 f, 262, 264
Bithynia, 55
'blood,' 46–8

Caesar, *see* 'Emperor'
Caesar's household, 226, 229
Caesarea, x, 19, 21, 75 f, 91 n, 92 n, 93 f., 102–8, 204, 211, 225 f, 259–61
Caligula, 12 n.
Carpus, 90 n
'carriages,' 94

INDEX

Castor and Pollux, 115 n
castra peregrinorum, 117 n.
Cauda, 111
Cenchreae, 70, 74, 181, 203, 244
charisma, 159 f, 243, 283
chiliarch, 6, 7, 99 f, 102, 105
Chios, 90
Chloe, 138, 149
chronology, xiii–xix
Church, St Paul's conception of the, 8, 179, 207–9, 214, 219, 222, 223, 224, 285, 287, 303
Cilicia, 4, 6, 21, 71, 99, *and see* 'Syria and Cilicia'
Cilician Gates, 39, 51
circumcision, 9, 10, 24 n., 26, 28, 40–4, 49, 53 f, 155, 175, 177, 181, 194 f, 202, 206, 209, 239, 295
Claudius, xiii, xv–xviii, 23, 59, 71, 105 n
Claudius Lysias, *see* 'Lysias'
Clement, 240
Clement of Rome, 137 n., 219, 231, 244 n, 256 f.
Cnidus, 110
collection, the, 52, 63, 87 f, 96, 104 n., 136 f, 140, 146, 150 f, 162, 163, 166, 181, 202, 233
Colossae, 7, 79, 203 f, 214–6
Colossians, Epistle to the, xix, 203–11
Communion, *see* 'Eucharist'
conversion of St Paul, xiii, xviii f, 11–17, 20, 100, 107, 176
coppersmith, 84 n.
Corinth, xvii f, 36, 64, 69, 70–3, 78 f., 82, 87, 95, 123, 129, 135–68, 169, 172, 173, 181 f., 189, 230, 233, 248, 261
Corinthians, Epistles to the, xix, 135–68
Cornelius, 22, 26, 28, 40, 43
Cos, 93
Council of Jerusalem, xiii f., xix, 26 f, 30, 40–50, 96 n., 170–3
Crescens, 254, 261
Crete, 110, 112, 244, 249, 254–6
Crispus, 72 f

Cross, the, *see* 'death of Christ'
cutting of hair, 74 f
Cyprus, 11, 22, 30, 50, 93, 109

Dalmatia, 254, 261
Damaris, 67
Damascus, xiii f, 13–16, 17, 18, 19, 29, 95, 100, 107
deacons, 11 n, 237, 243 f, 262
death of Christ, 10, 78, 125, 134, 153, 165, 176, 177, 181, 194, 197, 198, 208, 209, 223, 232, 238, 239, 248, 265, 267, 298–302, 303, 304, 307
Demas, 204, 210, 254, 261
Demetrius, 83, 84 n
demon, 49, 58 f, 68, 81, 159
Derbe, 37–9, 51, 52, 77 n, 78
Diana, 82
Dionysius, 67
Dorylaion, 55
doxology in *Romans*, 184–9, 192
Drusilla, xiii, 105, 106 n

elders, *see* 'presbyters'
election, 282, 284, 288
Elijah, 200
Elymas, 31 f
Emperor, the, 8, 106 ff, 118, 132, 226, 258, 273
Epaenetus, 183
Epaphras, -roditus, of Colossae, 203–5, 208, 210, of Philippi, 228 f, 232, 234, 236, 238, 241, 286
'Ephesian writings,' 82
Ephesians, Epistle to the, xix, 213–25
Ephesus, xiii, xviii f, 36, 74 n., 75, 76–86, 88, 91, 92, 98, 135 ff, 139–41, 143, 162, 173, 182 f, 188, 189, 226, 229–31, 244, 249, 254–6, 258, 259, 260
Epicureans, 65
Erastus, 82, 86, 139, 181, 229, 261
Esau, 199
eschatology, 10, 67, 78, 124, 128, 131–3, 155 f., 161, 165, 202, 203, 232, 240, 248, 265, 268–75

INDEX 315

ethnarch, 18
Eucharist, 11, 49, 89, 113 n, 150 f, 157, 159, 190, 304
Eunike, 53
Euodia, 232, 240
Euraquilo, Euroclydon, 111
Eutychus, 89
exorcism, 59, 81

Fair Havens, 110
famine, xiv, 23–6
Fatherhood of God, 265
Felix, xiii, 88, 102–7, 258
Festus, xiii, 16, 101 n, 106–8, 117, 259
flesh, fleshly, 161, 180, 198, 281 f, 290, 301
foods, idolatrous and other forbidden, 41 f, 46–9, 150 f, 156–8, 202, 206, 209, 250
fornication, -tors, 46–50, 137 f., 142, 150, 153 f., 280
Fortunatus, 149
Forum of Appius, 117
frumentarius, 109, 117 n

Gaius, 52, 83, 85, 87, 88 n, 181, 260
Galatae, the, 52
Galatia, 1, 27 n, 33, 34 n, 37, 45 n, 51 f, 77 n, 87, 168–70, 173, 205, 230, 261
Galatians, Epistle to the, xix, 168–81
Gallio, xv–xvii, 72 f
Gamaliel, 4, 100, 102 n
Gnosticism, 206, 251
God-fearers, 10, 35, 40, 62 n.
'Golden Rule,' the, 47 n

Hagar, 179, 297
haggada, 5
Hellenist, 6, 9, 11, 22, 40, 306
Hermes, 38, 169 n.
Hierapolis, 54, 203 f.

Iconium, 36, 38 f, 51, 52, 77 n, 78, 95
idolatry, idols, 7, 41, 46–50, 62 n, 150 f, 156–8, 159, 165
Illyricum, 63, 86

Incarnation, the, 178, 197, 232, 238, 267
Isaac, 179, 195, 199, 297
Ishmael, 179, 297
Isthmian games, 70

James, 11, 19 f, 24, 26, 28, 41–5, 49 n., 91 n, 96, 176 f.
Jason, 63 f.
Jerusalem, 5, 9, 10, 11, 17, 33, 103, 106, 107, 119, 174, 177, 255, 1st visit, xiii, xviii, 19–21, 22, 29, 176; 2nd visit, xiii, xiv, xviii, 23–8, 177; 3rd visit, xiii, xix, 30, 40–50; 4th visit, xiii, xix, 76; 5th visit, x, xiv, xix, 75, 82, 88, 91–4, 95–102, 104, 181 f, 202, 259–61; collection for the poor of, 87 f, 140, 146, 202; the earthly and the heavenly, 179, 297
Jesus Justus, 210, 254 n.
John the Apostle, 24, 26, 28, 176
John the Baptist, 35, 73–80, 275
John Mark, *see* 'Mark'
Judaism, -izers, 4, 10, 25, 31, 42–6, 53 n, 95, 96, 170–2, 174, 179, 205, 234–6, 239, 250, 296, 305
Judas Barsabbas, 44 f
Julius, 109, 114, 116 n, 117 n
Jupiter, 38 n
jus Italicum, 56
justification, *see* 'righteousness'

Kephas, *see* 'Peter'
Kotiaion, 55 n.

Laodicea, 54, 79, 211, 216
Laodiceans, Epistle to the, 215–7
Lasea, 110
Last Day, the, *see* 'Advent,' 'eschatology'
Lechaeon, 70
lex Valeria, 59
libertines, 235, 237, 239 f

INDEX

liberty, 48, 126, 153, 156-8, 177, 180, 202
lictors, 36 n, 59-61
litigation in heathen courts, 150, 152
Lois, 53
Lord's Supper, *see* 'Eucharist'
Lucius the Cyrenaean, 29
Luke, 1, 88, 120, 204, 210, 254, 260
Lutro, 110 n
Lycaonia, 37, 51, 53
Lycus, 204 f.
Lydda, 103
Lydia (district), 58, 79 n.
Lydia (woman), 58, 61
Lysias, 99 f., 102, 105, 107 n.
Lystra, 37, 39, 51-3, 66, 77 n, 78, 87, 95

Macedonia, 3, 30, 55-7, 63, 69, 71, 82, 86 f, 90, 119, 123, 135, 136 f, 139, 140, 143, 147, 164, 166, 167, 169, 173, 181, 229, 230, 254, 255 f
Man of Sin, Lawlessness, 131, 272 f.
Manaen, 29
Marcellus, 12 n
Marcion, 184, 186, 189, 215, 217
Mark, 30, 33, 50, 53, 204, 210, 255, 260
marriage, 49, 126, 150, 154-6, 271
Matala, Cape, 111
Mediator, 222, 262, 267 n
Melita, 112 n, 114 f.
Mercurius, 38 n
Messiah, -anic, 10, 16, 40, 101 n., 107, 118, 127 f, 199, 265, 268-74, 275; *and see* 'Advent,' 'eschatology'
Messina, 116
Miletus, x, 90, 91 n, 92, 261
millennium, 273
Mitylene, 90
Mnason, 94 f.
Myra, 75, 93 n, 109
Mysia, 55
mysteries, mystery religions, 7, 304-7

mystery, 161, 207-9, 224, 239, 303

Narcissus, the household of, 227
Nazarene, 103, 108
Nazirite, 74, 96-8
Neapolis, 56 f., 82, 86
neokoros, 83
Nero, 106, 120, 132, 257 n, 258
Neronian persecution, the, xv, 256 f
Nicomedia, 55
Nicopolis, 253 f.
Nympha, 211

Onesimus, 204, 210, 211-3, 214
Onesiphorus, 263
original sin, 291

Pamphylia, 33, 39, 54
Paphos, 31, 33
Parousia, *see* 'Advent'
parties at Corinth, 137 n., 138 f, 142, 144, 150-2, 159, 233
Passover, xviii, 75, 153
Pastoral Epistles, the, 241-64
Patara, 75, 91 n, 93
Pentecost, xiv, xix, 75, 82, 91, 96, 104, 135, 137, 140, 275
Perga, 33, 39
Pessinus, 52
Peter, ix, xiv f, 19 f., 22, 24, 26, 28, 40 n, 41-3, 49, 67, 137 n, 172, 176 f, 256 f, 275
Pharaoh, 199
Pharisee, -aism, 4, 8, 9, 12, 43, 101, 107, 239
Philadelphia, 54
Philemon, 211-3, 214, 225, 254, 260
Philip, 11, 22, 93, 204
Philippi, x, 56-61, 63, 86, 88, 91 n, 136, 215, 228 f., 230, 231, 234
Philippians, Epistle to the, xix, 225-41
Phoebe, 181, 183, 184, 192, 203, 244, 286

INDEX

Phoenix, 110
Phrygia, 33, 34 n. 37, 38 n, 51, 77 n.
Pilate. 12 n., 35
politarchs, 63
Pollux, see 'Castor'
Pontus, 71
praetor, 59–61
praetorian guard, *praetorium*. 117 n., 226, 228 f.
presbyters, elders, 25, 27, 51 n, 243 f, 263, 264
Primus, 115
Prisca, Priscilla, xviii, 70 f, 74 f., 78, 135, 182 f, 189
proconsul, xv–xvii, 31 f, 72
procurator, 102 f, 105 n, 108
prophecy, 3, 80, 129, 160 f, 243
prophets, 28 f, 94, 218, 223, 243
proselyte, 10, 11, 24 n, 28, 35, 40
proseuche, 58
psyche, psychic, 162, 279–81, 288, 305
Ptolemais, 93
public worship, regulations for, 150 f., 158–60, 245, 262
Publius, 115
purification, days of, 97
Puteoli, 116, 117 n.
Python, 58

repentance, 294
Resurrection, 10, 65, 78, 101, 104, 107, 119, 128, 134, 150 f, 154, 161 f, 176, 190, 193, 195, 204, 222, 239, 250, 265, 267, 268, 273, 298–300, 303
Rhegium, 116
Rhodes, 93
righteousness, 12, 35, 190 f, 193–6, 200, 284, 290, 293–5, 297
Romans, Epistle to the, xix, 182–203
Rome, ix, x, xv, xvii, xix, 3, 7, 82, 102, 107, 118–20, 211, 214, 215, 226–30, 235, 253, 254, 255, 260, 261; banishment of Jews from, xiii, xviii, 71

Sadducees, 101
Salamis, 30
Salmone, Cape, 110
Samaria, 26, 43
Samos, 90
Samothrace, 56
sanctification, 197, 294 f.
Sanhedrin, 2, 5, 13, 100–2, 107 n, 118 n, 259
Sarah, 179, 297
Satan, 1, 49, 64, 142, 167, 203, 271, 272
Sceva, 81
Second Coming, see 'Advent'
Secundus, 87, 250
Seleucia, 30
Seleucids, 5, 6, 7
Seneca, 73
Sergius Paulus, 31 f
shipwreck, 76, 112–4
shorthand, 122
sicarii, 99
Sicily, 112, 116
Sidon, 109, 116 n
Silas, Silvanus, 30, 44 f, 51, 59, 61, 63 f, 65, 68 f, 71, 74, 78, 123, 129, 174
silversmith, 83
Sinai, 18, 179, 296
slave, slavery, 155, 210, 211–3, 225, 226, 263, 264
Soloi, 31 n.
sonship, 221, 276, 278
Sopater, Sosipater, 87, 182, 260
Sosthenes, 73, 151
Spain, 202, 254, 256 f.
Spirit-filled persons, 150 f, 159–61
stake in the flesh, 1, 3, 163
Stephanas, 67 n, 149, 162
Stephen, 11–13, 21, 34, 67 n
Stoics, 65
St Paul's Bay, 113, 115
strangled, things, 46–8
strategoi, 59
stratopedarch, 117
sufferings, St Paul's, 77, 85 f, 165, 168, 180, 181, 224, 231
Symeon Niger, 29
synagogue, 5 n, 13, 22, 31, 34,

36, 44, 57, 62, 63, 65, 71, 75, 80, 89, 104, 118
Syntyche, 232, 240
Syracuse, 116
Syria, 74–6, 87, 88; Syria and Cilicia, 21, 30, 45, 49, 51, 169, 176

tabernacularii, 71 n.
Tarsus, xv n., 4–6, 19, 21, 22, 29, 30, 39
Taurus, 33, 39, 51
Tavium, 52
temple, the, 97, 98, 99, 101 n, 103, 104, 106, 272
tent-makers, 71
Tertullus, 103
theosophy, 205 f.
Thessalonians, Epistles to the, 123–35
Thessalonica, 57 n, 62–4, 69, 86, 87, 95, 123, 125, 128, 134 f, 233, 261
Three Taverns, the, 117
Tiberius, 12 n
Timotheus, Timothy, 30, 52, 53, 64 f., 68 f., 71, 74, 82, 86, 87, 123, 125 n., 126, 129, 138–40., 152, 162, 164, 182, 204, 208, 212, 229, 236, 237, 238, 241–4, 254, 255, 256, 260 f.

Titius Justus, 72
Titus, 23, 25 f, 90, 136, 142–5, 147, 163, 164, 166, 168, 177, 241 f., 244, 254, 255, 256, 261
tongues, 3, 80, 160 f., 243
trance, *see* 'vision'
Troas, x, 55, 82, 86, 88 f, 91, 136, 143, 164, 254, 259 f.
Trogyllium, 90
Trophimus, 87 f, 98, 260 f.
Tychicus, 87 f., 210, 214, 215 f., 225, 260
Tyrannus, 80
Tyre, 91 n., 92 n, 93

'Unknown God, an,' 66
Unleavened Bread, 88, 136

veil, 158
virgins, 150 f, 155 f.
vision, xviii, 3, 17, 20 n., 72, 89, 102, 112, 167
Vitellius, 12 n.
vow, 74, 97 f.

'Way,' the, 13, 78, 104 f.
'We'-sections, x–xii, 56, 61, 77, 86, 88
widows, 243 f., 263

Zeus, 38, 84

Old Testament references

Gen.	xv. 6	194	Ps	xiv. 1 ff.	194 n.
Exod.	ix. 27	293		xviii 49	202 n.
	xx. 11	38, 66		xix. 4	200 n.
	xxiv. 3–8	302		xxxvi. 1	194 n.
	xxxiii. 19	199		li. 4	293
Num.	vi 2, 5, 13–20	97		cxvii 1	202 n.
	vi 18	74		cxl 3	194 n.
Deut.	i. 31	34 n	Isai.	i. 2	34 n.
	xxvii. 26	178		vi. 9, 10	119
	xxx. 12 ff.	200		xi 2	283
	xxxii. 8	66		xi. 10	202 n.
	xxxii. 21	200 n.		xxv. 8	281 n.
	xxxii. 43	202 n.		xxxii. 1 f.	194
Ps.	v. 9	194 n.		xlii 1	283
	x. 7	194 n.		xlii. 5	66

INDEX 319

Old Testament references (*continued*)

Isai	xliv. 3	275	Joel	ii. 28 f.	275
	lix. 7 f	194 n.	Amos	ix. 11, 12	44
	lxv 1, 2	200 n	Hab.	1 5	35
Ezek	xxxvi 27	275		ii 4	178
	xxxvii 1–14	275	Zech	xiv 5	126 n.
	xxxix 29	275			

Readings of cod. Bezae (D) in the *Acts*, given in the footnotes

xi	20	22	xvii	4	62
	25	22		15	64
	28	23	xviii	3	71
xiii.	7	32		7	72
	8	31		16	73
	14	34		25	78
	20	34		27	79
xiv.	2	36	xix	1	76, 79
	7	37		9	80
	13	38		21	75
xv	2	43		34	84
	12	43	xx	3	87
	20, 29	47		15	90
	34	45		18	92
	41	51	xxi	1	93
xvi	10	55		16	94
	12	57		25 a	96
	13	57		25 b	47
	16	58	xxii	28	100
	39	60			

Map I

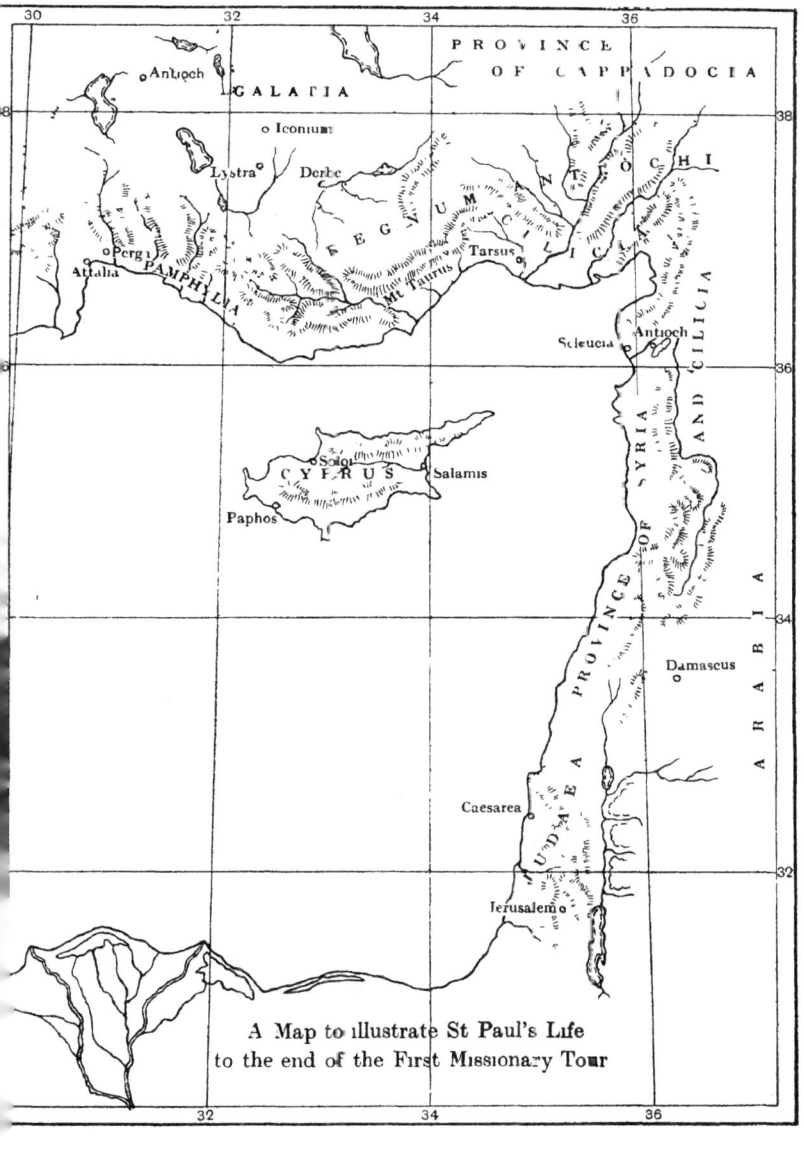

A Map to illustrate St Paul's Life to the end of the First Missionary Tour

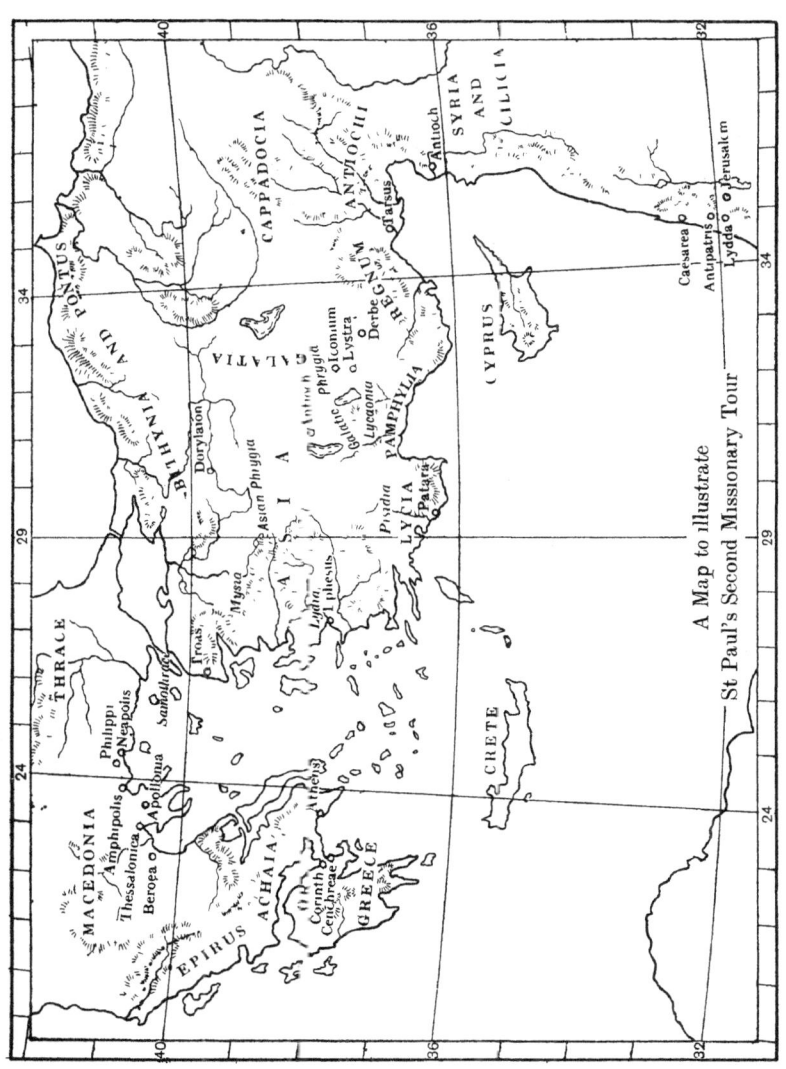

Map II

A Map to illustrate St Paul's Second Missionary Tour

Map III

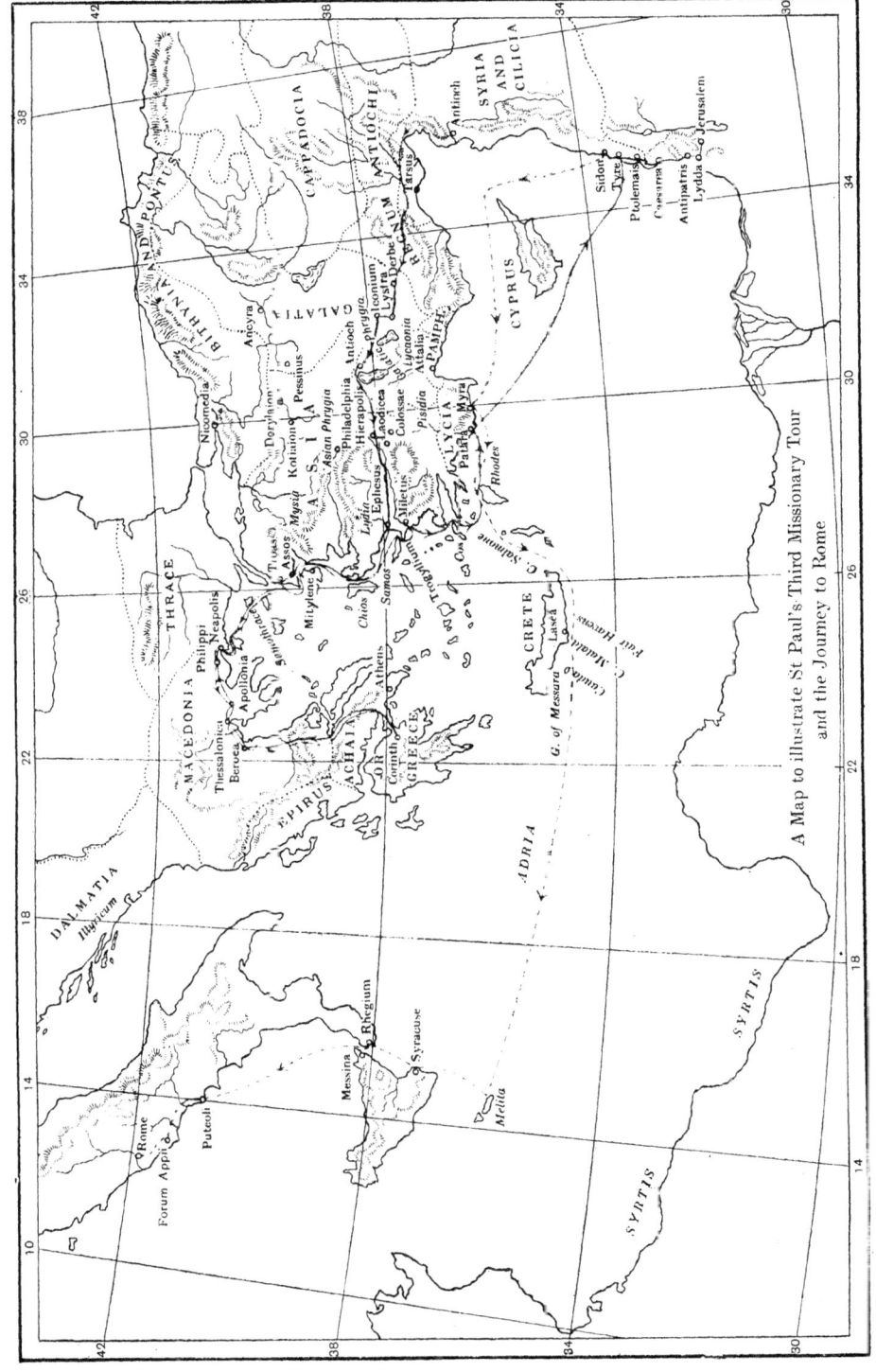

www.ingramcontent.com/pod-product-compliance
Lightning Source LLC
Chambersburg PA
CBHW071229230426
43668CB00011B/1360